Florida A&M University, Tallahassee
Florida Atlantic University, Boca Raton
Florida Gulf Coast University, Ft. Myers
Florida International University, Miami
Florida State University, Tallahassee
University of Central Florida, Orlando
University of Florida, Gainesville
University of North Florida, Jacksonville
University of South Florida, Tampa
University of West Florida, Pensacola

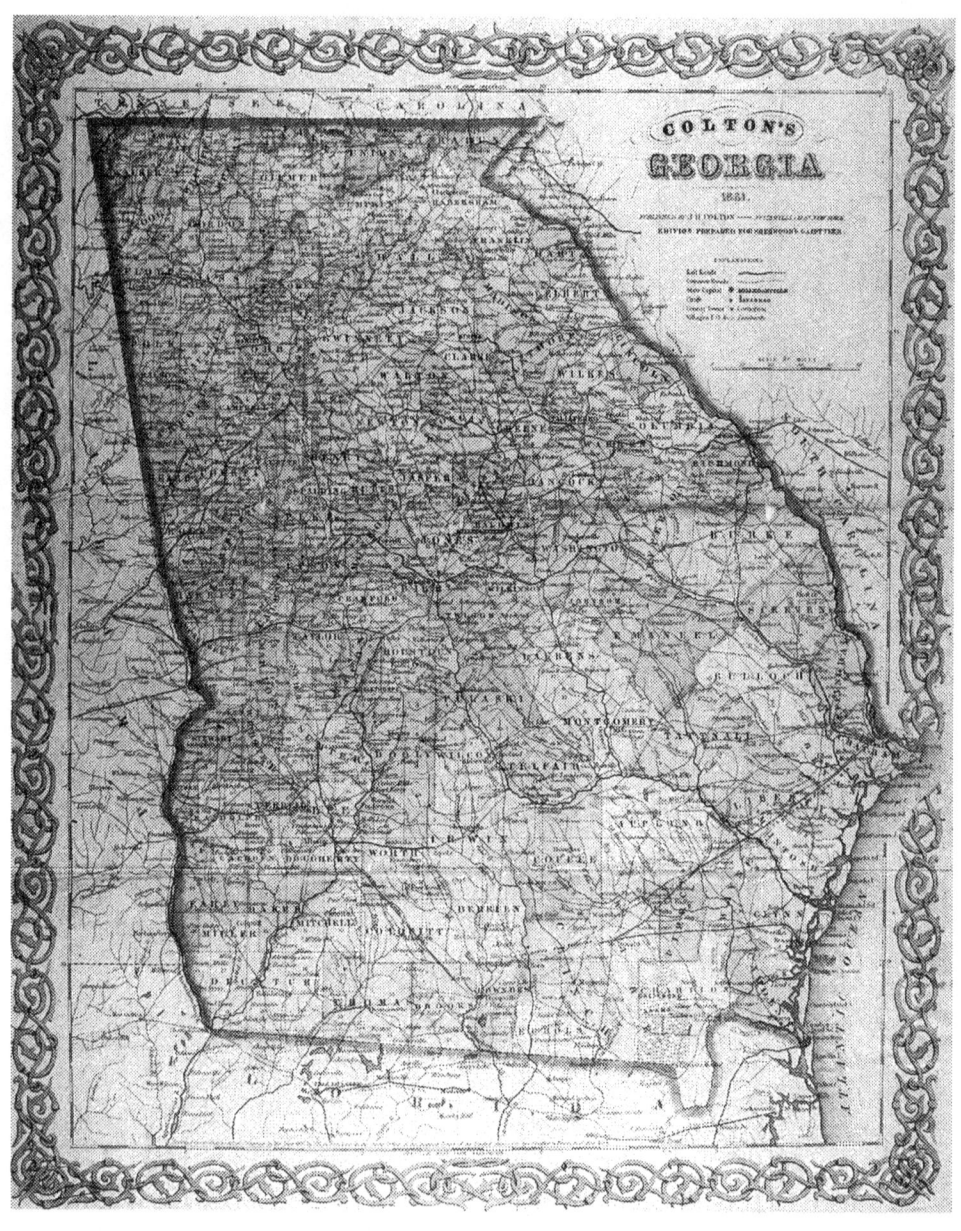

Georgia, 1861. Courtesy of Felix Hargrett Rare Book and Manuscript Collection.

Plain Folk in a Rich Man's War

Class and Dissent in Confederate Georgia

David Williams, Teresa Crisp Williams,
and David Carlson

University Press of Florida
GAINESVILLE · TALLAHASSEE · TAMPA · BOCA RATON
PENSACOLA · ORLANDO · MIAMI · JACKSONVILLE · FT. MYERS

Copyright 2002 by David Williams, Teresa Crisp Williams,
and David Carlson
Printed in the United States of America
All rights reserved

First cloth printing, 2002

First paperback printing, 2004

Library of Congress Cataloging-in-Publication Data
Williams, David.
Plain folk in a rich man's war: class and dissent in Confederate
Georgia / David Williams, Teresa Crisp Williams, and David Carlson.
p. cm.
Includes bibliographical references and index.
ISBN 0-8130-2570-2 (cloth: alk. paper)
ISBN 0-8130-2836-1 (Pbk.)
1. Georgia—History—Civil War, 1861-1865—Social aspects.
2. United States—History—Civil War, 1861-1865—Social aspects.
3. Social classes—Georgia—History—19th century. 4. Dissenters—
Georgia—History—19th century. 5. Rural poor—Georgia—Political
activity—History—19th century. 6. Plantation owners—Georgia—
Social conditions—19th century. 7. Georgia—Social conditions—19th
century. 8. Georgia—Politics and government—1861-1865.
I. Williams, Teresa Crisp. II. Carlson, David. III. Title.
E559 .W54 2002
975.8'03—dc21   2002027136

The University Press of Florida is the scholarly publishing agency for
the State University System of Florida, comprising Florida A&M
University, Florida Atlantic University, Florida Gulf Coast University,
Florida International University, Florida State University, University
of Central Florida, University of Florida, University of North Florida,
University of South Florida, and University of West Florida.

University Press of Florida
15 Northwest 15th Street
Gainesville, FL 32611-2079
http://www.upf.com

To our families, for their loving and patient support

Contents

List of Figures   ix

Acknowledgments   xi

Introduction: "A Rich Man's War"   1

1. "This Fuss Was All for the Benefit of the Wealthy": Secession and Dissent   8

2. "Far Greater Enemies to the South": Cotton Planters and Speculators   25

3. "God Help the Poor": Impressment, Hunger, and the Failure of Relief   45

4. "The Women Rising": Letters of Despair and Acts of Desperation   71

5. "Worse Than Slaves": Military Conscription   91

6. "Distemper of the Time": The Courts and Planter Privilege   112

7. "Very Improper Conduct": Slaves and Plain Folk   131

8. "We Are Fighting Each Other Harder Than We Ever Fought the Enemy": Georgia's Inner Civil War   151

9. "Don't Think There Is Much Regret for the Loss"   178

Notes   195

Bibliography   231

Index   247

Figures

1.1. Ladies encourage men to war 19
2.1. Notice to planters about cotton surplus 31
2.2. The *Shamrock* loading cotton 33
2.3. Kate Cumming, army nurse 36
2.4. Nelson Tift, Albany's founder 43
3.1. Plain folk bore the brunt of impressment 48
3.2. James Bush of Early County 51
4.1. Food shortage and soldiers' families 74
4.2. Women rioting for food 81
5.1. John Joseph Kirkland of Early County 93
5.2. Planter avoids military service 95
5.3. Order for missing conscripts to report 101
5.4. Georgia Militia, 1863 107
6.1. Hauled off to military service 114
6.2. Judge Richard Henry Clark 125
7.1. "Redeeming" deserters and escaped slaves 141
7.2. Vigilante "justice" 149
8.1. The Peace Society 155

8.2. Thomas A. Watson of Fannin County   158
8.3. David Snelling of Baldwin County   159
8.4. Dissenters offer stiff resistance   165
8.5. Layouts on the offensive   170
8.6. Victims of "guerrilla warfare"   175
9.1. Fugitives from slavery   181
9.2. Contrasting lifestyles of rich and poor   187
9.3. Sergeant William Andrews of Clay County   192

Acknowledgments

No work of scholarship is a singular effort. Never has that been more true than with this book. Those who contributed in some way to our efforts are far too numerous to list, and we thank them all, but a few deserve special recognition.

Meredith Morris-Babb, editor-in-chief of the University Press of Florida, and Gillian Hillis, our project editor, offered especially helpful advice and encouragement. So did those who read all or part of the manuscript's earlier incarnations: Cathy Badura, Anne Bailey, Lynn Corbin, John Crowley, Wayne Durrill, Lee Formwalt, William Freehling, Sharon Gravett, Stanley Harrold, Charles Johnson, Chris Meyers, Tracy Meyers, Randall Miller, Anastatia Sims, and students in a number of courses dealing with southern and Civil War history at Valdosta State University. Others who offered substantive support, tangible and intangible, were Alan Bernstein, Victoria Bynum, Ernestine Clark, Rex DeVane, Kathy Holland, John Inscoe, Jeff Jakeman, Patricia Mincy, Denise Montgomery, Larry Owsley, Jay Rickman, and Howard Zinn.

We are also grateful to staff members at the many repositories we visited. Among the most helpful and valuable were those of the Georgia Department of Archives and History, the University of Georgia Libraries, the Washington Memorial Library in Macon, and Valdosta State University's Odum Library.

Parts of this book were previously published in the *Georgia Historical Quarterly* and the *Journal of Southwest Georgia History*. We thank those publications and their sponsoring agencies for their kind permission to reproduce that material.

Finally, and most important, we thank our families, without whose support our work would not have been possible. It is to them that this book is dedicated.

Introduction

"A Rich Man's War"

On April 5, 1865, only days before the Civil War's end, an editorial appeared in the *Early County News* that read:

> This has been "a rich man's war and a poor man's fight." It is true there are a few wealthy men in the army, but nine tenths of them hold positions, always get out of the way when they think a fight is coming on, and treat the privates like dogs. . . . there seems to be no chance to get this class to carry muskets.

Such class-related sentiment was by no means isolated.[1] Throughout the Confederacy, plain folk expressed an increasingly antagonistic attitude toward the region's elite, especially the planters, as the war dragged on.[2] From its very beginnings, the war effort suffered from a rising tide of ambivalence, even hostility, toward not only planters but the Confederacy itself. Desertion and draft evasion were commonplace. By 1864, the draft law became nearly impossible to enforce, and most soldiers abandoned the ranks.

Not all dissent in the Confederacy had its origins in class resentment. Political alliances, ideological convictions, kinship ties, northern birth, shifting self-interest, personal animosities, or a combination of these sometimes played a role in dissent. Nor did refusal to support the Confederacy necessarily indicate a pro-Union stand, though disaffection and outright unionism were related in effect and often differed only in degree.³ Although general dissent in the Civil War South had various sources and differences in degree, class resentment played a major role in creating that dissent. It was clear to the plain folk that they suffered much more than the wealthy and well connected, many of whom seemed to profit from the war. Conflicting class interests, real and apparent, increasingly took their toll on plain folk's enthusiasm for the war effort.

Even before the Confederacy came into being, there were signs that a southern republic might have difficulty maintaining support among the plain folk. More than half the South's white population, most of whom owned no slaves, opposed immediate secession.⁴ Nevertheless, ambitious politicians and their slaveholding allies ignored popular disunity and forced secession on a reluctant South. One Texas politician insisted that conspiring colleagues had engineered secession without strong backing from "the mass of the people." A. P. Aldrich, a South Carolina politician and staunch secessionist, admitted that most plain folk were against it. "But whoever waited for the common people when a great move was to be made?" he asked. "We must make the move and force them to follow."⁵

Despite a general reluctance to secede, there was considerable enthusiasm for the war among southern whites after the firing on Fort Sumter and Lincoln's call for volunteers to hold the cotton states in the Union by force. Whatever their misgivings about secession, invasion was another matter. And, despite Lincoln's promise not to interfere with slavery, "fear of Negro equality," as one early historian of southern disunity observed, "caused some of the more ignorant to rally to the support of the Confederacy."⁶ But southern enlistment declined rapidly after the first major battle at Manassas, or Bull Run, as the Yankees called it. Many small farmers refused to abandon their families, and some already in the ranks deserted to help theirs.

The Confederacy's response to its recruitment problem was a clear indication of the role that class issues would play in the wartime South. In April 1862, the Confederate Congress passed the first centralized military conscription act in American history. As with the North's later draft, men of wealth could avoid service by hiring a substitute or paying a five-hundred-dollar exemption fee. In a letter to Governor Joe Brown, one Georgia resident asked, "Now who can afford to pay *that*?"⁷ The obvious answer was, of course, the rich.

Even worse in the eyes of plain folk, slaveholders who owned twenty or more slaves were effectively excused from the draft. This twenty-slave law was perhaps the most widely hated act imposed by the Confederacy, especially by poor soldiers already in the ranks. Said Private Sam Watkins of Tennessee: "It gave us the blues; we wanted twenty negroes. Negro property suddenly became very valuable, and there was raised the howl of 'rich man's war, poor man's fight.'" He continued, "From this time on till the end of the war, a soldier was simply a machine. We cursed the war . . . we cursed the Southern Confederacy. All our pride and valor had gone." When Jasper Collins of Mississippi got word of the twenty-slave law, he did not hesitate to desert. It was a clear signal to him, he told a friend, that the Confederate cause was a "rich man's war and a poor man's fight." Little wonder that desertion became an even greater problem for the Confederacy than for the Union.[8]

Another practice that helped turn Johnny Rebs against the Richmond government was confiscation of private property, or impressment. They resented Confederate officials forcing their families back home to give up a portion—sometimes a major portion—of their meager produce. That they had to sell at prices set by the government was just as galling. But it usually did not matter what the prices were, because all that these families got in exchange were promissory notes, usually unredeemable, or inflated paper currency that was nearly as worthless. Very often they got nothing at all, and neither did the soldiers for whom the confiscated goods were intended. Some impressment officers sold government produce on the open market and pocketed the proceeds.

After impressment officers took his horse in the spring of 1863, North Carolina farmer Samuel Holt sent an angry letter to the governor insisting that "the slave owners ought to bear the principal burden of the war, if not the whole of it." It was bad enough that they had "managed very *notably* to screen their *own carcasses* from Yankee bullets & have made it literally a *Poor-Man's War*. . . . The last act of this miserable farce is to send unsaddled partisan rangers or runaways—horseless dragoons and would be cavalry out upon the poor farmers of the county—to seize the best of the few remaining horses that they have to cultivate their crops." One Georgia woman complained bitterly that "the country is plum full of Cavalry . . . stealing all the time."[9]

As early as the summer of 1862, Virginia's *Richmond Examiner* reported the widespread feeling that the *"Yankees cannot do us any more harm than our own soldiers have done."* John Hagan, a south Georgia soldier, confirmed that assertion in a letter to his wife: "I believe our troops are doing as much harm in this country as the Yankees . . . and in fact where this army goes the people is ruined." He was certain that the Confederacy could never survive while handling its own people so badly.[10]

Plain folk bore the brunt of impressment, since they were easier targets than the more influential planters. And small farmers were more likely to grow food products, which was what the impressment officers most often wanted. For the planters, old habits were hard to break. They continued to devote much of their land to cotton while soldiers and their families went hungry. During the course of the war, planters committed the manpower equivalent of the entire Confederate army to cotton production.[11]

In the spring of 1862, a southwest Georgia man wrote to Governor Joe Brown about planters growing too much cotton and begged him to "stop those internal enemies of the country, for they will whip us sooner than all Lincolndom combined could do it." Most states put limits on raising cotton, but enforcement was lax and planters often ignored the law. Thousands of planters and merchants defied the Confederacy's cotton export restrictions and smuggled it out by the ton. With prices on the rise, many cotton producers and dealers were getting richer than ever. Some bragged that the longer the war went on, the more money they made.[12]

The inevitable result of cotton overproduction was a severe food shortage that hit women of the plain folk especially hard.[13] With their husbands off at the front and impressment officers taking what little they had, it was difficult for soldiers' wives to provide for themselves and their children. Planters had promised to keep soldiers' families fed, but they never grew enough food to meet the need. Much of what food they did produce was sold to speculators, who priced it beyond the reach of most plain folk. Desperate to avoid starvation, many women turned to stealing. As early as 1862, food riots began breaking out all over the South. Gangs of hungry women—many of them armed—ransacked stores, depots, and supply wagons searching for anything edible. Major urban centers like Richmond and Mobile saw the biggest riots. In Georgia, riots erupted in all the larger cities—Atlanta, Columbus, Macon, Augusta, and Savannah. Even smaller towns like Valdosta and Colquitt saw hungry women rioting for food.

In an open letter to the *Savannah Morning News,* one enraged Georgian was sure of where the blame lay. "The crime is with the planters ... as a class, they have yielded their patriotism, if they ever had any, to covetousness ... for the sake of money, they are pursuing a course to destroy or demoralize our army—to starve out the other class dependent on them for provisions." The letter spoke for a great many plain folk. It seemed increasingly obvious to them that they were fighting a rich man's war, which made the problem of desertion that much worse. One Confederate officer wrote home to his wife that "discontent is growing rapidley in the ranks and I fear that unless something is done . . . we will have no army. The laws that have been passed generally protect the rich, and the poor begin to say it is the rich man's war and the poor man's fight, and they will not stand it."[14]

Desertion became so serious by the summer of 1863 that Jefferson Davis begged absentees to return. If only they would, he insisted, the Confederacy could match Union armies man for man. But the soldiers did not return. Just over a year later, in September 1864, Davis admitted that "two-thirds of our men are absent . . . most of them without leave." Among Georgia troops alone, as many as 60 percent or more had deserted outright.[15]

Some deserters joined antiwar organizations that had been active in the South since the war's beginning. The Peace and Constitutional Society worked to undermine Confederate authority in Arkansas, as did the Order of the Heroes of America in southern Appalachia. Perhaps the largest such organization was the Peace Society, which was centered in Alabama and included members in Mississippi, Tennessee, Georgia, and Florida. Historian Walter Fleming estimated that by 1863 at least half of Alabama's able-bodied men were associated with the Peace Society. Antiwar sentiment was felt at the polls that year all across the South. Two-thirds of the Second Confederate Congress's newly elected members had opposed secession.[16]

Deserters also joined with draft dodgers and other anti-Confederates to form guerrilla bands, often called tory, or layout, gangs. They attacked government supply trains, burned bridges, raided local plantations, and harassed impressment agents and conscript officers. This internal civil war became so violent by 1863 that the editor of Milledgeville's *Confederate Union* wrote: "We are fighting each other harder than we ever fought the enemy." Three months later, another Georgian wrote to Governor Brown, "It is a certain fact that the Southern people are fast becoming as bitterly divided against each other as the Southern and Northern people ever has been." The man concluded his observations by insisting: "I have not written this letter to exaggerate these things. I only write such as I know to be true."[17]

Tory gangs were most active in the southern hill country and pine barrens, where they all but eliminated Confederate control by 1864. The piney woods of south Georgia and the mountains of north Georgia served as secure havens for those resisting the Confederacy, as did the Red River Valley of Texas and Louisiana. The same was true of Jackson County, Alabama, which seceded from the Confederacy and rejoined the Union in March 1864.

In southeastern Mississippi, Newton Knight led unionist guerrillas who controlled much of Jones County. They burned bridges, ran off impressment agents, and ambushed Confederate patrols. For much of the war, Knight and his men ruled the local countryside, popularly known as the "Kingdom of Jones." Years after the war, a neighbor recalled Knight's motives. Knight was, he said, "a poor man and didn't own any Negroes. . . . He felt that the [twenty-slave] law wasn't fair; that it enabled the rich man to evade service and that it wasn't right to ask him to risk his life for people who rated themselves so far above him."[18]

Louisiana's James Madison Wells, though a man of means himself, denounced the Confederate cause as a rich man's war and organized a guerrilla campaign against Confederate authority. From his Bear Wallow stronghold, Wells repeatedly led deserters and tories in raids against Confederate supply lines and depots. Joseph Sanders, leader of a tory outfit in southeast Alabama, made his anti-Confederate status official by accepting a lieutenant's commission in the U.S. Army.[19]

Compelling as it is, evidence of such widespread southern disunity has had a depressingly slight impact on the Civil War's popular image. In the audio-visual realm, the films *Tap Roots* (1948) and *Shenandoah* (1965) and the television miniseries *The Blue and the Gray* (1982) stand almost alone in suggesting that there were southerners who opposed the war. Such works continue to be overshadowed by *Gone with the Wind* (1939) and more recent popular productions like *North and South, Book 2* (1986) and *Gettysburg* (1993), all presenting an image of southern unity.

Much-applauded documentaries have done little better. *Civil War Journal* (1994–95) devoted not one of its many episodes to southern dissent. Despite the involvement of historians who surely knew better, the series posed no threat to the southern unity myth. Nor did Ken Burns's *The Civil War* (1990), one of public television's most celebrated events. Such ventures typically challenge few popular myths of any kind, which, to a great extent, accounts for their popularity.

Our fallacious popular image of Civil War America stems not only from a reluctance to deal frankly with class issues past or present but also in large part from an overemphasis on the war's military and political aspects. Studies of these aspects are crucial, to be sure. But focusing so much of our collective attention on battles and leaders tends to foster the myth of sectional unity, North and South, and to minimize dissent or to ignore it altogether. With their whimsical vignettes that purported to give a "common man's" view of the war but that failed to explore dissent among plain folk, Ken Burns and his associates only contributed to that problem.

Even in scholarly circles, which are immune neither to the influences of popular culture nor to market forces, the problem persists. Indeed, in recent years, several best-selling Civil War historians have gone out of their way to marginalize the impact of southern disunity.[20] Yet disunity and its class basis were clear to southerners during the war and were the subject of much contemporary discussion. After his army's engagement at Murfreesboro, Private Stephen Rutledge of the Army of Tennessee asked in his journal: "What is gained anyway? It is a rich man's war and a poor man's fight at best." Such attitudes contributed decisively to Confederate defeat, and some predicted early on that they would. Georgia native and Confederate senator Benjamin Hill warned before the conflict began that a divided South could not possibly triumph. Atlanta's *Southern Confederacy* was just as blunt in the fall of 1862: "If we are defeated, it will be by the people at home."[21] And so the Confederacy was defeated—not simply by Union armies but by arrogant planters, speculating merchants, corrupt officials, and by disaffected plain folk.

Perhaps nowhere can the divisive role of the southern class system be viewed more clearly than in South's keystone state of Georgia. Primarily an agricultural region, its population ran the socioeconomic scale from planters and lesser slaveholders down through landed yeoman farmers to landless tenant farmers and slaves. In addition to the rural farming folk, there were merchants, factory workers, skilled artisans and craftsmen, urban professionals, and industrial entrepreneurs. Most studies of Confederate defeat have focused on military strategy and tactics. But examining what went on behind the lines and the impact it had on plain folk attitudes can tell us even more about why the Civil War ended as it did.

1

"This Fuss Was All for the Benefit of the Wealthy"

Secession and Dissent

By 1860, Georgia was among the Cotton Kingdom's most prosperous states. But that prosperity was by no means shared by all its people. Many lived in conditions that were regarded even at the time as abject poverty. Of Georgia's one million residents, nearly half were slaves. The great majority of the state's free inhabitants were directly engaged in agriculture, but only half owned three or more acres of land. Most of the rest were tenant farmers, sharecroppers, or day laborers, all working land owned by someone else. A majority of landholders owned slaves, but two-thirds held fewer than ten. Many of these small slaveholders worked the fields along with their slaves and had a lifestyle not so different from that of nonslaveholding yeomen. It was mainly the planters and their families who benefited significantly from an economic system dominated by cotton and slavery. This planter class made up just 3 percent of Georgia's population.[1]

In the years after the Civil War, the planter image transcended fact to become potent popular myth. Romantically nostalgic films such as *Gone with the Wind* represent a Lost Cause cult that imagines the Old South as something of a cotton Camelot. If cotton was king, then the planter was its knight errant, sworn to protect the virtues of the kingdom. Beneath this image lay the less virtuous realitites of black enslavement, Indian dispossession, and plain folk oppression. Throughout the early nineteenth century, at the expense of the many, southern agricultural wealth became increasingly concentrated in the hands of a relative few.

Much of the planters' landholding gains of the 1840s to the 1860s came in the wake of the Panic of 1837, an economic upheaval that left only the most financially stable in continuing prosperity. Cotton prices fell dramatically and continued falling. Aspiring yeomen found it impossible to keep up with loan payments. Their land and slaves were repossessed and sold at auction, usually to wealthy planters. Some farmers were able to hold on to a few acres; others lost everything and fell into tenancy and sharecropping. When the cotton market finally recovered in the 1840s, affluent slaveholders held most of the Deep South's better agricultural land. By that time, most farmers found themselves trapped in a system of poverty from which there was little hope of escape.[2]

The gap between rich and poor continued to grow through the 1850s not only in Georgia but throughout the South. Planters bought up more and more land, forcing a rapid rise in land prices and making it nearly impossible for smaller farmers to increase their holdings or for sharecroppers to buy any land at all. Wealth in terms of slaveholding was also becoming concentrated in fewer hands. During the last decade of the antebellum period, the proportion of slaveholders in the free population dropped by 20 percent. Only the distribution of land and slaves to the heirs of deceased slaveholders kept social mobility from being far more limited than it was. By 1860, the 10 percent of people with the highest incomes in the cotton states held 53 percent of the region's agricultural wealth. The bottom half owned only 5 percent.[3]

For the most part, plain folk grudgingly accepted their socioeconomic status, but tensions were rarely far from the surface. Historian William Freehling, in a passage from his *Road to Disunion*, expresses those tensions well. A fictional account compiled from various nonfictional sources, Freehling's scene has a poor dirt farmer riding up the drive of a wealthy planter. The broad lane occupies more land than many farmers' cornfields, and the slave cabins that line it are little worse than the farmer's own home. After a brief discussion of politics, crops, and health, the two compare their plans for the day.

> *Oh, reckon this day will be like most days,* the planter answered. *Be directin' blacks and greetin' neighbors. In between, guess I'll read up yonder where it's cooler. Way nature meant it. Whites readin' and conversin' and*

directin' and blacks laborin' and sweatin' and servin'. Couldn't pay a white man to tolerate that blazin' sun. Nor could I pay a white man's daughter to suffer my boilin' ketchin.

The yeoman choked back rage. He stood the sun. Laboring fueled his dreams. *Ain't nothing nigger about sweatin'*, he thought. *And ain't nothing nigger about my darlin' cookin'.*

The planter's voice drawled on, slicing through such angry thoughts. *Gonna be readin' one of them fanatic's books today. Full of isms up north—anarchism and free-love ism. Crazy meddlers, think they're better than other folks. Think they can tell us how we should live. Think they can make niggers as wonderful as themselves.*

The yeoman nodded, resentments swerving. *Glad you gwine read it*, he said. *Don't know which I hate worse, a fanatic or a nigger. How'd you like to hev a nigger steppin' up to your darter?*

The slaveholder, relieved, smiled and waved farewell. *Wonder why he gave me that dark look*, the planter mused while watching the yeoman drive off. *Had a funny look when he first came too. Thank heavens these fellas are usually friendly. With a whole world invading, white folk can't be fussing.*[4]

But the pressures of war amplified class tensions and led to a good deal of "fussing" among whites—more, it turned out, than the Confederacy could withstand.

From the onset of secession, opinions of the crisis were mixed among the plain folk. Those who held a few slaves certainly saw Lincoln as a potential threat, despite his insistence to the contrary. And for lesser yeomen and poor whites, though they owned no slaves, they still had their racist pride. Would Lincoln really try to free the slaves, as secessionists claimed? Governor Joe Brown of Georgia, self-proclaimed friend of the common man, said it was true. Brown warned that poor whites would suffer more than planters if Lincoln ended slavery. Former slaves would, Brown insisted, "come into competition with [poor whites], associate with them and their children as equals—be allowed to testify in court against them—sit on juries with them, march to the ballot box by their sides, and participate in the choice of their rulers—claim social equality with them—and ask the hands of their children in marriage." Was this really Lincoln's intent? Of course, said Brown. The ultimate aim of the "Black Republican party" was to set the slaves free and place them on an equal footing with whites.[5]

Still, some plain folk were leery of secessionist motives. For years they had been told to think of themselves as the planter's equal. Joe Brown said they belonged "to the only true aristocracy, the race of *white men*."⁶ Kinship ties across class lines frequently reinforced that point. But the fact remained that plain folk did not live as planters' equals, and by the 1850s they could hardly hope to do so. Most blamed the planters themselves for that. It was just as clear to yeomen and poor whites that planters, no matter what they said in public, did not view them as equals.

Many planters, especially those from "old money" families, had indeed come to view themselves as aristocrats and the poor whites as little better than slaves. One planter, in a private letter to a friend, wrote of the poor whites, "not one in ten is . . . a whit superior to a negro."⁷ Most planters tried to keep such opinions concealed lest their hypocrisy be exposed. Occasionally, though, suggestions of planter arrogance slipped into print. In his 1854 defense of slavery, *Sociology for the South, or the Failure of Free Society*, George Fitzhugh insisted not only that slavery was "the best form of society yet devised for the masses" but also "that slavery, *black or white*, was right and necessary."⁸ Could white slavery be just around the corner? Some poor whites were beginning to think it might be. To many of them it seemed that one way or the other, whether under Republican or planter rule, they were condemned to occupy the lowest rung of the social ladder right along with slaves.

In 1849, a Georgia carpenter openly declared his opposition to slavery. Competition with slave labor, he believed, kept his wages low. In 1859, one poor Hancock County laborer confided to an acquaintance that if it came to a war over slavery, he was going to "black himself" and fight to end it. Without slavery, perhaps he could get better wages. That same year, a farmer in Taliaferro County was convicted of hiding a runaway slave for three months. The next year, yet another in Greene County was found making fake passes for slaves and "teaching them to write and cipher."⁹

Such class animosities had been building for some time. By the 1850s, despite their racist fears, resentment among nonslaveholders toward the slave system was on the rise. Hinton Rowan Helper, son of a poor North Carolina farmer, most forcefully expressed that resentment in his 1857 book, *Impending Crisis of the South*. Slavery, he pointed out, benefited only the few. Even worse, it suppressed industrial development, making the South little more than a colony of the North and keeping most southerners in poverty.

Could growing numbers of people like Helper be potential recruits for the Republican Party? Slaveholders dreaded the thought. One planter asked nervously, "If the poor whites realized that slavery kept them poor, would they not vote it down?" With Lincoln in the White House and discontent among southern plain folk on the rise, a truly national Republican Party might become a reality. One defender of slavery warned that there might soon be "an Abolition party in the South, of Southern men." Another frankly admitted, "I mistrust our own people more than I fear all of the efforts of the Abolitionists."[10]

And what of the slaves themselves? Though they argued otherwise, slaveholders knew very well that slavery did not come naturally to those of African descent. Slaves escaped; they resisted; they had to be controlled through fear and violence. Slaves wanted to be set free, and they believed Lincoln would do just that. How could they think otherwise with secessionists trumpeting throughout the South that Lincoln's ultimate goal was to free them? One freedman remembered that slaves had "hoped and prayed he would be elected. They wanted to be free and have a chance."[11] How much more difficult might controlling slaves be with Lincoln in the White House and expectations for freedom running so high?

More than the abolitionists, more than Lincoln himself, planters feared the South's plain folk and slaves. Control of both groups had always been hard. By the 1850s it was getting harder. A Lincoln presidency could only make it more difficult. Most planters feared that if the cotton states remained in the Union, their "peculiar institution" would be threatened. Outside the Union, controlling the lower classes might be easier and slavery might be safer. Other factors certainly helped fuel the crisis. Overestimation of abolitionist strength in the North, the issue of slavery's expansion, and personal political ambitions all played their part. But slaveholders' fear of their fellow southerners was a primary, though publicly unacknowledged, force driving secession.[12]

Even so, slaveholders were far from united behind the movement. Though most were disturbed by Lincoln's promise to end slavery's expansion, wealthier and more conservative "old money" planters tended to view secession as much more risky than remaining in the Union. With a greater stake in preserving the status quo, they tended to be more cautious than lesser slaveholders. Should withdrawal from the Union lead to civil war, success would depend on widespread support from the lower classes. Many planters wondered how long that support could last. Secession might actually hasten the end of slavery rather than preserve it.

This danger seemed clear enough to men like Alexander Stephens and Benjamin Hill, two of Georgia's leading planter/politicians. Stephens warned that, dependent as a southern government would be on plain folk, slaveholders could lose their grip on the course of events: "The movement will before it ends I fear be beyond the control of those who started it." Hill was just as certain that a divided South could not survive a civil war. The southern government would fall and slavery with it.[13]

Secession found its most enthusiastic support among the more numerous "new money" planters and lesser slaveholders. Their leaders were young up-and-coming lawyer/politicians trying to carve out a niche for themselves at the expense of the older establishment. Few were more ambitious than Columbus's Henry Benning. Young mavericks like Benning took up secession's banner and—to the dismay of more conservative colleagues—carried it high throughout the 1850s. It was this division of opinion among Georgia's most prominent politicians that set the stage for intense controversy over the issue of secession.

On November 20, 1860, less than two weeks after Lincoln's election, Governor Brown signed a bill calling for the election of delegates to Georgia's secession convention. Balloting took place on January 2, 1861, with the convention meeting two weeks later at Milledgeville, the state capital. Stumping for delegates began almost immediately after the bill passed, and it became clear that secession was not a foregone conclusion. Those who opposed it, who adopted the label *cooperationists*, held rallies throughout the state urging restraint among their fellow citizens.[14] Citizens at a "large meeting" in Crawfordville resolved that "we do not consider the election of Lincoln and [Hannibal] Hamlin as sufficient cause for Disunion or Secession." A mass meeting in Walker County expressed the same sentiment: "We are not of the opinion that the election of any man in accordance with the prescribed forms of the Constitution is sufficient cause to disrupt the ties which binds us to the Union." Rallies in Fayette, Gordon, Chattooga, Talbot, Meriwether, and many other Georgia counties declared the same.[15]

Harris County's local newspaper editor firmly stated that "we are a Union loving people here, and will never forsake the old 'Star Spangled Banner.'" To stress his point, he printed the names of 175 local men, all pledging themselves to "preserve the honor and rights of the South *in the Union.*" In Stewart County, a similarly "large number of citizens" attended an antisecession meeting. Union sentiment was so strong in neighboring Randolph County that secessionists were sure that the tide was turning against them. In a letter to Howell Cobb, one of the state's leading secessionists, they asked: "Where are all our speakers? We have done what little we can here but there is great need for missionaries [of secession] in every part of the State." They urged Cobb to take a short tour through southwest Georgia to bolster the secession cause. By late December, it appeared that antisecessionists might win the day. "All the masses of the people," wrote one Georgian, "are for the Union."[16]

On January 2, Georgia voters went to the polls to choose convention delegates. Accurate returns were hard to obtain, but within a few days the *Athens Southern Watchman* declared antisecessionists the victors "by a considerable majority." In fact, the popular vote was very close, with a likely majority of 42,744 opposing secession to 41,717 supporting it. That figure probably falls far short of expressing the antisecession feeling of Georgia's electorate. Voter participation was surprisingly low considering the gravity of the issue involved. Turnout was more than twenty-one thousand (20 percent) below that of the previous November's presidential election. Perhaps because of the cold and rain, voting was heaviest in and around urban areas, where opinions tended to favor secession. Alexander Stephens estimated that the bad weather cost antisecessionists at least ten thousand votes.[17]

There was an even more basic concern about how democratic the initial delegate nominating process had been. Some charged outright fraud. Shortly before the convention met, one furious voter accused Singleton Sisk, a Missionary Baptist minister, of cheating Habersham County out of its vote. In an open letter to the *Athens Southern Watchman*, he told how this "janus-faced expounder of the Gospel" had declared himself a Union man to gain the nomination of Habersham's antisecessionists. With their backing, Sisk was elected to the convention. "After the election, we find that he had privately promised the Secessionists that he would, in the Convention, support Secession." Sisk indeed betrayed his constituents and backed secession at the convention. Similar betrayals occurred among the representatives of at least twenty-eight other Georgia counties. In Campbell County, the fraud was so transparent that some who went to the polls declined to vote for any candidate.[18]

As early as December 22, 1860, a disgusted Thomaston editor complained bitterly that Georgia voters would not have a truly representative state convention:

> We do not believe that the character of the sentiments of a majority of the Convention will reflect the wishes of a majority of the people.

The delegates appear to be nominated by mass conventions assembled at the county sites; and it is plain that not half of the citizens attend these nominations. But few men living ten or fifteen miles from [the] county site go to such conventions . . . and as it is an admitted fact that the secession sentiment is much stronger in and around the cities than it is among the common people in the country, it is easy to see the advantage the "immediate secessionist" will have in the Convention.[19]

When the convention met at Milledgeville, Eugenius A. Nisbet proposed a test prosecession resolution to gauge the feeling of the delegates. Enough delegates who had been elected on a promise to vote against secession were enticed by the promise of "a slave republic" to pass the resolution by a vote of 166 to 130. The next day, with more delegates switching sides, the convention approved a secession ordinance 208 to 89. It could hardly have been surprising that the convention ultimately went for secession despite the popular vote. While little more than a third of Georgia's electorate owned slaves, 87 percent of the convention delegates were slaveholders. Setting down its justifications for secession, the convention listed first and foremost "causes of complaint . . . in reference to the subject of African slavery."[20]

In speaking for the secessionist cause just after Lincoln's election, Francis Bartow, a member of the General Assembly, had threatened "civil war in Georgia" if the convention did not vote to leave the Union. Robert Toombs had likewise expressed his determination to see Georgia out of the Union whether a majority of the people supported the move or not. "Give me the sword!" he demanded of his fellow Georgians. "But if you do not place it in my hands, before God *I will take it!*" Responding to Toombs's threat, an antisecession newspaper editor in Upson County wrote, "Let him take it, and, by way of doing his country a great service, let him run about six inches of it into his left breast." Such expressions of contempt for the fire-eaters were all in vain. By the time the convention met, Toombs, Bartow, and their powerful secessionist allies were so well organized that it was too late to stop them.[21]

After the final convention vote, the remaining unionist convention delegates insisted that the secession ordinance be ratified by a vote of the people. In calling for popular ratification, an Augusta editor reminded the delegates that previous conventions recommending alterations of the state constitution had sought the people's approval by ratification. But this convention's secessionist majority, sure that the people would overturn its decision, refused. Georgia, like the other seceding states, left the Union without submitting the issue to direct popular vote.[22] In February, Georgia representatives met with others from the Deep South in Montgomery, Alabama, to form the Confederate States of America.

News of secession and the Confederacy's formation touched off celebrations across Georgia and the South. But not everyone saw these developments as cause for celebration. For some it was a time of sober reflection. One Georgia man said of the merrymakers: "Poor fools! They may ring their bells now, but they will wring their hands—yes, and their hearts, too—before they are done with it."[23]

The question of whether secession would result in civil war had been on the minds of Georgians for months. In an open letter, a Decatur County man was so sure war would come that he referred to secessionists as "the suicides." Others were just as certain that they were nothing of the sort. The *Albany Patriot* assured its readers that the Yankees would never dare make war on the South: "In all honesty we can say to our readers, be not afraid. We will insure the life of every southern man from being killed in war by the abolitionists for a postage stamp." The editor of Upson County's *Pilot* was not sure what the outcome of secession might be, but he was glad his county had gone against it: "If the demon of civil war is to ravage our fields only to fertilize them with blood—we know our Upson Delegates will be able, at the last dread account, to stand up with clean hands and pure hearts and exclaim through no chattering teeth from coward consciences:—*'Thou canst not say we did it!'*"[24]

Uncertainty about the end result of secession reflected general ambivalence toward a military option. Common folk, North and South, were by no means eager for war in March 1861. But Lincoln was under intense pressure from his financial backers and other northern industrialists to keep the cotton states in the Union, by compromise if possible—by force if necessary. How else could they guarantee continued access to southern markets and cheap cotton?[25] The *Boston Herald* warned that the Confederacy would "impose a heavy tax upon the manufactures of the North, and an export tax upon the cotton used by northern manufacturers. In this way she would seek to cripple the North."[26]

Such arguments carried little weight among the northern working classes. Many of them had nothing against slavery in the South, only its expansion outside the South. Some were glad to be free of their political ties to the obstinate slaveholders. They certainly had no desire to put their lives in danger trying to hold the cotton states by force. One newspaper in Rochester, New York, reported on the difficulties officers had in getting recruits despite the availability of unemployed, able-bodied men by the thousands. "We hear a great deal of talk," said the editors, "among the ardent platform republicans about coercing the secessionists of the South by means of Northern soldiers, but the indications are that the fighting is to be done mostly with the tongue."[27]

How could Lincoln get the men he needed to make war on the Confederacy with such attitudes so prevalent? A military draft was out of the question; popular reaction might mean the end of the Republican Party. Lincoln considered issuing a call for volunteers, but that too was unrealistic. Not only would it be likely to drive more slave states out of the Union, it would also be political suicide in the free states. What Lincoln needed was an incident to fire northern patriotism and draw volunteers to the army. On April 12, 1861, the Confederate government gave him just what he needed by firing on the federal garrison at Fort Sumter.

When Lincoln subsequently called for volunteers to put down the rebellion by force, four more slave states—Arkansas, Tennessee, North Carolina, and Virginia—signed on with the Confederacy. Displays of southern unity were common on the local level too. In Georgia's Early County, Democrats and Whigs held a mass meeting on the Blakely town square, where they "buried the political hatchet." Judge James Bush, speaking for the Democrats, and Colonel James Buchannon, representing the Whigs, together promised an end to local political bickering. Henceforth all their efforts would be devoted to opposing the Yankees instead of each other. Near the close of the meeting, Judge Bush dug a hole under the courthouse steps in which he buried a hatchet to symbolically cement the agreement.[28]

In the wake of Sumter and Lincoln's call for an invasion, so many southern men rushed to military service that the Confederacy could not arm them all. Thousands of volunteers had to provide their own weapons or secure the backing of wealthy patrons. Like most Georgia units, the Miller County Wildcats were left to arm themselves "with every death-dealing instrument that could be procured." Each man carried a bowie knife along with an old rifle or shotgun. One elderly man who had tried without success to talk his son out of going to war finally gave in and presented him with what was surely a prized possession—a single-barrel shotgun. "I don't want any war," the old man told his boy, "but if you will go, here's old Betsy; take her and give the Yankees hell."[29]

Several factors account for the widespread surge of volunteering, fear of Yankee invasion among them. There was also regional identity, peer pressure, and a sense of adventure.[30] Many believed that the Yankees meant to free the slaves and grant them equality. Whatever their misgivings about the planters, most plain folk wanted none of that. Thousands of them took up arms to preserve their relative social status in the spring and summer of 1861. By May 7, Georgia alone had furnished over eighteen thousand volunteers for Confederate service, second only to Virginia.[31]

Even as mass volunteering and general excitement swept the country, there were signs that widespread support for the war, and for the Confederacy itself, might not last long. When vigilantes led by Harrison W. Riley threatened to seize the U.S. mint in Dahlonega and hold it for the Union, Governor Brown sent no troops to stop them. He knew sentiment in the region was with Riley and his gang. Union men in Pickens County flew the U.S. flag in front of the courthouse for weeks after secession. Randolph L. Mott of Columbus, a longtime Union man, kept the Stars and Stripes flying from the cupola of his home throughout the war. Some said it was the only place in Georgia that had never been out of the Union.[32]

Expressing popular sentiment in northwest Georgia's Walker and Dade counties, James Aiken wrote Governor Brown in February 1861 insisting that he and his neighbors would never submit to the secession convention's decision. The secession convention had taken Georgia out of the Union not for the good of its citizens, but for "those that owns lands and Negroes!" He begged the governor to allow Georgia voters to decide the issue directly, promising to abide by the outcome. But if Brown refused, there were 2,500 volunteers prepared to defend northwest Georgia's right to secede from the state and rejoin the Union. "If we cannot get it one way," he warned, "we know how we can get it at the point of the bayonet and the muzzle of the musket. We are just as willing as you ever seen mountain boys." Another Walker County man confirmed that there was talk of raising a company there "to defend the glorious Union."[33]

In nearby Cass (later Bartow) County, one citizen wrote a letter to Abraham Lincoln promising that local Union men were "ready to shoulder our guns" against secession. He estimated that sixty thousand other Georgians would do the same. Several men in the east Georgia county of Emanuel made it clear that they were among that number, saying they "would join Lincoln's army if it came to the push." From Fannin County

FIGURE 1.1. Despite the wave of volunteering that swept through Georgia in the spring of 1861, many young men were not eager to go to war. An item appeared in the May 27, 1861, issue of the *Columbus Sun* noting that to embarrass the reluctant, a group of well-to-do young women in the city had formed a Ladies' Home Guard for the "special protection of young men who have concluded to remain at home." (*Frank Leslie's Illustrated Newspaper*)

came word that "quite a number" there were prepared to defend the old flag and help "whip Georgia and the South back into the Union." The correspondent left no doubt what lay behind Fannin men's unionism: "They are not interested in the nigger question, [and believe] that this fuss was all for the benefit of the wealthy."[34]

Already some of Georgia's Union men were perpetrating violence against secession's symbol, if not against secessionists themselves. In the coastal town of Darien, M. B. Holland fired on the first Confederate flag raised there. So hostile were many Georgians and other southerners to secession that an Augusta editor warned in February 1861, "The greatest danger to the new Confederacy arises not from without, not from the North, but from our own people."[35]

Some Georgians who were not prepared to take up arms against secession still expressed doubts about its legitimacy. Governor Brown did not announce the results of the January 2 vote for convention delegates until late April, and that was only at the insistence of concerned voters. Even then he lied about the figures. Brown insisted that the secessionists had won by over thirteen thousand votes, when in fact they were almost certainly defeated by a margin of just over a thousand.[36]

With the Confederacy an established fact, most southerners were more concerned about how the war might affect the South in general, and themselves in particular, if it did not end quickly. The consequences of an extended conflict were evident enough to those on the front lines. In August 1861, when soldiers of the Fifteenth Alabama Regiment—many of whom were from southwest Georgia—arrived in Virginia and visited Manassas a month after the battle, they found hundreds of shallow graves scattered over the fields. Rain had washed much of the dirt away, and skeletal remains protruded from the ground. Hogs were feeding on the dead.[37]

It was not what the young men had expected to find. Few, in the immediate post-Sumter excitement, had allowed themselves to imagine what the horrors of war might really be like. But after Manassas, the soldiers had no choice. Little wonder that some soldiers, especially those from nonslaveholding families, began to reexamine their motives for volunteering. In late July, just ten days after Manassas, Joel Crawford, an enlisted man from Quitman County, wrote Governor Brown asking, "if after the signing of a written instrument binding the signer to go to the present war, if any signer thereof has the legal right to withdraw his name."[38]

Officers, who frequently came from the slaveholding ranks, did not have to ask. They could simply resign their commissions, and many did. On August 10, 1861, J. A. Maxwell of Blakely did just that in a one-sentence note to Georgia's adjutant general. In October, William Wood wrote home to Georgia from the Virginia front: "a great many of our commissioned officers are resigning and going home. . . . others say they will resign before they will stay . . . through the Winter." The option of resignation was not open to enlisted personnel.[39]

Such class distinctions were not lost on the men in the ranks, and the uneven treatment took its toll on morale. "The temper of the army is not good," wrote one Georgian from Virginia during the winter of 1861–62. "The troops widely feel the unjust oppression and partial hand that is laid upon them, and in my opinion the spirit of the army is dying." Corporal James Atkins of the Twelfth Georgia Regiment, also stationed in Virginia, clearly reflected the army's declining morale. After months of enduring oppression, he wrote in December 1861 that "reflection has modified my expressed view of patriotism." He had come to feel that it was "a strange virtue that clings to mere soil and in its defense will take the life of the dearest relatives; yet such is patriotism—*the love of dirt*." Four months later, Atkins deserted.[40]

Atkins was far from alone in taking the enlisted man's way out. Many did not wait as long as Atkins had. Some reluctant Johnny Rebs deserted even before the fighting began. In March 1861, four months before the war's first major battle at Manassas, two Marietta volunteers "took it into their heads to forego the honor and glory of serving the Confederate States upon the tented field, and without so much as saying to the officer in charge, 'By your leave,' took the back track from Griffin to Atlanta." In May, three men of Georgia's Second Infantry Regiment decided army life was not for them and headed home. Their commander offered thirty dollars each for their return. A month later in Virginia, two members of the Macon Volunteers deserted to the Yankees.[41]

Those who went home on legitimate leave often failed to return. In December 1861, one Augusta paper reported on the "undisputed fact that many of our volunteers, who come home on furlough to spend a few days or weeks, although in excellent health when they arrive, are taken ill while here." The editor speculated that perhaps "the change from the hardy habits of life in camp to the comparative ease and indolence of home, acts badly upon the system."[42]

Hundreds were leaving the ranks, and there were almost no new recruits to take their places. The volunteering boom of spring 1861 went bust by the fall. In October, word came from Greene County to the governor's office that "our people don't seem to be inclined to offer their services." That same month, Captain Edward Croft of the Columbus Artillery reported that it was almost impossible to find volunteers. In February 1862, W. H. Byrd of Augusta wrote to Governor Brown that he had been trying for two weeks to raise a company in what he called "this 'Yankee City,' but I regret to say every effort has failed." That failure did not result from a lack of potential recruits. The *Augusta Chronicle and Sentinel* noted a week earlier that "one who walks Broad street and sees the number of young men, would come to the conclusion that no war . . . was now waging."[43]

From rural Brooks County in south Georgia, C. S. Gaulden reported that "several large families of young men in this county have not sent out soldiers." F. S. Johnson of middle Georgia's Jones County wondered "how are the men to be got? . . . I have within a few days heard men say they would not go to the war; they had nothing to fight for and they would not go."[44]

Those who had slaves to fight for were just as reluctant to put their lives on the line. And the more slaves they had, the less willing they seemed to be. Some wealthy planters did lead front line units early in the war, and a few died in combat. But most were content to remain safe at home, especially after Fort Sumter made it clear that the conflict would be more than a war of words. Just a week after Sumter, the *Rome Tri-Weekly Courier* published an open letter from "One of the People," who reported that "there has been a withdrawing from the volunteer companies of men who have done their best to destroy this union." One Georgian who was himself a slaveholder chastised members of his class who were "doing nothing for the cause on which their *all* of earthly good depends. Surely such are slumbering over their interests or supinely hoping somebody will do their fighting for them."[45]

In spring of 1862, when the planters of Putnam County drew up a resolution calling on soldiers from the area to reenlist for the war's duration, the soldiers responded with a resolution of their own. "We are truly glad that those 'Planters' have at last waked up to the necessities of the times, and we only regret that they did not feel the same interest in their country when we were beating up for volunteers in their midst." They concluded by asking, "Can't the '*Planters*' of Putnam be induced, for their sakes, to come down and take our places for a short time while we go home to look after our *farms?*"⁴⁶

Men in the ranks became increasingly aware that their personal sacrifices were likely to be much greater than those of the southern elites. This class disparity became clear early on when the Confederate government, lacking weapons enough for all its volunteers, allowed those who could provide their own to enlist for only one year instead of three. That meant purchasing the expensive .577 caliber Enfield rifles, which few common soldiers could afford. Most volunteers were not informed until they reached the front lines that their shotguns and squirrel rifles would not do for military service. Many poor soldiers found that their one-year enlistments had suddenly turned into three. As historian Paul Escott put it, "the price of being a patriot was higher for the common man than for the rich man, three times higher to be exact." One volunteer unit, the Mountain Rangers of Meriwether County, would not pay that price. They refused to be enlisted beyond one year and disbanded in June 1861 before being mustered into service.⁴⁷

The price of service was equally high for families left behind. Interdependent as most women and children were on their menfolk, how would they survive without them? Who would work small farmers' land? Planters had little worry there. Aside from the fact that few were enlisting, their plantations were worked by slaves. As for taxes, they were going up on everything except slaves. As the 1861 state elections approached, these issues were uppermost in the minds of plain folk. In September, voters who signed themselves "Many Anxious to Hear" addressed an open letter to candidates of Floyd County:

> Please give your views concerning our present condition—about the war, and the cause of the war . . . and our present condition of taxation for the support of the war. Is it right that the poor man should be taxed for the support of the war, when the war was brought about on the slave question, and the slave at home accumulating for the benefit of his master, and the poor man's farm left uncultivated, and a chance for his wife to be a widow, and his children orphans? Now, in justice, would it not be right to levy a direct tax on the species of property that brought about the war, to support it?

A week later, the editor apologized for printing the letter, saying that this kind of talk might cause class division.⁴⁸ In fact, such letters did not cause division but simply expressed an underlying class resentment that had long been there.

With regard to help for soldiers' families, there were almost no relief agencies in Georgia. The few there were could hardly begin to cope with the rapid rise in destitution. As early as January 1861, one citizen raised the issue of soldiers' impoverished families in a letter to the *Macon Telegraph*: "Most of the members of the 'Jackson Artillery' have families. . . . Shall they suffer?" Like so many others, a Columbus man named Ogletree left his wife and three children "unprovided for" when he joined the army in April. One local newspaper insisted that such a price was too high for any family to pay and asked Columbus citizens to help with relief.[49]

Nor did planters seem to appreciate the sacrifices their poorer neighbors were making. From the heart of Georgia's cotton belt came a letter in May 1861 expressing a class resentment that signaled things to come. A Fort Valley woman wrote Governor Brown complaining bitterly of class disparities in the army and at home: "It appears that all the poor from here has gone and the rich remains who has the slaves. It is those in this place that has remain home who is benifited after the war. It is the rich. They have no mercy on the soldiers familys." Brown had assured Georgia's men that no soldier's family would suffer on account of military service; planters across the state had promised the same.[50] Their promises, however, were not being kept. Soldiers' families were already suffering from government and planter neglect. That neglect would only get worse, and its impact on the plain folk would have devastating consequences for the Confederacy.

2

"Far Greater Enemies to the South"

Cotton Planters and Speculators

As the war entered its second year, the gap between rich and poor became increasingly obvious. While the planters sacrificed luxuries and suffered inconveniences, the common soldiers' families and other plain folk faced a daily struggle just to stay alive. This situation was hardly a formula for unity among southern whites. When a "village belle" in Blakely, Georgia, said she "could get along without stockings so long as she had fashionable dresses," the editor of the *Early County News*, E. H. Grouby, labeled her and others like her "a set of ignoramuses."[1] As Grouby clearly recognized, most planters had little understanding of the plain folk's plight.

To make matters worse, planters continued to grow cotton even as the plain folk and the army faced starvation. Though the Confederate government had imposed a ban on cotton exports in an attempt to force recognition and intervention by Britain and France, planters continued to stockpile cotton for future sale. Many ignored the embargo and smuggled cotton out of the South. Most did not expect the war to last very long. But even if it went on for years, it could not last forever. When it was finally over, planters hoped to make millions selling their precious fiber to cotton-hungry textile mills in the North and Europe. With their vision firmly fixed on the promise of future wealth, southern planters failed to heed the warning signs that their shortsightedness was undermining the Confederate cause.

It might at first appear that the South should have been more than adequately prepared to feed its people during the war. Paul W. Gates writes in *Agriculture and the Civil War* that the ratio of hogs and cattle to humans in the South was double that of the North. But ratios can be deceiving. The livestock with which the South was to feed itself was usually inferior to that of the North. Hogs were variously described as "bony, snaked-legged, hairy wild beasts" and "long-headed, long-legged, fleet-footed 'piney woods rooters' used to depending on Providence for food." The cattle were no better. Free-ranging and thin, they were so small that they were referred to as "pony cattle."[2]

Adding to the South's potential food problem was the increasing dominance of cotton. With more and more land devoted to cotton through the 1850s, Georgia's livestock production was in decline. The corn crop was stagnant. During that decade, the oat crop dropped by more than half. So sparse was food production in some areas that huge shipments of meat and grain were brought in from the Midwest. One newspaper editor blamed planters who, more concerned with growing cotton, preferred to import produce rather than grow it. By the late 1850s, Georgia's comptroller-general lamented that, with regard to food, the state was "every day becoming more dependent upon those 'not of us.'" Many worried that Georgia might not be able to cope if food supplies from the Midwest were cut off by the war.[3]

Regions throughout the Confederacy faced similar problems, and newspapers were never short on solutions. Most suggested forsaking cotton entirely, at least for the time being. As early as January 1861, the editor of the *Macon Telegraph* urged planters to "Plant corn! Plant corn!" He was sure that if it came to war, double the supplies of corn would be needed for soldiers and civilians alike. "We must have large supplies [of corn], or poverty and suffering will come upon us like a strong man armed." The *Atlanta Southern Confederacy* recommended that planters raise huge herds of livestock and cultivate large crops of wheat and oats: "Too much of something to eat, and to feed the stock with, cannot be raised." The *Macon Telegraph* offered suggestions ranging from plowing up one-half of the cotton fields and replacing them with corn to alternating rows of cotton and corn.[4]

Planters responded with county meetings throughout the cotton belt, resolving to plant no more cotton than was absolutely necessary. Terrell County planters promised to plant cotton for home consumption only, deeming it the best method to ally England and France with the Confederacy: "Every bale of cotton made for shipment is a bonus to the Lincoln government—furnishing that infamous concern a bludgeon with which to break our own heads." A Sumter County planter suggested that only four acres of cotton per hand be planted and that any excess cotton be sold for the benefit of the soldiers. Some planters promised to do even better. In an article boldly announcing that "King Cotton was formally dethroned by his subjects of the county of Clarke," planters there pledged to produce no more than half an acre per hand.[5]

But planters' deeds seldom matched their words. Few took seriously any notion of reducing production, much less stopping it. One Atlanta newspaper provided a name and definition for planters who hesitated to grow corn instead of cotton: "The world is full of a class of beings called 'Old Fogies'—creatures who follow the old beaten tracks with their cumbrous routine, and will not learn wisdom by experience, the teachings of others, changes of circumstances, or revolutions, or what not." Even if cotton prices were high, the editor suggested that the "Old Fogies" keep in mind the rising prices of meat and produce. He was sure it would be just as profitable if not more so to raise foodstuffs. Yet another Georgia newspaper warned planters who continued to grow cotton, "Look out, Gentlemen, the public eye is upon you, as will soon be the public scorn unless you desist."[6]

That scorn was particularly severe among the soldiers, who constantly worried about how their families were getting along. A Macon soldier wrote to his wife back home: "All I fear now is that the planters will plant cotton instead of corn. . . . There is no use for cotton—none whatever. . . . I do hope the planters will not be so insane as to plant *any* cotton." When word of homefront hardships reached one Georgia volunteer, he wrote to planters through an open letter to his hometown newspaper: "All that we want for our watchful nights and life, is for them to stop the cry of hunger that comes to us from our families at home."[7]

Many Georgia planters were obligated by law to assist needy soldiers' families when called upon to do so. Planters became "bonded" when they agreed verbally or in writing to contribute supplies or sell them at reasonable prices to soldiers' families and to the government. After all, the soldiers—who came mostly from nonslaveholding households—were fighting to protect slaveholders' property. As they left their families behind, soldiers were assured by Governor Brown that they need not worry about their loved ones back home. The planters' bond was a guarantee that the soldiers' families would be cared for.[8] But as soldiers and their families quickly learned, it was easy for planters to ignore the stipulations of their bonding contracts.

A soldier's wife wrote to ask *Early County News* editor E. H. Grouby his opinion of bonded planters who grew more cotton than food and refused to support poor soldiers' families. Grouby called them "a set of lowdown, stinking rascals." Elizabeth A. Fields of Colquitt County wrote to Governor Brown, "The rich men that is sworn to sell soldiers families corn at government prices will not sell them a bushel." This troubled mother explained that she had a few hogs, but no corn to fatten them. Her husband was missing in action and believed dead. She continued, "I write with tears in my eyes for my heart is full of grief to think my all is gone."[9]

Though planters might forget their obligations to soldiers' families, cotton was something they wouldn't forsake. There was money in cotton, as the planters well knew. In April 1861, the *Columbus Times* announced that cotton was going for "the enormous price of 12½ cents per pound. It has not been so high for years." And prices continued to rise as the war went on.[10] Little wonder that Georgia planters, Robert Toombs prominent among them, refused to reduce cotton production regardless of the outcry. Some reports from the summer of 1862 had Toombs planting between eight and nine hundred acres in cotton. Committees of Public Safety in Cuthbert, Georgia, and Eufaula, Alabama—both near the Toombs plantation—issued resolutions condemning Toombs and a half dozen local planters for contributing to the South's worsening food shortage.[11] But condemnation could not compete with profits. The resolutions had little impact. "My property," responded Toombs, "as long as I live, shall never be subject to the orders of those cowardly miscreants, the Committees of Public Safety of Randolph County, Ga., and Eufaula.... you cannot intimidate me."[12]

Ironically, just a year earlier, General Winfield Scott, a southerner who had remained loyal to the Union, wrote Toombs asking him "to quit his rebel nonsense." Scott predicted that if the South continued on its independent course, it would eventually be starved into submission. In reply, Toombs sent an ear of corn by express to his old friend. Said one Georgia editor, "We consider this is one of Bob's best letters."[13] But now, unable to shake his addiction to cotton, Toombs was among the thousands of planters helping Scott's prediction come true.

Attitudes such as Toombs's make clear why food supplies were so low in Georgia by 1863. Grain could not be found within a 100-mile radius of Savannah. Few beef cattle were available anywhere in the state. North

Georgia had barely enough to feed local citizens, and Atlanta was competing with the army for produce from west and middle Georgia. The *Milledgeville Federal Union* placed blame squarely on "cotton bugs" who were ravaging the state's black belt: "We hear of several of these destructive insects in this neighborhood. In Baker county, it is said they cover a large extent of territory. If they cannot be destroyed any other way, the Government ought to set fire to their fields. These human insects are bent on destroying the Government. They must be wiped out."[14]

As early as spring of 1862, one indignant Georgian from Albany wrote to Joe Brown outlining the problem of cotton overproduction in his region and imploring the governor to do something about it. With "famine now stairing us in the face," he wrote, there were still many planters growing acre upon acre of cotton.

> We are in great danger of *Subjugation* to the hated government that we are resisting, *not* by the army of demons invading our country, but by *avarice* and the *menial Subjects* of King cotton. . . . I hear of one planter who is pitching 900 acres in cotton, the overseer of another told me he is going to plant 300 acres, another . . . 90 acres, another 300 acres, and two others full crops of cotton. And so it will be all over the state. . . . The country needs all the grain that can be raised, the producing forces, both in men and horses are greatly diminished, while the demand for grain is increased. I hope your Excellency will adopt some plan to stop those internal enemies of the country, for they will whip us sooner than all Lincolndom combined could do it.[15]

A Griffin man wrote to Brown warning him of planters who would "sink the Southern Confederacy for the sake of the everlasting dollar."[16]

Joe Brown was already well aware of the problem. He had only to pick up a newspaper and scan the headlines and editorials to confirm such observations. "The planters of Alabama, Georgia, Florida and the Carolinas hold the fate of the country in their hands," wrote one editor. "To them much is given, and of them much will be required. If they do not make very heavy crops of corn the present year, we can only see starvation and subjugation ahead." The *Athens Southern Watchman* insisted that cotton planters should be regarded as public enemies. Another desperate headline read: "MAKE BREAD—Never mind the cotton and tobacco." The short article was quick to point out that no one was frightened by the Yankees, but everyone was afraid of starvation. One Georgia woman warned

Brown of the worsening food situation and suggested a remedy: "Governor look to this and detail some good farmers to have bread made for the Confederacy if you don't it will soon wind up."[17]

Brown knew that support for the Confederacy among the plain folk was fragile. Many already saw planters as the source of their economic woes. Brown worried about what the consequences might be if the plain folk were forced to go hungry while wealthy landowners planted cotton. On February 25, 1862, in a private letter to his friend Linton Stephens, Brown admitted the obvious: "Our men cannot fight unless we can feed them and support their families at home." The way to do that was to "drop the cotton crop. The only question is will we do it? If we do not, in my opinion, we are ruined. If we do, our cause is triumphant. I speak plainly. There is no use in attempting to dodge the issue. We have to meet it." Brown was not at all sure that the issue would be met successfully. But he was sure on one thing. It was all up to the planters: "No class of our society is so wealthy and powerful as the cotton planters, and no other class has as much at stake. . . . I would appeal to them . . . to pause and reflect upon the vast responsibility which they are about to incur."[18]

Brown did just that in an "Appeal to the People of Georgia" that was published in virtually all the state's newspapers. He warned of the utter ruin of the Confederacy if cotton production were not curtailed: "We can never be conquered by the arms of the enemy. We may be by hunger if we neglect to husband all the resources for the supply of provisions, which a kind Providence has placed within our reach. Attempt to conceal it as we may, the fact is undeniable, that the great question in this revolution is now a question of *bread*. The army must be fed and their families at home supported, or the sun of liberty will soon set in darkness and blood, and the voice of freedom will be forever hushed in the silence of despotism."[19]

But all his urging fell on deaf ears. By fall of 1862, Georgia planters were growing so much cotton that the warehouses could not hold it all. In September of that year, the Columbus firm of Dillard, Powell, and Company ran this announcement in a local paper: "TO PLANTERS: OUR Warehouse being full, Planters will please stop consignments of Cotton to our care until further notice."[20]

When it became clear that the Confederate government would take no direct action against planters beyond the export ban, Joe Brown, like governors in other cotton states, moved to regulate production himself. In November 1862, he asked the General Assembly to impose a tax on "each quantity of seed cotton sufficient to make a bale of four hundred pounds

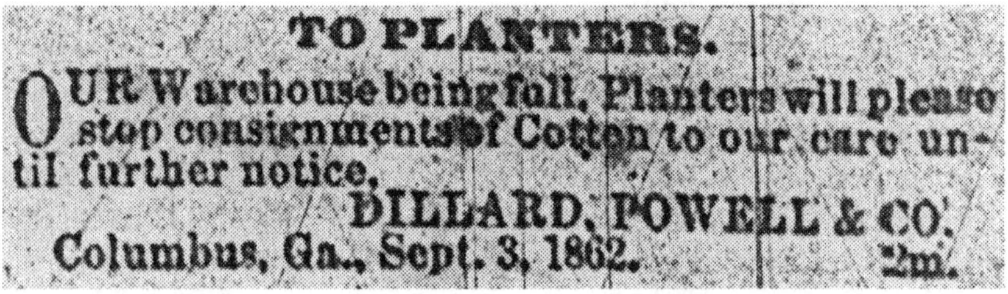

> **TO PLANTERS.**
> OUR Warehouse being full, Planters will please stop consignments of Cotton to our care until further notice.
> DILLARD, POWELL & CO.
> Columbus, Ga., Sept. 3, 1862. 2m.

FIGURE 2.1. Adding to the burdens of soldiers in the field and their families back home, planters grew so much cotton that the warehouses could not hold it all. The result was a food shortage so severe that it threatened to starve the Confederacy out of existence. One worried Georgian wrote to Governor Brown begging him to bring cotton planters under control, "for they will whip us sooner than all Lincolndom combined could do it." (*Columbus Enquirer*)

. . . produced next year . . . over what is actually necessary for a home supply." The assemblymen rejected Brown's suggestion of a tax on seed cotton. After all, many were planters and were not eager to place a tax on themselves. But they did make it illegal for anyone to plant more than three acres in cotton for each slave owned or farmhand employed. Any landowner who violated this law would be fined five hundred dollars for each acre of cotton beyond the three-acre-per-hand limit.[21]

The act inspired little fear among planters. Godfrey Barnsley, a prominent Bartow County planter, knew state efforts to curtail cotton production were in vain—and he knew why. In January 1863 he wrote to a friend, "some states have passed laws to limit the growth [of cotton] this year, but there is little doubt of a large area being planted under the stimulus of present prices." Barnsley was right. According to one report, "not one acre in fifty in the best corn district in Georgia was planted in corn." A frustrated Governor Brown responded by asking Georgia's legislature to restrict the cotton crop to only one-fourth an acre per hand and to "make it highly penal" for anyone to exceed that limit. The assembly refused and, despite continued urging from Brown, ignored the issue for the rest of the war. "If we are subdued," Brown pointedly warned, "it will be by starvation, and not by Lincoln's armies."[22]

In direct violation of state law and Confederate policy, "planters insisted," as one report put it, "on their right to grow unlimited amounts of cotton; to retain it for sale whenever they chose; and to sell it whenever, and to whomever, they chose." And it did not seem to matter who the buyers were. Planters and cotton merchants would sell to anyone, even the Yankees. Of the one and a half million bales that left the South during the war, two-thirds went to the North. Blockade-runners carried much of it to Nassau, where they sold it to buyers from New York, Liverpool, and other import centers. But a good portion made its way North by more direct routes, with government officials on both sides, civil and military, paid off along the way.[23]

Much of the smuggled cotton flowed directly north along rail lines to Atlanta and from there to Chattanooga. On March 12, 1862, came a report to the governor that two Tennessee men were in Macon buying cotton. "It is believed they intend to let the Federals have it." Two weeks later, the *Atlanta Southern Confederacy* published a letter warning that "uncompromising adherents to the Northern Government have been, for weeks, shipping cotton to East Tennessee. . . . Don't sell them your cotton. They are your enemies." It was not only Tennesseans engaged in the business. The *Confederacy*'s Chattanooga correspondent reported that "a few traitorous Georgians have a finger in the pie."[24]

Georgia's rivers also became highways of the illicit cotton trade. News circulated as early as December 1861 that cotton regularly made its way from Columbus downriver to the Florida port of Apalachicola, "where it is clandestinely conveyed to the enemy's vessels to be carried North." The next month, in January 1862, a hundred bags of cotton were found on a Chattahoochee steamboat headed south to the Florida coast. In March, a letter from Fort Gaines arrived on Governor Brown's desk describing the trade in considerable detail. Steamboats typically made their way up the Chattahoochee River loading cotton bales as they went, with Columbus their supposed destination. But somehow much of the cotton seemed to find its way to the Gulf port of Apalachicola, Florida. There it was transferred to vessels that took "pleasure excursions" out to see the blockading Union fleet, always returning with empty cargo holds. A few days later, Brown received news of cotton smuggling out of Albany and Bainbridge along the Flint River to the Gulf Coast. Much the same occurred along the Savannah River and the Ocmulgee-Oconee-Altamaha river system, Georgia's largest. As late as March 1865, the steamboat *Comet* was caught in Pulaski County on the Ocmulgee with "a cargo of cotton designed for traffic with the enemy." General Howell Cobb, commanding state and Confederate reserve forces in Georgia, was implicated in the affair.[25]

So rife was corruption that those engaged in the cotton trade conducted business openly with little fear of the law. Officials could nearly

Cotton Planters and Speculators · 33

FIGURE 2.2. Georgia cotton merchants regularly smuggled their product downriver to the Gulf port of Apalachicola on boats like the *Shamrock*—built in Columbus during the war—where it was transferred to oceangoing vessels for transport to Europe and the North. Some planters bragged openly that the longer the war went on, the more money they made. (Courtesy of Florida State Archives.)

always be paid to look the other way, and those who controlled transportation gave cotton shipments priority for a piece of the action. In March 1863, Albany had 100,000 bushels of corn rotting in its warehouses, while outbound trains loaded with cotton clogged the rails. "Is the Southwestern Railroad leaning to *favorites*, or speculating in the article themselves?" asked the *Albany Patriot*. Even wounded soldiers took a back seat to cotton. In November 1864, with Sherman's army bearing down, officers telegraphed Governor Brown from Macon about a state-owned train loaded with cotton: "We need the train to remove our sick from hospitals. I request your authority to use this train for the sick. . . . Please answer at once."[26]

Cotton smuggling was, according to one contemporary, such an obvious fact of economic life for Georgia planters that no intelligent person in the state could doubt it. Why would the South's planters and merchants provide cotton to clothe northerners while their countrymen went lacking? The simple fact was that the North paid better, and the planters knew it. Some reaped such profits from wartime smuggling that they were not eager to see the conflict end. In a private letter to a friend, Godfrey Barnsley made it clear that he feared a "terrific fall" in cotton prices if the war ended. Others openly bragged that the longer the war went on, the more money they made.[27]

So lucrative was the wartime cotton trade that in 1863 Joe Brown decided to get Georgia's state government in on the profits. The Confederate government did the same. Despite their previous insistence that planters grow more food, they encouraged the opposite by purchasing cotton and exporting it themselves. At one point, a single shipment of state-owned cotton loaded at Savannah and bound for Nassau contained over fifty bales.[28] State and Confederate officials knew that much of the cotton would reach the North. But for many planters and politicians, the war had become not a crusade but a moneymaking enterprise. Many plain folk were coming to think it had never been anything else.

Cotton's threat to the war effort had never been of overriding concern to the South's planters. By the war's midpoint, it was forgotten even by the common man's so-called friend, Joe Brown. But the plain folk could not forget. Both on the battlefield and the homefront, they knew that they were being kept hungry by those who benefited most from the war. Food was now a mark of social distinction. Malnutrition and starvation threatened thousands of soldiers and their families, while planters and politicians fed themselves nearly as well as ever. If southerners could not reverse that trend—if planters could not give up their addiction to cotton—then they were, as one editor put it, "not only a blockaded but a block-headed people."[29]

Planters' reluctance to devote themselves to food production contributed not only to hunger but also to an inflationary spiral that began to spin out of control soon after the war started. At first, few thought inflation would be a problem, since the war was expected to end quickly. Even after First Manassas, some scoffed at the North's blockade of the South and its supposed economic threat. Others were more farsighted. John B. Lamar, Howell Cobb's brother-in-law, wrote to the general in November 1861, "we can laugh at the blockade for a while if salt is $12 per sack." But he wondered what the impact would be if the blockade lasted another year. "Makes me hold my breath when I think of it." Less than a year later the blockade was tighter than ever, and salt was selling for $125 a sack when it was available at all. It had been only two dollars before the war.[30]

Such dramatic price increases for even the most basic commodities were not uncommon. Butter went from twelve cents a pound in 1861 to seventy-five cents two years later. By the end of the war it was five dollars or more. Corn that was two dollars a bushel in 1863 sold for fourteen by

February 1865. Bacon went from twelve cents to fifty cents a pound in the war's first year; by the end of the war, a pound of bacon was four dollars. Flour that sold for nine dollars a barrel before the war was going for four hundred by war's end. Coffee went to thirty dollars a pound shortly after the war began and from there to sixty and seventy dollars. The cost of more potent beverages was on the rise as well. Rum that was purchased for just seventeen cents a gallon in Cuba sold for twenty-five dollars after being run through the blockade. That was an increase of nearly 15,000 percent.[31]

Though the blockade contributed to rising prices, even more damaging to the economy was profiteering and speculation by planters and merchants. In his study of Columbus, Georgia, during the war, historian Diffee Standard concluded that the blockade was an excuse rather than a reason for inflated prices. The *Albany Patriot* reached the same conclusion. In November 1861, it ran an editorial entitled "The Blockade No Excuse." For months the editor had heard merchants blaming the blockade for high prices; however, he asserted that "there is dry goods alone within our southern limits sufficient to supply the wants of the people of the Confederate States for the next ten years to come. The blockade therefore is no excuse." In a private letter to a friend, one Georgia planter admitted as much. For some time, he wrote in April 1862, southerners had been "abusing the Yankees for extortion and speculation, but [we are] quite as bad ourselves."[32]

The inflation that hit so many so hard early in the war sprang largely from inducements of the market. Merchants kept a tight grip on food and clothing resources, selling only to those who could pay top dollar or holding out for even higher prices. Planters continued to focus on increasingly profitable cotton crops, leaving inadequate land for the levels of food production that Georgia and the South needed. Both groups took the same self-interested path that had served them so well before the war, following the dollar wherever it led. But in so doing, they left the interests of the plain folk—and ultimately of the Confederacy—far behind.

As early as November 1861, one Georgia man complained to Vice President Alexander Stephens that he and other "common farmers" were finding it difficult "to keep our heads above the flood of destruction" brought on by "the money thieves, those Speculators." If small farmers were ruined by speculation, the Confederacy would be ruined as well. Editor E. H. Grouby of the *Early County News* also saw the danger. Those who engaged in profiteering—"home Yankees," as Grouby called them—

FIGURE 2.3. Kate Cumming—an army nurse who served in Georgia during the war—criticized speculators for "making *piles* of money out of the misfortunes of their country." She expressed the feeling of many southerners when she wrote that speculators were murderers destined for hellfire. "If they only suffer one half the pangs of which they have been the cause, their case will be sad indeed." (Cumming, *Gleanings from Southland*)

were "by far greater enemies to the South and do more to injure her cause than ten times their number of Yankees in the field."[33]

Even before the war began, speculators tried to corner local markets. "Is there no boundary to their desire to accumulate money?" asked one editor in February 1861. "Will not the cries of widowhood and orphanage pierce their dull, cold ears?" The disgusted editor was sure that had southern speculators lived in "the days of Judas [they] would have taken the contract to betray the Savior for *fifteen* instead of *thirty* pieces of silver."[34]

As prices rose during summer 1861, enthusiasm for war began to ebb. After First Manassas in July, word of the true horrors of war reached citizens through newspaper accounts and letters home. And inflated prices came with rumors that the war might not end soon. That fall, commenting on widespread price gouging by speculators, the editor of Thomaston's *Upson Pilot* wrote: "They love Dollars and Cents, and nothing else. Money is their God—their country—their all!"[35]

In spring 1862, a woman from Griffin wrote an open letter to Georgians entitled "A Word to the Wise Is Sufficient." She insisted that speculators stop hoarding for higher prices and taking advantage of the disadvantaged. Fearing her letter would be taken as too outspoken, she wrote: "I am a woman, and am perhaps out of my proper sphere, if an interest in her suffering country can be out of a woman's sphere. I would keep silent, if the men were active, but many who remain at home, are so deeply immersed in the various schemes for money making that they seemingly pay little heed to the emergency of the times." The letter was signed, "A DAUGHTER OF GEORGIA."[36]

Such letters poured into the governor's office as well. Wrote one Athens man early in the war: "There is a good deal here held by speculators who will not even sell for present prices. . . . The poor are actually suffering." An Atlanta woman wrote of extortioners and the poor: "Even here in Atlanta, where there is an abundance of provisions, there is a great deal of suffering among the poor class in consequence of the high price of provisions and the low price of labor. . . . When the war first began I thought there was a great deal of patriotism among us, but, alas, where is it? Avariciousness has almost conquered it!" In fall of 1862, a Fort Valley widow related the grossly inflated prices in her region: salt was $125 per sack, flour $40 per barrel, sugar 75¢ a pound, and syrup $2 a gallon. "In the name of humanity must poor widows and helpless orphans be brought to suffering even for bread?" A year later, one Georgia editor wrote that "some reduction must be made in the prices now charged for the necessaries of life, or the poor must suffer this winter."[37]

A tightened market in grain, salt, bacon, and other products developed as fears of food shortages grew and the profits that could be realized from them became apparent. An open letter to the Georgia legislature in November 1861 predicted that the country would soon have "swarms of speculators who prey upon the Government and upon the people." That prediction was coming true. The superintendent of the Southwestern Railroad was inundated with so much cargo from speculators that he had problems completing his government shipments.[38]

It was not long before inflation and speculation began to take their toll on Confederate currency. With prices going up every day, government notes became increasingly worthless. Many Georgians abandoned the use of paper money altogether in favor of a barter system. Most were already accustomed to some degree of barter. According to one native, "cattle, cow hides, peas, pork, 'possum and potatoes were legal tender" even before the war.[39] But so serious was the inflation problem that livestock, farm equipment, corn, and cotton all became regular media of exchange by the war's second year.

Gadwell Jefferson Pearce, president of LaGrange Female College, advised a Troup County woman to "get all the thread you can. It is an article of necessity and good currency, vastly better than Confederate." Pearce knew what he was talking about. Newspapers throughout Georgia advertised items for barter, and yarn was one of the most common. In Early County, Joel Perry offered to exchange yarn for pork. Prices were running so high for yarn by December 1862 that a group of Bartow County women urged Governor Brown to seize control of Georgia's cotton and wool factories.[40]

The *Early County News* got in on the barter system when its editor began selling one-year subscriptions in trade for eight pounds of bacon, lard, or sugar. Thomaston's *Upson Pilot*, in an entry labeled "Anything for Pay," insisted it would take just that. "We will take in exchange for our paper, or in payment of old accounts: Fire-wood, Pork, Bacon, Beef, Mutton, Wheat, Flour, Corn, Meal, Potatoes, Butter, Chickens, Eggs, Peas, Oats, Fodder, Good Hay, Wheat Bran, Cotton Seed, Coffee, Salt, or '*Goobers*.'"[41]

The torrent of pleas from anguished citizens and the impact of inflation and speculation on the currency could not be ignored for long. In November 1861, the General Assembly passed a resolution calling for the governor to restrain speculation by "the most effectual means of accomplishing such suppression." A month later, the assembly took matters into its own hands, outlawing speculation in all sorts of basic commodities, including "clothing, shoes, leather, cloth of any kind, provisions, wheat, flour, corn, cornmeal, meat, bacon, hogs, cattle, salt, bagging, rope, and twine." Penalties for violation ranged up to five thousand dollars and three years' imprisonment.[42] Confederate officials also tried to address the inflation problem by appointing price commissioners in every congressional district. It was their job to fix prices on items deemed common and necessary. Even local citizens tried price fixing in an effort to ease their plight. A public meeting headed by M. T. Alexander and W. W. Fleming was held in Early County to regulate prices of homegrown produce.[43]

In the face of all efforts to curb it, profiteering continued to sap the South's economy and morale. Joe Brown was sure that speculators and profiteers were among the Confederacy's greatest threats but admitted that antispeculation laws were a "dead letter." Merchants simply ignored the law and continued their price gouging. This infuriated women like Kate Cumming, who criticized speculators for "making *piles* of money out of the misfortunes of their country." They were killing the poor with inflated prices, which, in her eyes, made them murderers destined for hellfire. "If they only suffer one half the pangs of which they have been the cause, their case will be sad indeed."[44]

Nearly every county's grand jury issued resolutions condemning the speculators. Critics called them "monomaniacs," "land sharks," "shovel-nosed sharks," "ground sharks," or "little taper-nosed, blue-coated, white-bellied coast sharks." Berrien County evoked the "finger of scorn" to point out all such men, and Dooly County poetically claimed that "like the Hyena they can only suck the blood of the Lyon."[45]

One such "hyena" was John L. McGregor of Blackshear. A British citizen, he refused allegiance to the Confederacy and claimed exemption from military service. He scoured Pierce County buying chickens, pork, syrup, sugar—"in fact what ever he can lay his hands upon"—at such inflated prices that local citizens could not compete. As the poor went hungry, McGregor shipped his purchases off to "we do not know where." J.H.B. Shackleford, an Albany merchant, was another accused speculator who imported northern products that he exchanged locally for bacon—bacon that he bartered to the army for sugar.[46]

Several Georgia newspapers reprinted an entry about one particularly callous speculator in the Confederate capital. Entitled "A Heartless Wretch," the story related that "a creature in the good city of Richmond told a poor woman, whose despair at his asking her seventy-five dollars for flour caused her to inquire of him what she was to do to live. 'I recon, madam, you will have to eat your children!' What a monster!" This story circulated widely in southern newspapers and may have been apocryphal. Literal or not, it reflected the attitude of many a speculator and the attitude of many people toward them. When an Atlanta woman accidentally ran over a pedestrian with her buggy, she was mortified, thinking she had hit a soldier. After a closer look, she recognized her victim as a locally well-known extortioner. She left the man in the street "regretting that her buggy wheels had not run over his neck."[47]

Despite their socially paternalistic self-image, planters were no more opposed to reaping huge profits at the expense of plain folk than were merchant speculators. Like their urban counterparts, planters commonly stockpiled foodstuffs to force higher prices on the open market. Initial market projections in 1861 set corn at one dollar per bushel, but few farmers would sell at that price. Jeremiah Wilson, who owned a plantation two miles outside Albany, had 2,000 bushels that he would not sell for under two dollars a bushel. Neither would John Jones of Dougherty County, who had 10,000 bushels. Captain Stow, a commissary agent sent to purchase food, had contracted with Dougherty County planters for 160,000 to 170,000 bushels of corn, but most of the planters never delivered. They held fast to their corn, anticipating that prices would soon rise from one dollar per bushel to five or six. Wrote Stow to his superiors: "You have no idea the number of corn-buyers in southwestern Georgia, mostly on speculation. They must be stopped in some way or our Army will suffer."[48]

In November 1861, one editorial called on the General Assembly to do something about such hoarding. "It is wrong and unpatriotic, and men should not do it; and our Legislatures should not allow it to be done." It did little good. The *Athens Southern Watchman* reported in April 1863 that "while hundreds are suffering for bread, there are many corn cribs in this county [Clarke], in Oglethorpe, Greene, Walton, Morgan, and all about, full of corn!"[49]

The crisis in corn prices was made even worse with those who could afford it still clamoring for whiskey. R. R. Hunt of Ellijay wrote in February 1862: "The distilleries have bought up all the corn and making it into Liquor our families must suffer for bread if it is not amediately stoped [it is] a worse scourage than Lincoln's army." Later that year, the General Assembly prohibited distillation of corn, wheat, rye, or other "spiritous or malt liquors" except for medicinal, hospital, chemical, or mechanical purposes. Anyone found guilty of illegal distillation could be severely fined. Half the money would go to the "informer"; the other half was entrusted to the justices of local inferior courts for support of soldiers' wives, widows, and children. But the law was easy to dodge, and some officials found great profit in overlooking unlicensed distillers. One county agent, supposedly buying corn for the indigent soldiers' families, instead took the corn to a distillery.[50]

Corn needed for starving families was continuously siphoned away by distillers who could pay more because their customers could. Hunt insisted that such men were a tremendous asset to the Union cause. "If they were acting as Lencolns agents the[y] could not fall on a better plan to favour him." M. Greenwood of Morgantown complained of the many stills in his area and of the men who were buying up all the corn and rye. Many of the men from his county were willing to report for military duty but believed that leaving their wives and children "to the mercy of a drunken set of men and extortioners is almost heart-rending." Greenwood and other volunteers threatened to destroy the stills if the government took no action. "If there is not something done, I am fully convinced that many of the soldiers' wives and families of the soldiers will suffer for bread to eat."[51]

Arch Smith of Lowndes County was one of many who complained of local planters refusing to sell what produce they had at prices plain folk could afford. "It is evident that they have enough," he insisted, "and are holding on for a rise in the price." In defense of such actions, planters frequently shifted the blame to speculators.[52] Some planters issued calls to organize "corn combinations" to set local prices. This was purportedly a defense against speculators but was actually a defense of their own inflated prices. If speculators were holding out for more, so the argument went, planters had to do the same. Critics called the combinations unpatriotic and ultimately harmful to plain folk and the Confederate cause. But one combination defender insisted that although "the wives and children, widows and orphans of the soldiers will suffer mostly by this arrangement . . . it is their misfortune to be poor and they must suffer the consequences."[53]

In January 1864, one corn combination, with members from Dougherty, Lee, Terrell, and Calhoun counties, gathered in Albany to discuss setting price controls on corn. David A. Vason, a prominent Albany attorney, offered a motion to accept government pricing as a regional standard. But planters knew that having their own prices tied to those of the government might restrict profits, and they roundly rejected Vason's proposal. Instead, they accepted a motion to average corn prices from the four counties and to restrict prices to no more than that average for the time being.[54] There were, however, no guarantees against future increases.

Nelson Tift, the chief opponent of Vason's plan, was in a unique position to profit from the war. By the 1860s, his financial and political interests extended in many directions throughout southwest Georgia. He had spearheaded attempts to draw the railroad to Baker and Dougherty counties and had sponsored legislation to clear obstructions in the Flint River for safe steamboat travel to the Gulf of Mexico.⁵⁵ He was one of the largest landowners in Dougherty County, and his Albany Bridge Company controlled the only dry foot crossing of the Flint River. He was also in negotiations with the Confederate navy for a lucrative commissary contract.

If the local corn combination had accepted government pricing, Tift's hands would have been tied, and the rapid growth that his real estate and infrastructure holdings enjoyed during the first half of 1864 would never have occurred. Instead, the combination's "average" pricing scheme allowed him to charge at or near his usual levels, and within three months Tift had built a complex of warehouses along the Flint River to fulfill his contracts.

At the center of this complex—and predating it by a decade—was the bridge house, a two-storied brick warehouse that served as the entrance to Tift's bridge over the Flint. The ground floor, containing Tift's private office, and the bridgekeeper's quarters were separated from one another by an arched passageway. Local farmers carrying goods to market had to go through this passageway after paying a toll. On the second floor was Tift Hall, Albany's frescoed dance hall and theater.⁵⁶

As a part of the commissary contract, Tift rented the bridge house to the navy for use as a slaughterhouse and converted the cellar into a meatpacking house. Large pens were erected at the rear of the building to hold impressed cattle and hogs. Adjacent to the bridge house was a three-storied, steam-powered wheat and grist mill, capable of producing one hundred bushels of meal and one hundred barrels of flour per day. To the left of the mill was a barrel factory, and between the bridge and the mill was a two-storied bakery. A soon-to-be-completed kiln for drying corn meal stood nearby, while a proposed tannery was delayed until the other buildings were completed. All of these newer buildings were built by ten slaves in a three-month period from locally milled lumber and handmade bricks.⁵⁷

Controversy soon swirled around the bridge house. To pay for his construction projects, Tift increased both the tolls on his bridge and his prices on corn and other supplies. He charged tolls twice on wagons loaded for market, once when entering town and again when leaving. And he began charging pedestrians to cross, who had paid no toll before the war. Popular opinion soon turned against Tift, and in March 1864, the Dougherty County Inferior Court declared Tift in violation of his charter. It ordered him to lower his rates to those fixed in his charter and to

FIGURE 2.4. Nelson Tift, Albany's founder, was such a notorious wartime speculator that the Dougherty County Inferior Court imposed pricing restrictions on him. Tift ignored the court order. His neighbors sued him, then threatened him, and finally burned his Flint River bridge house to the ground. (O'Donovan, "The Journal of Nelson Tift")

post those rates at the bridge house. Tift refused and the court, finding him in contempt, published its own rates and reinstituted the toll waivers.[58]

Tift ignored the court order and continued charging the increased rates, at times imposing different rates on similar vehicles. Albany's citizens had had enough. In June 1864, David P. Hill sued Tift and the Albany Bridge Company in Dougherty Superior Court for violation of his charter. But the controversy surrounding Tift's operations still did not end. Sales of grain and food commodities to the Confederate government continued, as did his inflated sales to the local citizenry. In March and April 1865, his sale of corn at sixteen dollars per bushel—six dollars above even speculation rates—brought scarcely veiled threats of retaliation, and citizens finally burned the bridge house to the ground.[59]

Nelson Tift was but one example of the planter-merchant-speculators who preyed on their neighbors all over Georgia and the South. They were clear evidence to plain folk that the struggle was a rich man's war. "The rich is all at home makeing great fortunes," complained a group of Spalding County women to Governor Brown, and "care nothing for nobody but themselves." "They can speculate of soldiers wives [and] make fortunes [on] them.... Just look at ther women & children that are begging bread ... they would see them pearish before they would give them one bushel of corn." A writer to the *Athens Southern Watchman* suggested that Lincoln commission such men as generals in the Yankee army "as they can accomplish far more than many of his Federal appointments."[60] Certainly they did as much to undermine Confederate morale as any Union general ever did.

3

"God Help the Poor"

Impressment, Hunger, and the Failure of Relief

Speculation by planters and merchants marked the starting point of what became a vicious encircling trap for the plain folk. Planters fed a lucrative market in cotton, devoting not nearly enough acreage to food production. Scarcity forced food prices up and speculation drove them even higher. Rampant inflation inevitably followed, making planters and smaller farmers even less willing to exchange what food they had for increasingly worthless Confederate currency.

By 1863, in a decision that would mark a turning point for southerners' attitudes toward the war and the Confederacy, the Richmond government determined that what it could not buy it would take by force. That summer the Confederate Congress passed a series of taxes on everything from occupations to incomes. The most significant was a 10 percent confiscation levy on such farm items as livestock, wheat, corn, oats, rye, hay, fodder, buckwheat, sweet potatoes, Irish potatoes, sugar, cotton, wool, tobacco, peas, beans, and peanuts. When even this tax-in-kind did not provide enough food to meet military needs, Confederate officials began confiscating these items, and anything else they wanted, far beyond the 10 percent level.

As food seizures became more frequent, so did complaints. Major M. B. Millen's October 1863 order to impress every hog in southwest Georgia's Mitchell County met with considerable displeasure. A local grand jury deemed the order "unwise, ungenerous, and unjust. Its execution would disorganize and demoralize the people." Even worse, said the jurors, it would "result in the starvation of the indigent." Impressment threatened the indigent of north Georgia as well. In an article entitled "Starvation in the Mountains," the *Athens Southern Watchman* reported that some people were living on roots and weeds: "Their means for making a crop this year are very lean—their oxen being impressed."[1]

One way or another, the burdens of taxation and impressment fell heaviest on the plain folk. Though planters resented taxation and confiscation as much as anyone, they usually had enough food on hand to satisfy tax collectors and impressment agents. Small farmers were seldom so fortunate. Few could afford to pay their taxes, much less turn over what little they had to the government. Officials were rarely welcome at yeoman farms, and as the war went on their jobs became increasingly dangerous. Impressment agents were beaten up, shot at, and sometimes killed. Joe Brown, an avid opponent of impressment by the Richmond government, warned that the practice and its "baneful operations" could only encourage opposition to the central government by producing an "evil spirit, bordering already in many cases upon open disloyalty."[2]

Brown was foremost among southern governors in his hostility to Confederate impressment. As early as 1861, when the Davis administration tried to seize engines and cars on the state-owned Western and Atlantic Railroad, Brown threatened to call out the militia to stop it. Davis thought it wiser to fight one war at a time and canceled the order. Two years later, when the Confederacy began general impressment, the Georgia General Assembly passed a resolution declaring it unconstitutional.[3]

As hostile as Brown and the assembly were toward Confederate impressment, they did not hesitate to impose it themselves. In fact, Georgia was one of the first Confederate states to begin impressment. One citizen wrote to a Georgia newspaper complaining of Brown's hypocrisy, pointing to numerous seizures by the state: "And yet this same Governor has made more noise about the legal and constitutional rights of the people than all the men in the Confederacy." William Scruggs of the *Columbus Sun* sarcastically observed that impressment "originated in this state with Governor Brown, who, of course, does everything according to the 'Constitutional' square and compass." Robert Toombs, who often joined the governor in opposing Confederate policy, wrote of his friend: "I see Brown has got him an impressment law too. How catching is thieving."[4]

Whether impressment was imposed by Georgia or the Confederacy, compensation for it was nearly always a point of argument. In October 1862, Confederate Secretary of War George Randolph asked Attorney General Thomas Watts for an opinion on the legality of impressment. Watts concluded that impressment was indeed legal as long as the government paid "just compensation." The problem was that impressment agents and property owners rarely agreed on what "just compensation" meant. President Davis tried to address the problem by establishing impressment committees to set prices. But inflation was so severe and committees met so infrequently that the government's fixed prices were always far below market value. By late 1863, the official price allowed for flour was half that available on the open market, and the government corn price was only a third of market value.

In most cases, farmers were lucky to get any payment at all for their impressed produce. Corruption was so rampant among impressment officers that it was not unusual for them to pocket government funds reserved for farmers. One Georgia farmer complained bitterly when he discovered that the government was paying fifty cents a pound for bacon. Confederate agents had given him only thirty-five. Sometimes farmers received a promissory note instead of cash, and very often they did not even get that. It was just as well, though, as the notes were nearly impossible to redeem. When one Georgia man tried to collect on a note that was ten months past due, he was met by a sign "placed up conspicuously in large letters, 'No funds.'"[5]

From south Georgia came reports in summer of 1862 that impressment agents were gathering cattle in Thomas and Brooks counties "without paying at all." The same was happening in north Georgia. John W. Cain of Whitfield County wrote Governor Brown complaining that "our army is taking our produces, our horses, cattle, sheep and hogs and very seldom pay anything." From Calhoun County, J.H.B. Shackelford wrote the governor that there were a great many soldiers in his region who "take the liberty to help themselves without money." William C. Humphreys of Clinch County told the governor that there was "a general system of stealing going on under the impressment act."[6]

Some officers sold confiscated produce on the open market and kept the money themselves. Duncan Jordan of the firm Lennard and Jordan, a small shoe manufacturing company in Cuthbert, complained to Governor Brown in November 1861 about the practices of government purchasing agents. He had been selling his shoes to them at low prices thinking they were going to the army. He later discovered that the agents were

FIGURE 3.1. Plain folk bore the brunt of impressment, mainly because they were easier targets than the planters. And impressment was often accompanied by depredations of all sorts. A seventy-year-old Bibb County man was threatened with a beating if he did not hand over his horse. An impressment officer shot and killed a man in Social Circle who refused to give up his cattle. (Ellis, *Thrilling Adventures*)

selling his shoes on the open market at inflated prices. Jordan suggested that the state make "application through honest agents" and void the contracts of "avaricious Speculators."[7]

Illicit trade in clothing occurred in the army as well. In the spring of 1862, uniforms made by women in Augusta and donated to their men at the front were "charged against the soldiers at full prices." Later that year, scandal rocked the War Department when quartermaster officers were discovered selling army food supplies to speculators and embezzling the proceeds. An Augusta man wrote to Governor Brown in December 1862 that army quartermasters in that city were "involved and complicated" with speculators. In September 1863, the *Columbus Sun* reported that "a Quartermaster is looked upon with a feeling of distrust in almost every community."[8] By 1864, the *Early County News*'s masthead called for death to, among others, "RASCALLY GOVERNMENT OFFICIALS."

Distrust of government agents, state and Confederate, had been widespread for some time. As early as the fall of 1861, a farmer wrote to the *Athens Southern Watchman*, "I have never entertained the shadow of a doubt as to our success—our whipping out all the Yankees that can be produced—but God knows how we shall escape the *corruptions* of our own Government, and the *leeches and sharks* of our own people." Another exasperated Georgian was sure that there was only one route of escape, and he begged Governor Brown to take it: "Do for God's sake put an end to this unrighteous war. We shall be eaten up by Confederate Office holders and Speculators."[9]

Congress responded by making it illegal for the public to buy military supplies from enlisted men but said nothing of officers. Small wonder that the act hardly put a dent in the problem of corruption. It served only to emphasize the South's pervasive class divisions. One Georgia editor denounced the legislation for its blatantly elitist overtones:

> Why is it not also against the law to buy any of these articles from Quarter Masters, Commissaries, &c., when it is a well known fact that many of these swoll head gentry steal a great deal of this kind of Government property which they have in their possession, to be distributed among the needy Soldiers, sell them, and pocket the money? There is more rascality, according to the number, among officers than privates. Why are not officers bound up as tight as privates? There is altogether too much *favoritism* shown to little jackass officers by Congress.[10]

When confiscated produce made it to government depots without being sold off by corrupt impressment agents or quartermasters, it frequently went to waste through incompetence or neglect. It was not uncommon either for produce to rot in government warehouses or for the Quartermaster Department to deliver inedible food to the troops. In March 1863, the *Columbus Times* reported that while thousands faced hunger every day, over half a million bushels of corn were rotting in government depots throughout southwest Georgia. Albany alone had fifteen storehouses filled with corn, much of it already ruined and the rest soon to be.[11]

Those presenting themselves as government agents were not always what they appeared. Farmers often tried to redeem promissory notes only to find that they had been swindled by imposters. Hundreds of scoundrels posing as impressment officers roamed the southern countryside swindling farmers out of their harvests and livestock. The problem became so bad in Georgia that the General Assembly mandated ten years imprisonment for anyone engaged in confiscation without authority to do so. Governor Brown favored an additional punishment of "thirty-nine lashes on the bare back," but the legislature thought imprisonment sufficient.[12]

Still, because enforcement was lax, the situation only worsened. Layout and deserter gangs dressed in army uniforms roamed the countryside taking what they pleased. The *Sumter Republican* wrote that "government agents, or persons claiming so to be, who are thick as bees in this county, are seizing wheat at the mills." The *Augusta Chronicle and Sentinel* reported in 1864 that northeast Georgia was overrun by uniformed impressment companies claiming without written authority to be part of General Wheeler's command. In October, John Bryan of Appling County wrote the governor complaining about his horses being seized. Bryan reported that "when asked by what authority they done so Sergent Pratt presented his Gun and Said that that was his warrant for so doing." The next month, Governor Brown finally issued a proclamation authorizing local officials to hunt down these "predatory bands . . . and shoot them down whenever they find them."[13]

Even when impressment was done under state or Confederate authority, it was often accompanied by depredations of all sorts. Local agents occasionally used their power of impressment to victimize political or personal enemies. Soldiers' wives or widows were the most frequent targets, since their husbands were dead or hundreds of miles away. Sometimes abuse did not end with simple confiscation. A seventy-year-old Bibb County man who had sent five sons to Confederate service, two of whom were killed, was threatened with a beating if he did not hand over his horse. An impressment officer shot and killed a man in Social Circle who refused to give up his cattle. "Let these outrages be stopped," demanded the editor of the *Atlanta Southern Confederacy*. "We advise the people to resist them." So did the editor of the *Early County News*. Otherwise, he said, "our military officers will soon think they own the whole country."[14]

James Bush headed a meeting of Early County citizens who warned that violent and corrupt impressment officials were so numerous that they would "ultimately alienate the affections of the people from the govern-

FIGURE 3.2. James Bush—author David Williams's great-great-great-grandfather—headed a meeting of Early County citizens who warned that violent and corrupt impressment officials threatened to "alienate the affections of the people from the government." One of the county's richest planters, Bush contributed to that alienation himself by refusing to deal in Confederacy currency. (From the collection of the late Helen Kirkland Daniels, Miller County, Ga. Photograph in possession of David Williams.)

ment." They were right. Reflecting such alienation was a letter that Nancy Mann of Harris County sent to her brother, encouraging him to desert. She did not want to lose a member of her family to a cause she felt was not worth defending. "There is so much rascality carried on in this confedracy," she complained, "untill I think some times I do not no what will be come of the people and nor the confedracy and I do not care much."[15]

Though no member of any class held either impressment or taxation in high regard, plain folk knew that the wealthy did not contribute their share. Soon after Congress levied an income tax in April 1863, it became obvious that wealthy men would not willingly part with their riches. So many refused to file tax returns that one Milledgeville citizen called on the state's superior court judges "to give the subject in special charge to their Grand Juries. . . . Our Government is entitled to support from the men who have been skulking from the field, while our brave boys have been pouring out their blood like water to protect their ill-gotten property."[16]

In response, the state levied a nominal penalty that was rarely enforced. Such superficiality had a devastating effect on morale. In February 1864, a citizen wrote to Joe Brown warning him of "strong Union feeling" among plain folk in southwest Georgia. The inequitable tax system had much to do with such dissent. It was apparent that "poor people has to pay all the tax and do all the fighting, while the gentlemen and their sons are loafing over the country."[17]

Impressment's lack of equity was just as obvious. Agents typically sought out the most vulnerable targets first—the farmsteads of the plain folk. Only when these farms were stripped bare did agents turn to the plantations. Even then, planters were reluctant to part with their surplus. Some used political connections to avoid impressment. Others simply had themselves appointed impressment agents—and profited by it. Mary Lane of Wilkes County complained to Governor Brown that William Sneed, a local slaveholder and impressment agent, was feeding confiscated produce to his slaves.[18]

Some planters hid their supplies to avoid impressment. A Georgia soldier recalled how planters "would hide their wagons under straw piles, and carry off their horses where you cannot come at them. . . . Some of these men [are] rich—worth fifty thousand dollars." One Georgia planter stashed at least a thousand bushels of corn in a large crib hidden deep in the woods on his plantation. "What kind of a man can he be?" asked the local newspaper editor. "Is he a friend of the country? No; for no man who is will, at such a time as this, hide his corn from suffering Soldiers and their families." The editor insisted that the planter ought to be lynched. "He is a meaner man, by far, than any Yankee that ever invaded our country."[19]

As reluctant as planters were to give up their produce and livestock, they were even less willing to part with their slaves. In 1862, after Fort Pulaski fell to the Federals, state officials began impressing slave labor for work on the Savannah fortifications. Though the state promised compensation for slaves killed or injured in government service, slaveholders staunchly resisted slave impressment. A group of Lee County planters led by C. M. Irvin, among others, drew up a nine-point resolution announcing their determination to resist slave impressment. Others acquiesced but demanded compensation. William Castleberry of Clay County wrote to Governor Brown protesting that he received no pay for his slaves' services. In a public letter addressed "To the Planters of Georgia," Governor Brown seemed puzzled that so few had responded to his call for slaves. He reminded planters of their stake in the Confederacy and of their earlier promises to support it: "I will not believe that there was a want of sincerity in your professions of liberality and patriotism."[20]

That slaveholders were promised pay for lost slaves only reinforced growing class antagonism. E. H. Grouby of the *Early County News* gave voice to many of Georgia's angry plain folk when he asked, "If a man of means is to be paid for a negro that dies while doing Government work, why should not a poor man or woman be also paid for the loss of a son while fighting for the country?" If anyone were to be paid, he insisted, it should be the plain folk, "instead of the rich man or woman who has lost a confounded negro, for which the poor people are now fighting. But giving poor people their rights in this country has long since 'played out,' and so, we suppose, the poor will have to 'grin and endure' whatever the wealthy are a mind to require. So wags the world!"[21]

The aversion of planters to making sacrifices led increasing numbers of plain folk to conclude that the conflict was a rich man's war. The wealthy, wrote a group of Spalding County women to the governor, "don't care what becomes of the poor class of people" as long as "they can save there niggroes." When Robert Toombs used political connections to have the slaves on his southwest Georgia plantation exempted from impressment, one local newspaper lashed out. "We believe Toombs, because he is rich, does pretty much what he wants. . . . if he were a poor man he would be hanged." Recognizing the class disparities of impressment, the editor concluded that "a *poor* man in this world has no more showing than a blind dog in a meat house with a dozen starving Yankees after him."[22]

The inequities of impressment greatly contributed to the rising poverty and hunger that plagued common folk. Early in the war, destitution struck the lower classes of the Confederacy with such cruelty that it forced many poor soldiers' wives to provide for themselves by any means available. Abandoned and hungry, many women became beggars just to keep their families alive. Leaving children at home for days or weeks at a time, they roamed the countryside pleading for food. Sympathetic railroad and steamboat men occasionally provided transportation, but most often the women made their way on foot. Some planters gave the women nothing; others gave what they could. But even the more generous viewed these unfortunates with a measure of contempt. One planter called the starving women "perfect nuisances."[23]

Some desperate women turned to prostitution. It was not uncommon for men of wealth and power to demand sexual favors in return for money, clothing, or food. One Columbus man wrote that women in unfortunate circumstances were "sometimes offered assistance at the sacrifice of their honor, and that by men who occupy high places both in church and State." Other women turned to relief committees supported by city councils. In Savannah, the city council voted to appropriate several thousand dollars to purchase provisions for needy families, and a "committee of ladies" helped distribute the goods. The pride that ran deep in most families made them reluctant to ask for assistance. The council felt that these people would trust women committee members and allow them to ascertain their needs on a confidential basis.[24]

Issues other than pride contributed to the difficult and confusing poor relief process. Frequently, men joined companies from a county other than the one in which they resided. Which county was responsible for aid to his family? The *Macon Telegraph* discussed such a predicament in 1863. B. Blair of Taylor County joined a company in neighboring Bibb County since none was forming in his own at the time. His family applied for aid in Taylor, but they were denied because the company was organized in Bibb. The clerk of Taylor County's relief fund refused to bend the rules. A concerned citizen wrote, "The one [county] takes care of the families of those who join its company, scattered perhaps all over the State, and none other; the other assumes charge of all resident families, regardless of the company in which they serve, and none other; so that between them, many needy families are left entirely destitute, of whom the Blair family is but an example." If all counties were as inflexible as Taylor and Bibb, deep suffering was inevitable for poor soldiers' families.[25]

As conditions grew worse, editors increasingly called on affluent citizens to support the poor. Throughout 1861, the *Columbus Sun* frequently reminded west Georgia citizens to care for the soldiers' families.[26] Athens's *Southern Watchman* asked its readers to remember the families of the volunteers.[27] "Give to the Poor!" read the heading for an article in the *Macon Telegraph*.[28]

Early the next year, in February 1862, the *Milledgeville Confederate Union* called on wealthy men of Baldwin County to "COME UP WITH YOUR MONEY!" Soldiers' families were suffering, and the editor reminded planters of their obligation to help: "It is for you and your property that tens of thousands of poor men are now fighting. . . . What are the rich men of Baldwin doing? Nothing. Wake up from your slumber." But many did not awaken, neither in Baldwin County nor in all of Georgia. In May 1863, the *Union* editor wrote: "There are many men, in every county in the state, who have fallen short of their duty. . . . When called on to make subscriptions to aid a poor disabled soldier, or help a soldier's suffering family, they have turned the back of their hands." The editor doubted that Georgia's upper classes would ever change their ways: "To expect such miserable abortions of humanity, who have been a living lie for more than two years, to give in their property at anything like its value in Confederate money is to expect heat from ice or light from darkness." The editor was right. As late as March 1865, the *LaGrange Reporter* had to remind Troup County planters of their obligation to provide corn to needy families in accordance with their state bonding contracts.[29]

Meat, particularly pork, was also a subject of concern for many soldiers' families. As one editor wrote in 1863, there was a great demand for pork, but much of it was being hoarded for higher prices. Citing an earlier selling price of thirty cents a pound, the *Athens Southern Watchman* noted: "We suppose those who have it expect to get *a dollar per pound for bacon* next summer. God help the poor!"[30]

In an effort to supply meat to the poor, Confederate and state governments had ordered livestock impressment in the war's first year. But the system was so fraught with excess and corruption that it hurt more than it helped. Impressment officers were authorized to take only 10 percent in cash or in kind, but they often took the last morsel of food and the last horse, mule, or milk cow. If small farmers were not already poor when the impressment officer arrived, they often were by the time he left. One newspaper reported that an impressment officer stopped a soldier's wife driving a wagonload of bacon into Augusta and took her entire supply: "Such acts as these, by officers, will not strengthen the affections of the party wronged either to the official or the parties under whom he holds his commission."[31]

When beef or pork was not at hand, some turned to less traditional sources of meat. In March 1864, the *Atlanta Southern Confederacy* asked its readers: "DO YOU EAT SAUSAGES?—If you do we have a word for your ear and a fact for your memory. A large dog was killed in this city last week and his skin was found in the possession of a butcher." The editor supposed that some of his readers had already eaten "dog venison." He could not resist a tongue-in-cheek suggestion that this might explain "the terrible 'growling' at the high prices of meat."[32]

Leather goods were also scarce in Georgia. "The article of leather for making shoes has reached enormous prices," wrote W. C. Cale of Lumpkin County. He attempted to purchase leather to make shoes for the wives and children of soldiers but found that raw leather had jumped from thirteen cents a pound to two dollars or more. Cale insisted that there was leather enough available and that such price gouging was unnecessary. He suggested that unless inferior courts were empowered to purchase shoes or leather at reasonable prices for the widows and wives of soldiers, they would suffer terribly in the coming winter months. Writing on the outside fold of Cale's letter, Brown responded by saying that he had no power to authorize the courts to insist that tanneries sell leather at particular prices: "The legislature may do something when it meets."[33]

Even firewood for cooking, curing meat, and warming the household became a scarce commodity, hoarded like any other item of value. By early 1862, the shortage was so great in Atlanta that, on his own, the superintendent of Georgia's state railroad began procuring wood for soldiers' families and the indigent. In November, Augusta's *Chronicle and Sentinel* urged the city to organize wood distribution to Richmond County's poor before the onset of colder weather. A year later the situation had not improved. In October 1863, the *Milledgeville Confederate Union* editor wrote that "the present prices of wood foreshadows great suffering among the poor for wood during the coming winter." He suggested that the inferior court of Baldwin County make preparations to raise a county tax to supply wood for the poor and called on the wealthy not to forget their poor neighbors: "Will not those in authority attend to this business before they hear of families freezing to death in our midst?" Some counties had already levied relief taxes, but as a letter in the *Atlanta Southern Confederacy* pointed out, there was rarely a systematic method for dispersing money or supplies to needy families. The writer suggested appointing committees in each ward to organize relief efforts: "Let them visit every family, and relieve the wants of those who are entitled to it."[34]

An equally pressing need was for thread to make clothing. This need was felt by both rich and poor, but there were wide degrees of difference. Planters' wives and daughters, accustomed to silks and other finery, sometimes had to settle for homemade dresses, or "homespun" as they were called. With most of the vital ports blockaded, fashionable silk dresses and hoop skirts were quickly becoming unobtainable. But to some elite young ladies of the day, style in clothing still meant everything. In 1861, one young lady calling herself "Jennie Freedom" responded to an editorial about hoops worn under the more prominent ladies' dresses. The editor had suggested that young ladies, "old maids," and children *not* wear hoops because of the shortage of material to make the undergarment wiring. "Miss Jennie" would hear none of it: "Wouldn't my new silk look a *fright*, all *tucked up* to keep it out of the mud! And then, if it were not for hoops, how could I and my two dear class mates fill up a whole pew at church and keep out all common folks from jamming down by us?" She was afraid of what the "common folks" might overhear if the girls happened to "whisper a little." She declared that she would wear her hoops as long as they were fashionable and if "awkward pedestrians" did not like it they could step out of the way.[35] Aside from fashion, her reasons for wearing hoops were clear—to keep the "common folks" at a distance.

Upper-class women were increasingly encouraged to forgo some of their prewar luxuries. Milledgeville's *Confederate Union* reported that President Jefferson Davis, during a trip through Jackson, Mississippi, tipped his hat to a southern lady wearing a homespun dress. He expressed pride at seeing an upper-class woman doing her part for the cause by wearing a dress made with her own hands instead of imported fine silk. With such an approving nod from the Confederacy's leader, what southern woman would hesitate to do the same? After all, "a homespun dress well made, and snugly fitted to the form, is truly beautiful." More women should wear homespun and, according to the editorial, "thus prove to the world that the Southern woman's principle and patriotism are not subordinate to the pride of the eye."[36] For many common folk, it was hardly a matter of pride. It was a matter of having something, *anything*, to wear.

The great difficulty was obtaining cloth to make homespun dresses, trousers, and blankets. T. M. Furlow of Americus wrote to the governor of factory misdeeds in his area and throughout the state. Cotton and woolen materials were increasingly hard to come by. Manufacturers charged outrageous prices to those wanting to make clothes and blankets, either for soldiers or themselves. Furlow suggested ways Brown could stop such speculation and warned, "If you do not do it, I would not be surprised to see the people rise in mobs and put it down themselves."[37]

Julia Fisher of Thomasville, writing for several women in her county, complained that there were no factories in the area and that it was difficult to purchase cotton cards.[38] The women were willing to spin and weave thread into blankets for soldiers and clothing for families at home, but they had no materials. Even when factory thread was manufactured locally, it was sometimes difficult to get. Bartow County factory owners claimed that the governor had "seized" their goods and that they could not sell at any price. The women petitioned Governor Brown for help. They told Brown about their husbands, brothers, fathers, and friends suffering on the battlefront, and that they wanted to make uniforms and blankets for them. "We suffer when we know they suffer," wrote the women. "We are unable to relieve them as the stony hearted owners of factories have placed the materials of clothing beyond our reach."[39]

Troup County women also suffered. An anonymous letter complained of one local factory's unwillingness to sell cloth or cotton cards at reasonable prices. The writer asked, "How is a poor soldiers wife to clothe her children when she has no cards?" She further complained of the factory employing able-bodied men who should have been in the army. She suggested that the men be sent to the front and that women be hired in their places. That way the women's families would have some means of support.[40]

Even those women fortunate enough to find work were at risk of losing their jobs if the business moved or shut down. In Savannah, many poor soldiers' wives and daughters were employed by the government to sew clothing and tents. But as Yankee blockaders choked off access to the port city, businesses moved inland, leaving Savannah's poor "needle women" without jobs. One concerned citizen asked, "Cannot the work be distributed—a portion to Savannah as to other cities—and thus help those whose condition is rendered dependent exclusively on the patronage of the government?"[41]

Perhaps worse yet was being employed at government work and receiving no pay. Martha Russell of Augusta, who had three children working at the state arsenal, was upset because they had not received their wages. "I am poore and desolate and I stand in neede of money and I cant get a sent and I wish you would try and get it for me," she wrote Governor Brown.[42]

Factory owners holding government contracts to employ "needle women" had ample opportunity to skim wages. Some paid their workers barely half the contracted wages, keeping the rest for themselves. These profit-making scandals, taking advantage of the government and the poor, drew the attention of the *Columbus Sun* in spring 1863:

Only think of it. A sleek speculator growing rich by the labor of the poor half famished needle woman, who gave up her husband as a sacrifice on the altar of our country! A man who forcibly wrests from the hands of starving children that which is to make him rich! A man who will deliberately rob the widow and orphan of their daily bread, that he may add to his opulence. A man who professes not only to be a patriot, but also a christian, who would deliberately drive the poor sewing woman to choose between a life of shame or an ignominious death by starvation! How dare such a monster look his fellow man in the face without cowering in very shame? The milder forms of villiany, such as treachery, and counterfeiting sinks into insignificance when compared with such enormities.[43]

Despite the increased profits flowing into the pockets of southern industrialists, wages were generally low in most areas, even from the war's outset. In October 1861, a "poor mechanic" wrote the *Athens Southern Watchman* complaining that when he could find work at all, it did not pay nearly what he got before the war. With prices on the rise, he wondered how he was going to support his family. He was not alone. The paper's editor knew that many local workers faced similar hardships. The only thing he could add to the man's "words of truth and soberness" was "God help the poor day-laborers."[44]

Working conditions were just as appalling as wages. In some cases, they were deadly. With labor readily available, few industrialists saw much point in spending money on worker safety. The result was that throughout the war, Georgia's urban newspapers were filled with reports of fatal industrial accidents. One of the worst occurred at Augusta's Confederate States Laboratory, where gunpowder was made. In August 1864, eighteen thousand pounds of powder exploded at the work's granulating mill, killing nine employees. The concussion stripped all the leaves from neighborhood trees and broke windowpanes in all the surrounding buildings. According to one report, the victims were "blown to atoms. Hardly a vestige of them remaining. Portions of the bodies were found hanging on the trees—a most shocking spectacle."[45]

Children in the labor force were even more imperiled. Because they were usually unskilled and economically less valuable, they often performed the most hazardous jobs. Martin Reilly, who worked at a Savannah foundry to support his widowed mother, was blinded in one eye when molten lead splattered his face. A falling timber killed John Henry, a boy of fifteen, at Oglesby's Mill near Augusta. His father had died earlier working at the same mill. Jack McElrath and John Madden, aged twelve and fifteen respectively, were horribly mangled when an artillery shell they were working on exploded at the Columbus Naval Iron Works. Both suffered through more than an hour of agony before they died.[46]

Facing dangerous conditions and low wages, one group of working women chose to strike for higher pay. In October 1864, the "female operatives" of Augusta's powder works walked out after being refused a two-dollar raise to supplement what was by then a "paltry" five-dollar-a-day wage. The owners opted to advertise for new workers, but they offered barely a living wage. As one newspaper noted, "It is rather a criminal sort of economy which arranges a schedule of pay upon a calculation of the minimum amount of food it requires to sustain a human life."[47]

Along with other sources of working-class anger—high food prices among them—a controversy over trade unions and black labor sparked unrest in cities throughout Georgia. When the General Assembly considered a bill outlawing trade unions and strikes in April 1863, white workers throughout the state howled in protest. They saw it not only as a move by industrialists against collective bargaining but also as a first step toward placing them in direct competition with slaves. In an open letter to their legislators, one group of enraged mechanics wrote: "We feel sirs, that you would rob our childrens mouth of their last crust. We feel that you would grind us down to poridge and rags. We feel that you would have us gravel in the dust beneath your aristocratic tread." They spoke for many common folk when they charged that the Confederate Constitution had been "formed solely for the benefit (socially and pecuniarily) of the aristocrats," giving poor whites "no rights that are not guaranteed to the negro." White laborers, especially skilled workers, were sure that if the anti-union bill passed, "the wealthier classes would attempt to apprentice a lot of negroes, and place them in the various machine and workshops (thus placing the negro on an equality with the white man)."[48] Many working-class whites saw those in power as a threat to their economic and social status, perhaps as much so as northern abolitionists, further entrenching the attitude that this was a "rich man's war."

Thousands of Georgians, men and women alike, wrote to state newspapers and the governor's office about desperate conditions among the plain folk. Most depressing was that much of the suffering was avoidable, arising from little more than incompetence or neglect. One man wrote to

Governor Joe Brown with news that Irwin County's court reports of indigent families were not "just and true." He listed the names of needy women, and the number of children in their households, that county officials had ignored. Francis A. Dorris wrote that the Milton County courts refused to let women draw relief rations more than once, and that her provisions had been taken by passing soldiers, leaving her without food for her family.[49]

Where some soldiers took what they wanted, others shared what they had with hungry civilians. In early 1864, General Joseph E. Johnston, commanding Confederate forces at Dalton, refused to share his army's rations with even the most destitute. An officer stationed there tried to offer as much help as was in his power, violation of policy though it was. "But," he wrote, "the supply of subsistence in the hands of the department is barely adequate to the subsistence of the army."[50] Concern for hungry women and children and the priority placed on them varied from official to official. Concerned or not, there often was not enough food available to meet either military or civilian needs. Cotton was still king.

To cope with continuing local food difficulties, county inferior courts were charged with handling the collection of taxes and distribution of goods according to each county's relief policy. Several counties established means for collecting money for support of indigent families, but conducting and enforcing such operations was difficult. In April 1864, J. D. Hammack, clerk of Taliaferro County's inferior court, wrote Governor Brown of promises made and not kept. Many of the county's men had entered service early in the war, and now their families were destitute. The men had joined believing "liberal promises from men of wealth that their families should be amply provided for." But those promises had "not been fully complied with." Hammack noted that the inferior court had tried to provide relief, but food was so scarce that there were few provisions available. Bacon was especially hard to come by. "The farmers in the County have little . . . and when you find one who could spare it, he dislikes to sell it to those families, because others can afford to pay higher prices."[51] By others, he meant planters and speculators. In a bidding war for food, poor soldiers' families were inevitably the losers.

Sometimes, local relief policies themselves were contradictory and offered little help to soldiers' families. In July 1861, a group of leading citizens met at Valdosta to discuss relief for Lowndes County's poor. Headed by R. A. Peeples, the men voted to ask the county inferior court to consider collecting a property tax for the support of volunteer soldiers' families in need and to procure clothing, blankets, and food for soldiers. One man suggested that soldiers' property should be exempt from such taxation, but Captain B. F. Mosely and J. W. O'Neal spoke up against the idea. With little debate, the motion was adopted to levy a tax on all property, including that of soldiers. Such relief efforts, whether intended to offer any real help to soldiers or not, ultimately did little good for the destitute. Later in the war, hungry women raided a government depot and a store in Valdosta.[52]

Problems with indigent assistance arose across the state as various municipalities engaged in belated, uncoordinated, and often self-defeating efforts to relieve the poor. In the war's second year, Savannah's citizens called for a system for relief. The editor of the *Savannah Republican* wrote, "The poor have been fed and clothed in other cities, and it can, and *should* be done in ours." Some voluntary contributions had already been made to the poor, but some citizens called on the city to impose a tax for their benefit. One newspaper noted that collected funds were not evenly distributed and were an "uncertain charity of the benevolent." It was not "charity" to support families sacrificing their men to the war, wrote the editor. It was simply their "just dues."[53]

A movement to establish stores for the poor began in Atlanta and spread to Columbus, Milledgeville, and other cities in 1863. The *Macon Telegraph*, hoping to spark a reaction, asked its readers, "Why should other cities and towns of Georgia be ahead of Macon in this provision for the more indigent classes of the community?" Unfortunately, many well intentioned plans never materialized. Savannah's call for the establishment of a cost-free market for soldiers' families in 1864 elicited only a "feeble response" and was abandoned.[54]

Like their urban counterparts, Georgia's rural counties also faced problems with voluntary contributions. It quickly became obvious that there were not enough volunteers to meet the need. When Clarke County's inferior court issued bonds to the amount of five thousand dollars for the relief of volunteers' families in June 1861, a local editor wrote, "This was a move in the right direction," but that "the idea of raising funds by voluntary contributions was not a good one." It seemed that many wealthy men were "penurious and closefisted," not willing to contribute a single penny.[55] Plans were made to relieve the poor from general county funds.

Other counties adopted similar plans to help the poor. Sumter County's superior court minutes from October 1863 reported that 279 soldiers' families received relief funds from which monthly payments totaled nearly twenty-eight thousand dollars. Six dollars went to each wife and two dollars to each child except to boys ten years of age and older. Parents of soldiers having no means of support received two dollars. Muscogee County's grand jury appropriated sixty thousand dollars for the relief of the poor, which was an amount additional to the state's thirty-three thousand dollars and a private relief association's one hundred thousand dollars.[56]

The cries of the indigent became so persistent that they forced the state government to take increasing notice. Letters poured into Governor Brown's office, each as heart-wrenching as the last. There were desperate tales of children having no bread or meat, of widows trying to provide for their young children while planters and county agents turned them away. In February 1862, a Georgia woman wrote to Brown: "I hope before many days we will have better times than we have now. For, if we don't, what will become of us all? We have the war to support and nothing to support with, for the provisions is so high and no money that people can't get it if they don't make it at home. And when the men all leaves, who will make support for the soldiers and the rest?"[57]

Governor Brown was soon arguing that justice and necessity called for tax reform not only by local governments but by the state as a whole. The General Assembly responded by making poor families exempt from property and poll taxes, while tax rates on the wealthy increased tenfold during the war. By 1864, disbursements from Georgia's state treasury focused mainly on welfare. More than half the state's budget that year was marked for indigent relief. But inflation took its toll on the public as well as the private sector and seriously hampered relief efforts. As early as December 1862, the wholesale price index was already seven times what it had been at the war's outset.[58]

Other difficulties plagued the relief system as well. Once a state or county agent procured items for poor relief, there was no guarantee that they could be delivered in a timely fashion. Two men in north Georgia's Dawson County wrote in 1863 about such a problem. Their court agent had received about eleven thousand dollars for indigent families from the state and had gone to middle Georgia to buy corn. However, he had not been able to obtain transportation for the corn. Three months had gone by and still no corn. It was a mystery because adjoining counties had bought and received corn since the Dawson agent had purchased his supply. The two men writing the letter believed the agent had done "his duty," but there were women in the county in desperate need of relief, "and if they are going to get any help it is time they had it." Whether the corn did not make it to Yellow Creek due to dishonesty is open to question, but such episodes eroded trust in court officials. A year later, Wiley Knight of Blackshear wrote Governor Brown that the inferior court of Pierce County "does not make an equal distribution of the money given by the State for the benefit of indigent families." Knight asked the governor to help him get a list of people who were supposed to receive help and the amount of funds given to the inferior court for distribution. "I believe," he wrote, "there is something rong, and I can detect it if you will assist me."[59]

Very often, problems with relief arose from miscommunication. In May 1862, the state relief agent in Miller County wrote to Governor Brown asking for clarification on how he should distribute the salt ration. "The salt which by your order was sent to Miller County has come to hand," the agent wrote, "and there is great need of it." But, he continued, there was "some difference of opinion" over who should receive it. Was it for the families of all soldiers then in service or only for those in service when the order was issued? And did the order include both Confederate and state troops, or only one group? If only one, which one?[60]

Salt procurement was no minor concern. Without salt, meat could not be cured and preserved, and hides could not be tanned for use in leatherwork. Salt had been imported before the war, but Lincoln's blockade had cut off outside supplies. To meet the crisis, Governor Brown began contacting various city officials and militia officers across the state about gathering the salt supplies on hand. One dispatch to Colonel Robert May of Augusta, who was also the city's mayor, read, "Take in custody for State from dealors having Stocks two thousand sacks of salt for the State and see that none goes out of the State."

To the mayor of Columbus, Brown wrote, "See to it that not another sack of salt is shipped out of the State from your City." Private citizens and the Confederate government began producing salt along the Gulf Coast early in the war, much of which was shipped up the Chattahoochee River to Columbus. But the supply was never adequate, and costs increased dramatically. In some Georgia towns, prices soared from fifty cents to ten dollars a sack. As early as December 1861, M. H. Sandwich of Thomaston wrote Brown of the poor in his county being unable to pay the exorbitant prices for salt. Their county agent had traveled to Savannah to purchase salt but had "returned without any as he could not procure it [for] less than $10 per sack." One citizen from Macon warned the governor of possible unrest and mob action if he did not release a portion of the seized salt: "They say they will take it by force as they must have salt to save their pork."[61]

It was no small task for Governor Brown to get salt and arrange for its distribution. In December 1862, he instructed officials to supply one bushel each at a cost of five dollars to families in specific counties in northeast Georgia and in Dade County to the northwest. Brown chose those counties because they had furnished large numbers of troops, their families were generally poor, and most were far removed from rail lines. But there was no guarantee that once orders were issued, county officials would follow them. Though the governor set the prices, local officials found it easy to inflate those prices and pocket the difference. Brown had run into the same problem earlier that year in south Georgia. Thomas and Joshua Griffin, assigned to distribute government salt in Valdosta, had sold it at more than twice what the state allowed and pocketed the difference.[62]

Corruption and mismanagement in distributing aid hampered state relief efforts all over Georgia. George W. Cleveland, acting justice of the peace for Miller County, wrote Governor Brown that "there must be something wrong somewheare." Apparently the families had not drawn relief funds for several months, and the county agent reported there was "no money on hand." Cleveland worried about the possibility of someone "swindling" the money. "Please answer this as soon as it comes to hand and let Justice be done to the Brave soldiers suffering wives and children." John Cain of Whitfield County expressed concern that the county agent would not give aid to several destitute women because their names did not appear on his schedule.[63]

Just as state agents could not always be counted on for competence or trustworthiness, justices of inferior courts frequently mismanaged poor relief at the county level. J. Paine of Quitman wrote the governor about women in Colquitt, Berrien, Clinch, Echols, Pierce, Ware, and Appling counties who needed food. Paine noted that the inferior courts were doing nothing to relieve the suffering families as they were bound by law to do. Women told Paine that they had received no assistance since the war began and accused court officials of using government funds "for their own private purposes." Paine stressed that he was no planter and that his only interest in the matter was to relieve suffering.[64]

Tales of corruption, incompetence, and cruelty among county agents flooded Governor Brown's office. H. W. Blake of Hog Mountain in Hall County told of local justices who refused to distribute funds to soldiers' widows and wives, and gave them only "Bread to eat and no meat. . . . I sincerely hope that the decision of the Inferior Court may never reach our Brave Men from this County that there wives and children should be compelled to live on bread alone." Alfred Harris, an elderly Dahlonega man with sons in the army, complained that Lumpkin County's inferior court refused him "any of the Benefits of publick Corne so liberally apropriated by the State to this County."[65]

From neighboring Dawson County, Sarah Hudlow—an enfeebled seventy-three-year-old widow with children and grandchildren in the war—wrote that local officials of "the meanest carrecter" were misappropriating state corn. She begged the governor "to inquire into this bisnes for it is not manege rite for some draws corn that orte [ought] not." Hudlow had applied for the badly needed corn herself but had been turned down: "If I dont git help from the government I shal have to suffer if not pearish." Enraged citizens from Fannin County called on the governor to remove their inferior court justices "for want of energy, incapacity, [and] misapplication of the public fund corn."[66]

Some local men did try to help. One concerned citizen wrote the governor about suffering in Burke County. G. R. Brown had been asked by poor soldiers' families to be appointed as their agent. With no one to act on their behalf or make complaints to the courts, the families had been allowed to suffer. Thread and yarn appropriated by the governor for needy families "was not obtained by one third," and the women were in need of someone to "protect them against swindlers." Others, like John Bachlott, worried also about widows who had lost their husbands before the war. They, too, were in need. Had their husbands lived, he argued, they likely would have joined the army. The widows should, therefore, be allowed to draw rations with soldiers' wives and widows. "Now if your Excelency don't let them in to draw corn thay must starve but I now you will."[67]

Women whose husbands had deserted, or were suspected of having deserted, were likewise often deprived of needed supplies. John Booth, an inferior court judge in Ware County, wrote the governor asking if "indigent families who there husbands has Deserted from the Service and will Not Return whether those families is intitled to the fund or not?" William Sumner of Swainsboro in Emanuel County asked the same. He told the governor that families of deserters in his county were "destitute of subsistence. Even bread and thare husbands in the bushes."[68]

Rebecca Paxton of Pickens County wrote Joe Brown in April 1864 about her situation. She had not heard from her husband for some time, and rumor was that he had "gone to the Yankees." A local official, believing the rumors, took her one mule and the only corn she had to make bread for her children. She asked for advice or some kind of relief and ended her letter by apologizing for her boldness in writing directly to the governor.[69]

Needy women were usually uncomfortable interrupting the governor's busy schedule with their letters. Some did not want their husbands to know of their complaints. Mary Lane wrote from Greenville of her destitute condition and asked for relief. She did not want her husband told that she had written the governor about "my being with out some thing to eat for it would trouble him so much. I want him to do all for his country he can."[70]

It was not uncommon for women to sign a petition or letter to the governor as a group, hoping that protesting in numbers would add strength to their pleas. Two soldiers' wives from Whitfield County dictated a letter to Governor Brown about their desperate condition and signed an "X" in place of their names: "We are willing to bear all that is possible but when our poor children calls to us for bread and we have none to give them the case is harrowing beyond description." With winter approaching, they hoped for a favorable reply from the governor so they would not have to suffer the cries of their hungry children. In the spring of 1864, seventeen Heard County women signed a petition describing their condition: "They can't get or draw any thread, corn, cards, meat or any thing of the like."[71]

As individual letters or collective petitions, the cries for relief poured into Brown's office. Mary A. Clemmons wrote of having to feed her children bread three times a day and having no meat. "Mr. Brown," she wrote, "we are not commandid to live by bread alone—we want bacon to go with the bread." In October 1864, Martha Tyler of Lowndes County wrote, "we are destitute of food and clothing and without help we will suffer." Her husband had been in the army a year and drawn no pay. Now she was asking for her husband to be discharged.[72]

Soldiers' wives often asked for their husbands' release from military service, if only for planting or harvesting. Many women had small children who were not yet old enough to help in the fields. One sympathetic captain wrote of conditions in Colquitt County after visiting there in February 1865: "I am sorry to say that nearly all of the families in that County are almost wholly destitute of any and all the articles of subsistence." He recommended that soldiers be allowed to return home to plant crops. If not, "*famine* will be the *inevitable* result." He complained that one local planter had a surplus of corn but refused to sell it, saying that soldiers' families could not pay half its worth. Even with the war drawing to an end and people hungry all around him, the man still held on to his corn hoping to sell it to those with means to purchase the highly priced staple of life.[73]

In October 1862, the *Augusta Chronicle and Sentinel* published a letter that described conditions in the governor's home county of Cherokee this way: "There are hundreds of families without salt, or leather, or thread to cloth themselves and their children, without wheat and but half crops of corn." The letter said that most of those suffering were women and children whose menfolk had gone to war—a great many of them dead or wounded. In response to this letter, perhaps currying favor with the governor, Judge Richard Lyon of Newton in southwest Georgia wrote Brown and offered one thousand bushels of corn for the people of Cherokee County. Lyon also offered to make contracts with area planters for food supplies since corn was "abundant" in the area. The state, however, would have to provide transportation.[74]

Brown sent a letter to justices of inferior courts in twenty-two north Georgia counties, including Cherokee, notifying them of the available corn. The corn was divided into portions according to each county's population as recorded in the 1860 census, with Cherokee and Cobb counties receiving the most at only seventy-two and seventy-five bushels respectively. But Brown left it to the county agents to arrange transportation, or they could opt to sell the corn where it was stored. Brown warned the justices that "it will not probably bring half as much where it is, as it would cost you to buy the same amount of corn in your county."[75]

In December 1862, the General Assembly adopted a resolution asking railroads to ship corn at half rates if it was purchased for destitute families. Regular rates would apply for speculators. In a few cases, railroads shipped corn bound for the poor free of charge. Unfortunately, some railroad owners preferred the profits that came from shipping cotton instead of food and fodder. In southwest Georgia, where Richard Lyon had his plantation, area farmers stored corn in warehouses in and around the railhead of Albany. But the corn frequently sat for weeks, wasting away as cotton was shipped out. In early 1863, several southwest Georgia citizens complained that bushels of corn by the tens of thousands were rotting in local warehouses.[76] It was one more source of frustration for starving families, and another source of class resentment.

As conditions worsened, editors urged local relief societies, often composed of well-to-do women, to continue their good works. By 1863, some of them had disbanded. In Americus, a citizen asked of that town's relief society, "Why is it that the ladies of Americus have abandoned that good work of 'feeding the soldiers' daily at the depot?" The women had been feeding returning soldiers as they made their way home. "Reorganize your Society at once, and commence the good work again." Signing the letter "Z.," the writer left one hundred dollars at the local newspaper office for the society to use in purchasing supplies.[77]

Early County's Soldiers' Aid Society had also become silent. The women had enthusiastically collected money and clothing at the war's start, but their efforts waned as the war continued. "What has become of the Soldiers' Aid Society of Early County?" asked editor E. H. Grouby in March 1864. "We haven't heard anything of it lately. We hope our noble ladies have not concluded to cease their efforts to assist our brave Soldiers." Grouby's admonishment spurred the society to renewed action for a short time, but its efforts came to little. A few months later, Grouby published a list of the meager contributions received by the Soldiers' Aid Society. "It is with *shame* for our citizens that we publish it," he wrote, "for there are many, *very many*, in our county who are well able to give *bountifully* who have not contributed a cent, while those who have, have given a very small mite." Grouby announced that he would no longer publish meeting dates of the society since the area's contributors had turned "too *infernal stingy* to give anything to those who are fighting for their all." He advised the Soldiers' Aid Society to "hang up the fiddle and the bow, for the people are too infernal hardhearted and selfish to give a poor Soldier a mouthful to eat."[78]

Confederate currency was so weak by late 1862 that planters would hardly sell food to the poor, much less give it away. In November of that year, J. B. Adair of Paulding County wrote to Governor Brown complaining that several local men were hoarding "considerable quantities" of corn. He singled out one for special censure: "Bennett Cooper of this County has about fifteen hundred bushels, more than sufficient to answer his purposes and refuses to sell a grain for anything except gold or silver, swearing that he has as much of the *damned* Confederate money as he wants." James Bush, one of Early County's wealthiest planters, refused to deal in Confederate money at all.[79]

A southwest Georgia soldier's wife wrote to the *Early County News* complaining bitterly of hunger caused by planters hoarding and refusing to take currency. They would, however, take what little the poor had in exchange for food. "This is the only way many Soldiers' families in this county can get anything to eat," wrote the distraught woman. "Love nor Confederate money won't do it." Editor Grouby added that such men "should be drummed out of every respectable community, and sent heels over head to Yankeedoodledum, where they properly belong."[80]

To many, it seemed the height of hypocrisy for planters to turn down Confederate currency. Not only had a majority of them pushed for secession, but now they were largely responsible for the currency's inflation. The *Athens Southern Watchman* announced, "Some hard cases have come to our knowledge recently of men who were very active in bringing on the war, and who now vehemently urge its prosecution, and yet refuse to receive Confederate money in payment of notes given by poor men." "Such men," said the *Turnwold Countryman*, "are whetting a sword to cut their own throats." The editor knew that if the currency broke down, the government would fall with it.[81]

Planters and speculators hoarding corn, yarn, and other essentials quickly eroded not only the economy but also the sense of enthusiasm that many had felt at the war's outset. Plain folk began to realize that class lines determined who would get those precious items and at what prices. It was just as apparent that they were being marched off to war while, for the most part, planters remained safely at home. Like so many others, one Georgia woman wrote to Governor Brown complaining that poor men had gone off to do the fighting while rich planters stayed at home. Even worse, she wrote, planters refused aid to needy soldiers' families. She ended her letter by begging the governor to "forgive me for writing this and tear it up for those people [the planters] would be as hostile towards me if I were in favor of Old Lincoln."[82]

Suffering women wrote to their husbands as well. After a visit to the Army of Tennessee, a Macon citizen wrote home to the *Telegraph* about the soldiers' concerns: "Our wives write us that corn cribs and smokehouses are locked up, and planters say they have nothing to sell, when at the same time, they are hoarding up provisions until speculators come along to give high prices."[83] Such letters would become more frequent and more desperate as the war went on.

4

"The Women Rising"

Letters of Despair and Acts of Desperation

Written words were powerful tools in the hands of Georgia's women, barely literate though many of them were. They put fears and frustrations down on scarce sheets of paper, often in homemade ink, and sent them to far-removed locations in hopes that their husbands were still alive to read them. Women from both the plain folk and the planter class shared concerns ranging from possible slave insurrections to having no bread for starving children. They flooded government offices with letters begging mercy for themselves and their menfolk. Poorer women asked for husbands and sons to be relieved from duty to return home and help on the farm. Plantation wives asked for furloughs for their men so they could protect their property from layout gangs and their women from unruly slaves. The differing concerns of women from the upper and lower classes were clear in letters received at the governor's office.

Jane Eubanks of Columbia County wrote to Governor Brown about needing men detailed to control local slaves. There were four hundred slaves in her vicinity and few white men to keep them subdued. "What will become of the females and not only for them but the stock." She worried that slaves might kill all the livestock and steal provisions.[1]

In December 1863, Mrs. John Green of Burke County wrote to Brown about the lack of white men in her area, with so many of them having been called away by the draft. She insisted that it was the governor's duty to sustain a police force for the protection of Georgia's "planting interest." Mrs. Green insisted that Brown must "see to it, that [the planter] class of citizens are protected, & not left to meet a fate worse than death." Green made much of the fear that slaves could induce when left unsupervised. The letter's last page finally made her purpose clear. It was her own husband for whom she was asking detail duty. What better choice than Mr. John Green to be placed in charge of a police detail in Burke County to oversee the slaves?[2]

Neither Eubanks nor Green was alone in wanting protection from possible slave rebellions. Women of Schley County petitioned the governor for the assignment of a man from their county who kept a pack of "Negro dogs" that he used to hunt escaped slaves. Julia A. Brooks of Brookville gathered signatures for a petition to have her husband, B. F. Brooks, detailed to conduct slave patrols. William Mansfield of Stewart County asked the governor to consider leaving men in his area to protect against "the worst of insults" and "impudence" exhibited by slaves. With the First Conscription Act in April 1862, he feared that the county would be drained of white males.[3]

In April 1862, W. M. Nichols of Stephens County wrote Governor Brown that though he had considered joining the army as a colonel, "it has been thought more patriotic in those that are left in this neighborhood to remain at home, than to go to the war."[4] Nichols added a few lines about a sick wife and his eleven plantations in the immediate area needing his supervision. He dropped a few names of those that he thought might be familiar to the governor who would support his rationale for staying at home.

Mrs. Richard B. Hill of Early County penned a letter to the governor requesting an exemption for her husband. It seemed he had charge of his mother's and sister's plantations and had just sold his own to purchase other lands. Of course, he would need to remain home to take care of the transaction. Mrs. Hill pointed out that "only the enrolling officers need know of your exemption," suggesting the matter be kept confidential. Brown responded that it was not in his power to grant her request, since he had no control over the enrolling officers of the Confederacy. However, if her husband joined a state company, Brown could detail him at home as an overseer, where he could conveniently take care of his pending purchase and ease his family's fear of being left alone with the slaves.[5]

Also fearful of slave insurrections was Francis B. Tillery. She requested that her husband be exempted from duty because of his ill health and because she would be left alone if he went into service. "I am in the midst of hundreds of negroes," Tillery wrote Brown, "and they have bin making there threats that when all the white men all went of in the war that they was going to kill the white women and children and take possession of there houses."[6]

Mrs. Mitchell Jones of Brooks County likewise asked for her husband's release. She wrote that a slave conspiracy, organized by a local white man, had been discovered and that one of her slaves was involved. She asked that her husband be allowed leave to come home and administer proper punishment, even though the Quitman jailer had already thoroughly beaten the slave and placed him in the county jail. Still, Jones feared more slave unrest. "I believe," she wrote, "I would rather fall into the hands of the Yankees than the Negroes."[7]

From early in the war, some suggested that one way to head off slave rebellion might be to put slaves in the army, especially those held by "speculating" planters. Mrs. C. J. Owen of Putnam County, upset that wealthy planters in her county were "heaping up money on sufferings of the poor," insisted that "rich speculators and extortioners should be compelled to send a part of their negros to fight." That would not only provide more men for the army but would also reduce the numbers of local slaves and the possibility of slave rebellion. As it stood, she wrote, slaves were being used only to "uphold their aristocratic owners who are nothing but Vampires."[8] In the face of mounting public discontent, slaveholders countered that slaves would make poor soldiers and continued insisting on their need for white supervision.

Plain folk expressed different concerns when asking for exemption or release from service. Pauline L. Wheeler of Columbia County considered Brown a "friend of the poor" and asked for her son's release. She had already lost her husband and two other sons to the war, and having no slaves, she needed help on her small farm. She described her work of hauling corn and wood, cutting crops, going to the mill, tending stock, and going for a physician when necessary. "Not having my son with me to do these things, I live in a state of some perplexity and vexation which is enough to drive me into insanity." The long hours of worry and work drove some women to their graves. In October 1864, soldiers' wives of Baker County petitioned the governor to allow one of their men to remain at home to make spinning wheels and build coffins. A clerk in the governor's office summarized the contents on the folded petition, underlining for emphasis the words "build coffins."[9]

FIGURE 4.1. The food shortage took a heavy toll on soldiers' families. They lived on what little they could grow and hide from impressment officers or beg from men of privilege. One Columbus resident lamented that poor women were "sometimes offered assistance at the sacrifice of their honor, and that by men who occupy high places in church and State." (*Harper's Weekly*)

The worsening condition of their families was clear enough to the soldiers. Letters from home described the struggles of destitute wives, who were often pleading for their husbands to come home. Mary Brooks was left with three young children, a baby not yet weaned, and a farm to run near Greenville. She wrote to her husband, Rhodam, "I never get any rest night or day, and I don't think I will last much longer." She was running low on bacon and salt as well as money with which to purchase them. "It is money for everything," she said, "so you may know it is getting low with me." Most soldiers had little or no money to send home. Enlisted men went without pay for months at a time. One Georgia soldier wrote home about officers in his regiment receiving their pay while the enlisted men got none. In protest, they laid down their arms until the payroll arrived.[10]

The soldiers wanted to come home just as badly as their wives wanted them to, but it was difficult for an enlisted man to get a furlough. William Asbell wrote from his station in Decatur County that none of the men were getting furloughs, and there was "no telling" when they would. A month later, furloughs were still unavailable. Some had better luck getting leave, if only for a few days. In 1862, G. W. Huguley asked for leave after receiving word that his child was ill, possibly dying. Describing his wife as being in a "wreched & desolate condition," Huguley wrote: "I must see my Bebe. I must go to my wife."[11]

Second Lieutenant G. Foster of Vann's Valley in Floyd County got equally frightening news from home. His wife wrote of someone breaking into their house while she, suffering with pneumonia, slept on a pallet in front of the fireplace. It was not an isolated incident. There had been other burglaries in the area. The whole family was suffering from sickness, and she was worried about staying home with thieves running rampant: "My Deare Husband I cant rite you the worst of it. . . . I want you to come home by the middle of next week." That was on March 6, 1862. By March 10, Foster had an eight-day furlough. After receiving a furlough, however, there was no guarantee the concerned soldier or officer could get home. One captain stationed near Savannah in 1862 got a five-day leave of absence, but no transportation was allowed.[12]

If furloughs were hard to get, discharges were nearly impossible to come by. One Georgia private said of his commander, "This damned general won't give you a furlough or a discharge till you are dead ten days, and *then* you have to prove it." William Andrews, a sergeant of the First Georgia Volunteers, recalled a soldier who found that the only way to get out of the army was to shoot his left hand off. "That," wrote Andrews, "ended his soldiering."[13]

One thing that alienated poor soldiers almost as much as the government's inability to care for their families and its refusal to allow them to do so was the ease with which wealthy officers got furloughs and discharges. The higher one's rank and the greater one's wealth, the easier it tended to be. As one Johnny Reb put it: "A general could resign. That was honorable. A private could not resign . . . and if he deserted, it was death."[14] That was no exaggeration. In 1864, a regiment of Hardee's Corps stationed at Dalton, Georgia, was forced to witness the firing squad execution of sixteen deserters. The commanding officer had each deserter tied in a kneeling position to a cross at the head of an open grave. All were shot through the head.[15] The right to act according to the dictates of one's conscience was a privilege that the South's self-styled aristocracy reserved for itself.

Failing to get permission from the army for their men to come home, thousands of Georgia women turned to Governor Brown for help. A flood of despairing letters poured into the governor's office. They told of sickness at home, only sons being taken away, husbands needing to take in crops or mend fences, and the occasional mention of an overzealous evening of drink that led to the enlistment of an impaired husband. Once word of the firing on Fort Sumter in April 1861 had spread, good cheer and whiskey flowed freely in Georgia's taverns as men gathered to talk of war or to enlist. One Atlanta woman wrote Governor Brown a few days after Sumter that she wanted her husband released from service because "he was under the influence of liquor when he did enlist—and now he regrets it very much." She had already written to President Davis, but he had instructed her to write the governor of the state in which her husband had enlisted.[16]

Such letters became more common as the war continued and more men died. Susan Thurman of Lumpkin asked Brown to declare her husband exempt from service. All his brothers and brothers-in-law had been killed in the army, and he was needed at home to help their widows and children. A Decatur County woman, Mrs. Aliff Williams, wrote to Brown on behalf of her brother. He was home on sick leave suffering with bronchitis and chronic asthma and was unable to return to duty. "Besides," she wrote, "he is a poor man with a wife and a hand full of little children [and] a widowed mother."[17]

Brown received another letter from a poor woman in Stewart County who had lost her husband, two brothers-in-law, and a brother to the war. She had one brother left, and he was in the army sick with typhoid fever, measles, and a "hacking cough." She begged the governor to discharge her brother so he could recover and care for his three children. "Their Mother is dead," she wrote, "and his Mother is a widow and not able to do anything for them."[18] Despite such heartbreaking pleas, few enlisted men who could walk and carry a rifle were allowed to leave the army.

That became painfully clear to one Georgia woman who had sent ten sons to the army. Mildred Bone of Bogg's Chapel wrote General Robert E. Lee on April 7, 1863, asking for a furlough for one of her sons to help with planting crops. Lee replied by commending her on her noble devotion of ten sons to the service. He wrote that he needed every good soldier available and denied her request: "If we allowed all to return who are needed at home we should soon have no country and no home." Lee sympathized but felt sure that Bone's kind neighbors in the "patriotic State of Georgia" would not allow her to suffer.[19]

Lee's response demonstrated how little he knew, or cared to acknowledge, about conditions on the homefront. Suffering had long since become a way of life for thousands of Georgia women. Catherine McDonald of Sumter County, a widow for some years before the war, needed assistance in writing a letter asking that her sixteen-year-old son be allowed to stay home and help her on the farm. She had already lost two sons in battle. One son-in-law was in a Yankee prison and the other was at the front. Her household consisted of nine children and six grandchildren. To add to her difficulties, McDonald had fallen and broken her right arm. She had someone write the letter for her; then she marked an "X" by her name. "Can she be allowed to keep the lad at home for a while at least," the letter read, "or is it the policy of the state to subject the widow and her children and grand children to suffering and starvation in order to have the services of a mere boy in the ranks?"[20]

Letters from soldiers to their families were filled with regret at not being home and advice on what to do until their return. In November 1863, William Asbell wrote to his wife, Sarah, from Camp Cobb in Decatur County: "I have received both of your letters and was glad to hear Through them that you are all alive but sorry to know that the children are sick on your hands when I cannot be there to assist you with Them." William told Sarah to feed their hogs corn once a day and potatoes the rest of the time. "If the children are not able to dig the potatoes," he said, "fence of a portion of the patch for [the hogs]." As the weather grew colder and food ran low, William wrote his wife, "You had better try and sell one or other of the horses . . . as you are scarce of Provisions. You will have to do the best you can."[21]

For many women laboring under the burdens of inflation, impressment, sick children, and absent husbands, their best was simply not good enough. Thousands of petitions from women all across the South describing their desperate situation and begging for relief poured into Richmond. Typical of these was the following, dated September 8, 1863, from soldiers' wives in Miller County: "Our crops is limited and so short . . . cannot reach the first day of march next. . . . But little [food?] of any sort to Rescue us and our children from a unanamus starveation. . . . We can seldom find [bacon] for non has got But those that are exzempt from service . . . and they have no humane feeling. . . . I tell you that with out som grate and speadly alterating in the conduckting of afares in this our little nation god will frown on it and that speadly."[22]

They received no help from the Davis administration. Worse yet, military officials denied their husbands the opportunity to help. Family deprivation was not generally considered a valid reason for furloughs. They would have done Miller County's women little good in any case. Just a day after they signed their petition, the Miller County Wildcats were captured at Cumberland Gap, Tennessee, and spent the rest of the war in an Illinois prison camp.[23]

Letters to men at the front also detailed the horrible conditions their women faced at home. These letters were filled with such gloom that thousands of men began leaving the ranks. Knowing the inevitable impact of such letters, one Georgia editor wrote in August 1861, "If you feel sad, don't write at all, rather than write in a sad strain."[24]

Despite the many warnings, women continued to send their tear-stained letters to loved ones in the field. In April 1862, Eli Hurst, stationed at Camp Jackson, Savannah, received word from his wife in Thomas County that the fence around his land had been destroyed by fire, leaving crops exposed to the livestock. He requested an eight-day leave of absence so he could mend the fence or make arrangements for someone else to do so.[25]

In early 1863, one soldier received a letter from his wife, who told of her suffering and begged him to come home. After several days of reading and rereading the letter, he abandoned his post. Soon he was captured, tried, and convicted of desertion, then executed by firing squad. Wrote one commentator about the man's wife, "She inconsiderately brought her husband to a dishonorable death and refuses to be comforted." He chastised women for writing such sad letters and closed with an ominous: "Wives! mothers! beware what you write to your sons and husbands in the army. A thoughtless and imprudent letter may lead to discontent, desertion and death."[26]

Times were indeed trying for families left at home. Jason L. Dupree, a Putnam County miller, wrote Governor Brown about his family's condition and begged for an exemption from service. Like so many others, he was deeply worried about the well-being of his wife and three children. Dupree was reluctant to leave his poor family "to the cold sympathies of the world." He continued in his letter, "please think the matter over, imagine a man's feeling to go to the bedside to take leave of his sick wife whom he had nersed so long, the children clinging to him to stay."[27]

It was for many men the greatest struggle they faced during the war. As one soldier wrote in October 1863 in response to his wife's letter: "Dear Wife, I would like to bee thare with you in youre sickness to waite on you as it is I cant. I want you to take care of yourself as i want to see [you] more in this life and if we are note permited to meete nomore in this life I doo hope that we will bee prepared to meete in thate uper and beter world where there, there will bee no more parting of wives A[nd] husbands And children fathers And mothers."[28]

When soldiers found a quiet moment to answer letters, they poured their hearts onto the paper wishing for better times. Many chose to desert, feeling that their family's survival was more important than the Confederacy's. What would be the point of victory if there were nothing left at home? To many, letters from home were proof enough that desertion was a necessary and honorable act, especially since they believed that the wealthy were acting so dishonorably toward soldiers' families. Letters sent to the governor and to the battlefront contained not only news of destitution but also news of class resentment. Such class resentment helped to further divide and define a soldier's sense of honor and duty from that of his commanding officers.

Written expressions of homefront hardships sometimes took a poetic turn. In the spring of 1863, Georgia newspapers circulated this heart-wrenching verse. It was a reminder of the sacrifices made by soldiers' families and a general cry for help.

The Widow's Appeal

Stranger, have you corn?
Can you my wants supply?
My infant, early born,
Needs succor, else 'twill die.

At Crampton, where the skies
With bullets were o'ercast—
There my loved Charlie lies,
And sadly breathed his last.

I cannot, will not steal,
Me loved one to supply.
Will you my sorrows heal?
Refuse me and I die.

The days are sad and drear,
Since Charlie left me alone,
I'm a stranger, pilgrim here,
To Heaven I make my moan.[29]

The poem was also a gentle admonishment. Its assumption that women would not resort to theft was more wishful than real. By the time it saw print, Georgia women had already begun taking matters into their own hands. As early as June 1862, a group of soldiers' wives in Bartow County descended on Cass Depot and demanded cotton. They needed only a small amount and intended to pay, but the agent refused to deal with them. That would not be the end of it. Returning later that day, the women "called for the Agent as a witness of their doings, and cut the rope from one bale, took what they needed, and marched very quietly home with it." In November, a "party of Ladies . . . driven by necessity" raided a Cartersville store.[30] With desperate times calling for desperate measures, many others soon followed their example.

Cities throughout the South saw the same kind of disturbances in early 1863: Salisbury, North Carolina, on March 18; Mobile, Alabama, on March 25; and Richmond, Virginia, on April 2. Other riots took place in Lafayette, Alabama; Abingdon, Virginia; Archer, Florida; and Sherman, Texas.[31] Georgia too saw robberies and riots that spring. They would continue through the rest of the war.

Widespread outbreaks of looting hit the state's northern and central urban centers first, where deprivation was most concentrated and keenly felt. Raids later spread south, occurring mainly along rail lines where food was stockpiled. Most took place in the spring after winter supplies had been exhausted. Speculators were the rioters' prime targets in the larger cities like Atlanta, Columbus, and Savannah. Government warehouses and depots frequently bore the brunt of attacks in smaller towns like Valdosta and Colquitt. In the rural areas of Early, Miller, and Pierce counties, planters felt the women's wrath. Near the towns of Marietta, Thomasville, and Forsyth, women attacked wagons loaded with food or other necessities.[32]

Most of the women were driven by hunger and destitution. Some may also have had political motives in mind. All certainly knew, consciously or not, that the market system of goods distribution had left them wanting. By the spring of 1863, in what amounted to an open display of class conflict, desperate Georgia women aimed to impose greater equity on the system.[33]

FIGURE 4.2. In March 1863, a band of Atlanta women—led by "a tall lady on whose countenance rested care and determination"—stole two hundred dollars worth of bacon at gunpoint. Similar incidents occurred in Savannah, Macon, Augusta and Columbus. Smaller towns like Valdosta and Colquitt also saw hungry women forced to robbery and riots. (*Frank Leslie's Illustrated Newspaper*)

March 16, 1863, saw about a dozen women raiding a store on White Hall Street in Atlanta. Their leader, "a tall lady on whose countenance rested care and determination," asked about the price of bacon. When she heard it was a dollar a pound, she said that the women in her group were wives and daughters of soldiers and could not afford to pay such prices. To demonstrate her seriousness, "this tall lady proceeded to draw from her bosom a long navy repeater, and at the same time ordered the others in the crowd to help themselves to what they liked." They cleared the room and made off with nearly two hundred dollars worth of bacon. A few weeks later in Cobb County, just north of Atlanta, a black man driving a wagonload of goods to Marietta was robbed of several bales of yarn by a "gang of women" who forcibly took three to six bunches of yarn each.[34]

On April 10, a number of women entered a store near Augusta's Upper Market and asked about prices for shoes and calico. The proprietor sensed mischief afoot, so he closed his store due to "pressing business" elsewhere. The women moved to another store but took nothing and dispersed after authorities came on the scene. They arrested one man for "telling the women they did perfectly right." One Augusta newspaper labeled the women "Amazonian warriors" even though the mob never turned violent.[35]

A few days later, Columbus newspapers gave accounts of that city's "seizing party." On April 11, a group of women numbering about sixty-five rallied at the intersection of Broad Street and Franklin Street (now Fourteenth Street) and marched down Broad Street "to raid the stores of speculators." Armed with knives and pistols, the rioters shouted curses as they went. They first struck George A. Norris's dry goods store and "commenced helping themselves to whatever they wanted." Police arrived in time to disperse the mob before it could reach other stores. A man named "Shanghai Brooks," described by the press as a vagabond, was arrested for encouraging the women. Seven months later, Columbus women warned the governor by letter that they would again organize a mob and take provisions if they received no relief. Brown forwarded the letter to Muscogee County's inferior court justices, "requesting them to take such action in the premises as the court might think proper."[36]

Milledgeville women seized items from a dry goods store on the morning of April 14, 1863. They dispersed only when Judge L. Harris promised that if they would end their march and return the goods, they would get immediate relief. The women did as Harris asked and received funds from the city treasury. Macon saw its women rioting that same month. In what one editor called "The Women Rising," a crowd armed with pistols and knives attacked "Rosenwald & Bro." store on Second Street to seize calico and other supplies. The proprietor grabbed one of his assailants, wrestled a bowie knife from her, and retrieved two bolts of calico. The other women escaped with their loot.[37]

Later in April, a band of twenty-eight women, most of them armed with pistols and knives, robbed a freight wagon headed from a factory in Butts County to the rail depot at Forsyth. The editor of the *Macon Telegraph* called on "the good old county of Monroe to nip this dangerous business in the bud." Sensing class animosities reflected in this and similar incidents, the editor emphasized that protection of private property for both elites and commoners was at stake: "The rich can better afford to be robbed than the poor, and when that game is set afoot the poor will be the greatest sufferers." But from the perspective of plain folk, the rich had robbed them through speculation and impressment. They saw themselves as taking back only what was, in a general sense, theirs by right.[38]

Most newspaper editors did not share that view, at least at the outset of rioting. The *Athens Southern Watchman*'s editor warned of dire consequences should women continue their miscreant ways. "Every body and every thing we hold dear," he feared, "would be involved in one common ruin." A few weeks later, the editor refused to publish a letter defending riotous action, suggesting that those who supported such acts were "in favor of an abrogation of all government.... Why, Hell itself, with all its horrors, has never descended to the degradation of mob violence." Still another newspaper, labeling the rioting women "of the baser sort," suggested that the rioting crowds receive an "application of the Hydropathic principle from the noozle of a Fire Engine."[39]

Some editors were quick to suggest that no respectable woman would participate in such lawlessness. Some dismissed hunger as a motive for the riots. Said one editor, "The class composing the mobs are of the lowest—prostitutes, plug uglies ... and those who have always been a nuisance to the community, and who are not in a perishing, or even suffering condition, for want of food." Another editor wrote that the raiding parties were made up of loafers, vagrants, prostitutes, professional thieves, and jailbirds instigating riots under the pretense that they were driven by "stern necessity." Others accused mobs of working with the Yankees to throw citizens into "a state of confusion, consternation and terror."[40]

The editor of Turnwold's *Countryman*, in assessing the rioters, perhaps most clearly reflected the patriarchal prejudices of his day: "Women do not transgress the bounds of decorum so often as men, but, when they do, they go [to] greater lengths. . . . for with reason somewhat weaker, they have to contend with passions somewhat stronger. Besides, a female by *one* transgression forfeits her place in society forever." According to this editor, a woman's modesty was her greatest asset; if she engaged in stealing and rioting, she forfeited her heavenly "ornament." "If an angel falls," he insisted, "the transition must be to a demon."[41]

Yet another editor believed that the female raiders must be "under the control of cowardly, villainous men, and by them instigated to the commission of these robberies." But that was no excuse for women to behave in such a dishonorable way: "let not the seizers with stripes and gold lace escape." Some thought that men might be more directly involved. One editor likened the riots to those of the French Revolution, "inaugurated by women and men dressed in women's clothes." Insisting that food was bountiful and no family was starving, another editor urged authorities to crack down on "the worthless beings."[42]

Still, it was clear that female violence, though localized, was hardly isolated. In April 1863, with riots breaking out all over the state, the *Athens Southern Watchman*'s editor looked for the root cause of the disturbances. He concluded that ultimate blame lay not with the rioters but with self-interested elites, especially speculators, who cared more for profit than patriotism. In a passionately worded editorial, he begged the well-off to change their ways: "In the name of our beloved country—in the name of outraged humanity—in the name of that religion they profess to reverence—in the name of the God they pretend to fear—we call upon these men to change their policy before it shall be too late! Our sun may yet set in anarchy and blood."[43]

As reports on raids and riots filtered through Georgia newspapers in the spring of 1863, sympathy for the indigent and destitute became more widespread. So did the riots. When asked why she participated in the Augusta disturbance, one woman said, "We heard that they had raised the red flag all over the country, and people only had to go and take what they wanted." Women throughout the state, driven by the same red flag of hunger and deprivation, imposed what some called "mobocracy" as they took up knives and pistols, raiding depots, warehouses, and stores.[44]

At the height of the spring riots that year, the Confederate Congress passed a joint resolution urging that planters, "instead of planting cotton and tobacco, shall direct their agricultural labor mainly to the production of such crops as will insure a sufficiency of food for all classes, and for every emergency, thereby with true patriotism subordinating the hope of gain to the certain good of the country." But planters ignored the resolution and continued, as one Georgia editor later put it, to "carry their patriotism in the *pocketbook*." Efforts to employ soldiers' families in major urban centers helped ward off riots after 1863, but with planters unwilling to change their ways, hunger and destitution remained serious problems.[45]

In the summer of 1863, eleven Pickens County women—said to be unionists—stormed a tanyard at Talking Rock. According to one report, they "helped themselves to as much leather as they could well carry off." They boasted of having protection from menfolk home as paroled prisoners of war and threatened to raid other businesses. One local merchant wrote to Governor Brown begging him to stop the riots and to protect the community from those "who have not our cause at heart."[46] But the riots did not stop. Food was too scarce and hunger too rampant.

In the late fall of 1863, starving women rampaged through Thomasville for the "purpose of supplying themselves with goods." Threats of further violence caused such fear among city officials that they called for help from as far away as Lowndes County, fifty miles to the east. Thannie Wisenbaker, a Valdosta resident, later remembered when the town's home guard

> was ordered to Thomasville where some great excitement was reported. My! Such preparation in getting ready for the trip! Everything that they imagined they might need was gotten ready. Old muskets, used in the war with the Indians, shot-guns and such old pistols that they had on hand, were readied. . . . The men rushed hurriedly from place to place, pressing into use every horse and mule available, until at last they rode off to Thomasville. But alas! For their hopes and dreams of meeting and subduing the enemy. When they arrived in Thomasville, they learned, to their utter chagrin, that some soldier's wives had threatened to break into the government commissary to obtain food for their hungry children.[47]

It was the only time Valdosta's home guard was ever called to service.

At its December session, the Thomas County Superior Court called the riot a "disgraceful act" and warned that "all such misguided females" should refrain from "unlawful demonstrations in the future." Driven by continuing hunger, women did not always heed such warnings. Some months later, six Thomas County women armed with rifles stopped a wagon and stole its cargo of corn. Ineffective as they were, warnings like those from Thomas County's superior court were usually the extent of legal recriminations.[48]

Another wave of rioting struck Georgia in the spring of 1864, this time focused on the state's southern half. In April, newspapers reported a "daring robbery" in Savannah near the old City Market. A number of women entered the stores of A. F. Mira on Whitaker Street, John Gilliland on Congress Street, W. and R. McIntire on Saint Julian Street, and a Mr. Stroup on Bryan Street, helping themselves to bacon and other items. Mira was preparing to sell the women bacon but was forced into a corner while they helped themselves. One of the McIntires offered the women rice and sugar free of charge, hoping to avoid a general ransacking. His gesture appeased the women. They moved on to Gilliland's store, where they stole all his bacon. Gilliland tried forcibly to retrieve some of his pork, but most of the women escaped with their plunder.

Sheriff Cole of Chatham County arrested three women and placed them in jail. Mary Welsh, charged with taking bacon from Gilliland's store, was turned over to the magistrate for prosecution. Anne McGlin and Julia McLane were charged with disorderly conduct. In the end, none of the women were prosecuted. There was too much popular sympathy for them, especially since they were soldiers' wives. Store owners Gilliland and Mira later applied for reimbursement from Savannah's City Council. Gilliland asked for $250; Mira wanted $210. The council tabled their requests.[49]

On April 19, E. Yulee of Stockton wrote Governor Brown that "thirteen women made their appearance here armed with pistols and knives and demanded admittance to the depot containing the provisions collected as tax in kind." Three guards at the depot tried to "pacify" the women, but they shoved the guards aside, broke open the door, and took over one hundred pounds of bacon. Yulee believed that these women would steal more supplies now that they knew they could "seize them with impunity." He suggested that the civil courts might offer a remedy, but "unfortunately these are now silent in the middle of our troubles." Most of the governor's incoming correspondence was read by clerks who wrote a short description on the outside of envelopes or letters for faster processing. Yulee's letter was marked "women outrages."[50]

Just to the west of Stockton, Lowndes County saw more female lawlessness that month. A group of Valdosta women marched on a local store and tried to buy cotton yarn, but the proprietor refused to take Confederate money. He would, however, trade for bacon. Having no bacon to exchange, the women "forcibly took all the yarns in the store." In the same neighborhood, a dozen or more women—at least one armed with a pistol—broke into a government warehouse and stole a wagonload of bacon.[51]

At about the same time, the small Lowndes County settlement of Naylor had troubles of its own. A mob went on a rampage "for the purpos of taking of spun yarn cloth and bacon." Among the participants were three members of Union Primitive Baptist Church. Hetta Peters, Rachel Chitty, and W. S. Peters came under the "displeasure" of the congregation for their role in the riot. According to church minutes, "W. S. Peters cleared himself; Hetta Peters confessed and was forgiven with joy." Chitty, apparently unrepentant, refused to answer the church summons and was turned out of the congregation.[52]

Campbell County Justice of the Peace B. D. Smith found himself in an uncomfortable situation in May over the issue of women taking impressment into their own hands. In a letter to Governor Brown, Smith outlined the circumstances that led two men to accuse him of "up holding the women presying provisions." The men in question were trying to avoid conscription by having Smith call elections for bailiffs and running for the positions themselves. Once elected, they would not have to report for duty. To force the issue, they had tried to frighten a sixty-one-year-old bailiff into quitting his post. But neither Smith nor the bailiff would be intimidated. In retaliation, the two men accused Smith of supporting women who forcibly took what they needed. He denied the accusation but wrote, "I did not blame the women." Smith told of a gentleman who was "staying at home" only to profit from a war in which he refused to fight. Though the man was well aware of how badly soldiers' wives needed provisions and had "a right smart to spair, he would not let them have it neither for money nor work but was speculating on it." Careful not to alarm the governor, Smith noted that the women's actions were peaceful. He refused to call the impressment a raid, insisting that no such incident, with all its violent connotations, had ever taken place in Campbell County.[53]

Destruction of property was usually not a part of the women's plans for justice. But there was at least one raid that resulted in severe property damage. In June 1864, a number of armed Pierce County women broke into a storehouse, "carried off several wagon-loads of bacon, and burned some houses." These women boasted that they had plenty of men—including deserters hiding in the Okefenokee Swamp—who would back them up should they meet resistance. According to one source, "the people of property were much alarmed"—so much so that one "prominent citizen" took the train from Blackshear to Savannah and personally reported the attack to military authorities.[54]

As the war entered its final months and the plight of Georgia's women grew more desperate, they continued their robberies and raids. During the winter of 1864–65, soldiers' wives and children were regularly seen stealing livestock in Early and Miller counties. One man who signed himself "A Stock Raiser" placed a notice in Blakely's *Early County News* demanding that the thievery stop. He insisted that he had already given generously to local relief efforts and was sorely disappointed in the women. He threatened to publish their names in a later issue of the *Early County News* if they did not stop their criminal ways: "What would your husbands and fathers think if they should see your names in a public print as *stock stealers*?" John Davis of Miller County, a well-to-do slaveholder and stock raiser, complained about women stealing his sheep's wool. The sheep were being caught, sheared, then released back into the woods. He too warned that unless the women stopped their "nefarious business," he would have their names published in the local paper. Besides, Davis insisted, these apparently desperate women were not needy at all. It was simply, he said, their nature to steal: "They are now acting as they always would have done, had they the same opportunity."[55]

Such attitudes were common among the upper classes. As early as 1862, Godfrey Barnsley, a wealthy Bartow County planter, complained that "the character of the population here . . . is growing worse." "Thieving," he said, "in no small way" was among their character flaws.[56] Few planters acknowledged the obvious link between desperate circumstances and desperate acts. But ignoring the problems of cold and hunger only made them worse.

In February 1865, fifty women raided the government depot in Colquitt, the seat of Miller County. Armed with axes, they broke open the doors and took close to fifty sacks of government corn, or about one hundred bushels. It was reported that the women were soldiers' wives and that the justices of Miller County's inferior court were to blame for their conditions. In an open letter, one local resident accused the justices of being more focused on their own concerns than on the well being of the destitute women and children. The accusations of callousness did not stop with local officials. State officials, including Governor Brown, were also at fault. Singling out the governor, the writer stated that he had always thought of Brown as a "complete demagogue" and an "out and out humbug" looking after his own interests. The *Augusta Chronicle and Sentinel* shared the writer's sentiments, especially about the lack of proper administration of poor relief. Commenting on the Colquitt raid, the editor wrote: "The Government has lost the corn. Would it not have been much better to have given it freely to the sufferers? We think so."[57]

Among the women's staunchest supporters were deserters or soldiers home on furlough. In March 1865, Hart County soldiers formerly of the Army of Tennessee arrived home and were appalled at the destitution they found. Realizing that no help was coming from the county's inferior court justices, these men raided a local gristmill and distributed sacks of government flour to about fifty women.[58]

In the spring of 1863, Daniel Snell of Harris County had written home to his wife, Sarah: "You spoke of a riot in Columbus. . . . it is no more than I expected. I understand there was also one in Augusta. . . . What will become of the women and children with the food situation?"[59] Many soldiers wondered how their families would get along in their absence. Others knew all too well. Said one man serving in the Army of Tennessee: "I have been in all the battles of the West, and wounded more than once, and my family, driven from their home, and stript of everything, are struggling in Georgia to get a shelter and something to eat. . . . little sympathy is shown my suffering wife and children—they are charged three prices for what scanty accommodation they get, and often are nigh starvation. We might as well be under Lincoln's despotism as to endure such treatment."[60] Like so many others, he was ready to give up the fight and go home.

Thousands of southern men faced the dilemma of whether to allow their families to die at home or to risk death themselves by deserting. Despite the danger, soldiers deserted by the thousands. Presenting their rifles as furloughs to anyone who dared challenge them, soldiers made their way over hundreds of rugged miles to help their starving families.[61] Some never made it. Many of those who did were dragged back to the army in chains. Sergeant William Andrews of Lee's Army of Northern Virginia wrote that it was "an everyday occurrence for men to get letters from home stating that their families are on the point of starvation. Many a poor soldier has deserted and gone home in answer to that appeal, to be brought back and shot for desertion."[62]

The way the soldiers saw it, they had very little choice. If the government could not care for their families, they had to; their first duty was to their wives and children. Even soldiers with no families starving at home had great sympathy for those who did. William Andrews, a bachelor, insisted that he too, faced with the same choice, would desert. "Thank God," he wrote, "I have no wife and children to suffer on account of an ungrateful government."[63]

5

"Worse Than Slaves"

Military Conscription

Family hardships, hunger, and class resentment all contributed to an early general decline of enthusiasm for the war. So weak was popular support by the spring of 1862 that officials in Richmond feared the war might soon be lost. The army needed men badly, but few would willingly come forward. Willing or not, as far as the government was concerned, they had to come.

In April 1862, the Confederate Congress passed the First Conscription Act, giving the president authority to force young men into the military. Under the terms of this act, commonly known as the draft, white males between the ages of eighteen and thirty-five became subject to involuntary military service. To induce men to enlist before the draft went into effect, the government offered a cash bonus to those who volunteered and allowed them to serve with units of their choice. With prior warning that the Conscription Act was imminent and fearing they would be drafted in any case, thousands of reluctant men volunteered in March and early April.

One such volunteer was John Joseph Kirkland of Early County. A small slaveless farmer, Kirkland had a wife and five children when he enlisted as first corporal with the Early Volunteers in March 1862, a few weeks before the draft began. He was thirty-three, only two years short of exemption. His younger brother Jacob joined the Early Volunteers as well and two months later died in Virginia. John Joseph had the heartbreaking duty of escorting his brother's body home to their mother. A year after that—having fought through the Peninsula campaign, Second Manassas, Sharpsburg, and Fredericksburg—John Joseph was nearly killed himself when his right leg was shattered at the Battle of Chancellorsville. His leg was amputated just below the knee.[1]

To plain folk, the most offensive provisions of the Conscription Act were those allowing moneyed men to hire a substitute or simply pay the government an exemption fee. Equally offensive was the infamous twenty-slave law, which virtually excused planters from the draft. Though few officials seemed to realize it at the time, this single law defined the nature of the war for many southerners. From 1862 until the conflict's end, the attitude that it was a "rich man's war and a poor man's fight" was so pervasive that some wealthy gentlemen saw no point in pretending otherwise. One member of southwest Georgia's gentry ran an advertisement in the *Early County News* that read "WIFE WANTED—by a young man of good habits, plenty of money, good looking and legally exempt from Confederate Service."[2]

Not only could planters have themselves exempted from the draft, they could get their overseers off as well. Congress had initially made overseers exempt, but the outcry among plain folk had forced repeal. It hardly mattered. President Davis had the authority to exempt them himself, and he did so under pressure from influential planters. In spring of 1863, Dougherty County planters demanded in a collective petition that Davis exempt their overseers. So did David Barrow, who owned several plantations in southwest Georgia. In a private letter to one of Davis's military aides, Barrow listed the names of his overseers and insisted that "the President can exempt these men. . . . get him to have them exempted from conscription." Davis did just that and more. He directed his secretary of war to suspend conscription of all overseers in southwest Georgia.[3]

Overseers were not the only commoners to whom exemptions were extended. While conscription policies excused the mentally or physically disabled from service, they also exempted those deemed essential to social and economic stability: state and Confederate employees, contractors, shoemakers, tanners, blacksmiths, wagon makers, millers, millwrights, and employees of wool and cotton factories and paper mills. Occupational status had to be demonstrated to the satisfaction of enrollment officials,

FIGURE 5.1. John Joseph Kirkland of Early County—a small farmer and author David Williams's great-great-grandfather—had a wife and five children when he enlisted as first corporal with the Early Volunteers in March 1862, a few weeks before the draft began. He was thirty-three, only two years short of exemption. A year later he was nearly killed when his right leg was shattered at the Battle of Chancellorsville. The leg was amputated just below the knee. (Courtesy of Martha Bush Kirkland, Miller County, Ga.)

who sometimes required an unofficial fee for the service. Exemptions did not extend to conscientious objectors.[4]

Elite southerners, of course, supported the exemption system. By their reasoning, it protected the select few to whom the Confederacy looked for fiscal, political, and social leadership. It also allowed those skilled workers who could supply the military with weapons, clothing, and transportation to remain where they could best serve. Was it not obvious, the elite argued, that unskilled commoners serve where best they could—on the battlefront? But those commoners—the great majority of the South's people—saw the act in a different light. To them, upper-class justifications aside, one thing was perfectly clear: money and social standing protected men who wished to avoid a bloody death on the firing line.

When one Georgia farmer was drafted, he complained bitterly to a neighbor: "They've got me in this war at last. I didn't want to have any thing to do with it any how. *I* didn't vote for Secession—but them are the ones who have to go & fight now—and those who were so fast for war, stay out." Plain folk expressed similar attitudes throughout the state. "The people of Georgia regard the draft as disgraceful," George A. Mercer insisted. Even those already in the army complained about conscription. Young Edward Harden wrote from his post: "The army here is in great excitement. . . . I find everybody opposed to this tyrannical conscription law." William Andrews and five other men of the First Georgia Regiment hanged a conscript officer in effigy as a way to "make our intentions known to them. . . . It was never found out who done it and that was the last thing heard of a conscript officer coming to our camps."[5]

Plain folk were especially upset that planters were virtually exempt from the draft. One enraged Georgia soldier wrote to the *Atlanta Southern Confederacy*, "for God's sake don't tell the poor soldier who now shivers in a Northern wind while you snooze in a feather bed, that it is *just* and *right* that the men, who Congress has exempted, should enjoy ease at home, amassing untold riches, while *he* must fight, bleed, and even die."[6] Another Georgia trooper called planters

> the most contemptible of all our public enemies. . . . These fellows talk loudly about *their* constitutional rights—that no body has a right to say how much cotton they shall plant and intend to put at defiance the law and the authorities. But listen again and you will hear them loud for the enforcement of the Conscript Law. Oh, yes! Their negroes must make cotton and whilst doing it the poor men must be taken from their families and put in the Army to protect their negroes. Was ever a greater wrong, or a more damning sin, perpetrated by men or devils?[7]

Another Georgia soldier suggested that "owners of twenty hands . . . ought to be made to fight for their property or ought to be deprived of it."[8] The inequities of conscription turned many against not only the Confederate government but also the state for permitting it. A. W. Millican of

FIGURE 5.2. Shielded from the draft in various ways, legal and illegal, planters who wished to avoid military service had little trouble doing so. "Their negroes must make cotton," complained one Georgia soldier, and "the poor men must be taken from their families and put in the Army to protect their negroes. Was ever a greater wrong, or a more damning sin, perpetrated by men or devils?" (*Harper's Weekly*)

Dirt Town in Chattooga County wrote a biting letter to Governor Brown in June 1862 asking why he was not protecting Georgians from "the centralized military despotism at Richmond." "Why didn't you hang the first minion of Richmond that called himself a Conscription officer for treason against the Government [of] Georgia?" Millican insisted that if Brown were not going to defend his people from Confederate oppression, he should tell them how they might do it themselves: "You will very much oblige many men in Georgia if you will assist them in finding out whether they are *citizens* or *slaves*." Someone in the governor's office scribbled on the back of the letter "Impertinent and disrespectful. No answer." The answer seemed clear enough to one Georgia soldier who wrote home that "Georgia freemen who voluntarily put their necks in the yoke in response to this country's call are to day slaves—nay, worst than slaves—bruts—chained under the yoke of military discipline & must abide their time."[9]

Compulsory military duty was, in fact, nothing new in Georgia. The state had used a form of conscription to boost militia enrollments for home defense, and state laws required all eligible white males to serve on local slave patrols. But until the Civil War, a national government had never exercised such powers. Instead, requisitions were made for state troops in time of war, requisitions that could be refused by state governments. With the Conscription Act, the Confederate government sought to bypass the state and act directly on the citizen to form a national military under Confederate, not state, control.[10]

Many in the Confederacy regarded the Conscription Act as an ominous sign of a government bent on stifling personal freedoms, much as the United States government had been accused of doing. If the Confederate government could assume such sweeping powers over its citizens, could a complete denial of personal liberty, even a declaration of martial law, be close at hand? Although conscription had been passed by a civilian body, the Confederate Congress, its enforcement was left to the military. State leaders immediately recognized the constitutional implications of such centralized power. Governor Brown considered the act "a bold and dangerous usurpation by Congress of the reserved rights of the States and a rapid stroke toward military despotism." Yet, while Brown argued that the centralization of military power in the hands of President Davis would "cripple or destroy the civil government of each state," Georgia's Supreme Court disagreed. In its November 1862 *Jeffers v. Fair* decision, the court ruled that the Confederate Constitution allowed for the creation of a national army, while placing no specifications or limitations on how the government raised it. Voluntary enlistment was preferable, but limiting enrollment methods lessened or negated the power.[11]

As to the state's argument that Confederate control of military enlistment violated state sovereignty, the court ruled that the national government's ability to raise an army in no way conflicted with a state's ability to raise or maintain a state force. The former was constitutionally limited to external, or offensive, actions, while the latter could be called only in time of invasion or insurrection, strictly defensive actions. While men could be enrolled in state and local forces, they remained citizens, unremoved from the general population. They were able to go home at night and maintain their professions during the day. They remained citizens and were still subject to the duties required of all citizens, including national military service.[12]

The court's ruling was a huge blow to state rights advocates. It accepted the authority of the Confederate government over state governments, of Confederate interests over state interests, and of a Confederate military over state and local forces. Fear grew that as the Confederate army drafted men from state forces, no one would be left for local defense. But the issue of Confederate conscription's legality was settled. State and local officials were expected to swallow their state rights pride and enforce the Conscription Act as well as its exemption policies. Not all were willing to do so. Men like Judge Thomas W. Thomas of Elbert County—the first of Georgia's superior court judges to rule conscription unconstitutional—continued to order Confederate enrollment officers arrested throughout the war.

As the fighting wore on and enrollment difficulties only became worse, Congress passed a Second Conscription Act in September 1862 and a third in February 1864. In both cases, the age requirements for conscription were expanded; with the third act, all white males between seventeen and fifty were subject to the draft. Each successive year saw a greater uproar over exemptions and details. Classes of exemptions were extended, then limited, then revoked. What had been a legal exemption under an old act might be eliminated by a slight rewording in subsequent acts. Men who thought they were exempt, or who thought they had been discharged, could suddenly find themselves being chased by a conscription officer.

In November 1862, Peter L. Thomson of Quitman County posed a simple question: "Am I a deserter?" It was a question that many soldiers asked during the course of the war. Thomson had enlisted in Georgia's Second Battalion Partisan Rangers in September 1862 but quickly hired A. S. Edgerly, an exempted schoolteacher, as his substitute. For his services, Thomson paid the teacher the princely sum of $2,700 to serve in Thomson's stead for three years or until the end of the war. But only one month later—with sources of available men dwindling—Congress passed the second of its three conscription acts, this one extending the draft to men between the ages of thirty-five and forty-five. While the second act expanded the list of exemptions, it tightened eligibility requirements. For example, a teacher must have been actively teaching for at least two years before he could gain an exemption. Edgerly's qualifications as a substitute were now in question. If he were not acceptable under the new law, Thomson would either have to report for duty or pay out another, possibly higher, fee for a new substitute.[13]

Confusion, corruption, and resentment plagued the substitute system from the start. Men frequently sold themselves as substitutes, deserted, then sold themselves again. Some operated individually; others were handled by brokers who ran what one Georgia paper called "a traffic in white human flesh—a blood-money speculation."[14] More devastating to the Confederate cause was the legal ability of moneyed men to hire substitutes in the first place. In May 1863, the *Milledgeville Confederate Union* pointed out what had been obvious to plain folk for some time: "The rich have it in their power to hire a substitute, whilst the poor man has not the power to avail himself of that privilege, for want of means. . . . Verily Solomon was right when he said: 'The poor is hated even of his own neighbor; but the rich hath many friends.'"[15]

Indeed, plain folk who wanted to avoid Confederate service or wanted to stay close to home had few legal options. Some sought light military details, such as those of enrollment officers, police patrollers, commissary agents, physicians, or impressment officers. Civil and judicial offices at all levels offered sanctuary, but most of these positions went to the well-to-do. Political favors and newly created offices brought many well-connected men relief from service, so much so that the *Southern Recorder* wrote, "it is discouraging to witness with what eagerness these offices are sought in every county by able bodied young men without families, hoping thereby to procure an exemption from the military duties demanded of them by our bleeding country."[16]

The ease with which wealthy men were "skulking" was one of the chief causes of discontent. "The bomb proof places they hold were, in most cases, bought with money—yes! Bought with money!" wrote the editor of Augusta's *Chronicle and Sentinel*. His words reflected the outrage of thousands when he lashed out against those who bought their way out of combat: "They do not intend to pass sleepless nights and encounter dangers for the cause—not they! . . . is it any wonder that the masses are fast losing confidence in their Confederate leaders?"[17]

Plain folk hardly needed newspapers to point out the obvious. They saw it often enough for themselves. The citizens of Grooverville in Brooks County knew that W. R. Joiner had gained an exemption based solely on a petition signed by "some few special friends and some Ladies and a great many little children who cannot sign their own name." But officials rarely questioned a petition backed by the local gentry. In fact, Brooks County's inferior court, without authority to do so, commonly granted exemptions to wealthy men. Clinch County's H. B. Hill gained an exemption as a doctor even though he had given up his practice, refused to see patients, and spent most of his time speculating. "We think it hard to give up our fathers and young brothers," the citizens of Stockton wrote concerning Hill, "and have such an able bodied healthy man as he is allowed to remain at home who does nothing but is an injury to the county buying up all the provisions for speculation which poor women and children are needing."[18]

Even before the draft, some men of means like Thomas S. T. Knight of Brooks County, perhaps sensing that conscription was on the way, headed off front-line duty by raising their own military units and offering them for service at safe locations. Knight, an inferior court justice, preferred militia or state guard service at Georgia's coastal defenses and raised a cavalry company for that purpose. "We wish to remain at home," he wrote to Governor Brown, "and drill subject to your order at a moments notice to march to any point on the co[a]st of Georgia or Florida."[19]

After conscription went into effect, an officer's commission with state forces provided a safe haven for those with the money and connections to secure it. Governor Brown made this clear in June 1862 when he told his state troop commanders, "in case any [Confederate] enrolling officer attempts to arrest you, or any other commissioned officer under you . . . call out immediately such military force as you may need for the purpose, and place such enrolling officer under arrest." Brown was prepared to make war on the Confederacy itself to keep his officers at home. Plain folk hardly appreciated the gesture. In September, a Columbia County woman wrote complaining of "protection given to shirkers." She told of wealthy, able-bodied men being granted positions as state troop officers for the sole purpose of shielding them from Confederate conscription. Poor men, she said, who had no money to buy state commissions, were the ones forced to leave wives and children and fight for rich men's liberty. That remained true even after Congress, responding to the rage against substitution, repealed the substitute law in December 1863. No longer able to hide behind his paid substitute, Jefferson Thomas, a well-connected slaveholder in Richmond County, secured a commission in the state militia and remained at home on call.[20]

Legal options for avoiding service were usually available at prices only the wealthy could afford. Most southern men could not outfit their own military units, nor could they buy high-priced black-market exemptions. Political and military offices were usually reserved for the well connected. The majority of Georgia's soldiers, as with the majority of all Confederate soldiers, did not qualify for exemption under the twenty-slave law. Most owned no slaves at all, a fact that surprised some of their Yankee counterparts. Colonel James Nisbet, a former Georgia slaveholder, paraphrased this quote in his postwar memoirs: "It was a perplexing thing to the Northern mind that these people who owned no slaves, who were put out of the pale of slave-holding society (as they thought) should have accepted with so little question the leadership of the slave-holder."[21]

Nisbet, like so many of his class, chose to ignore the obvious. Most poor nonslaveholding soldiers did question slaveholders' leadership. They questioned why they were being forced to fight for a way of life that was not theirs while most of its beneficiaries remained at home. They questioned why their families starved while food rotted in warehouses and cotton was smuggled out. Such questions led many southerners to ignore enrolling officers. One newspaper noted that not a single man appeared at the April 1862 enrollment in Savannah and listed 199 names of absentees.[22]

In Franklin County, popular resistance made conscription efforts useless. In Augusta, persons unknown set the enrolling office afire. In Putnam County, the *Turnwold Countryman* warned of threats against a local conscript officer named Gallaway: "We would regret very much to see these threats carried into execution. . . . we trust that Mr. Gallaway will resign." Another conscript officer was nearly killed when he tried to draft men at Fort Gaines. Threats to his life became so serious that he fled the state. Draft resistance was so widespread that General Howell Cobb was sure it would take the whole Confederate army to enforce the draft.[23]

Thousands of letters poured into state and Confederate offices requesting exemption from the draft. Potential draftees cited a number of reasons why they should be excused. Isaac Bush of Colquitt asked for exemption on account of "my ankles swelling." For B. J. Smith of Cuthbert, leaving home would mean leaving his "large warehouse" with three thousand bales of cotton unattended.[24]

Those who could not get draft exemptions outright tried to avoid military service by other means. When the Confederacy made county officials exempt, such positions became the focus of heated campaigns. Thirty-one Washington County men offered themselves as candidates for the local inferior court. In Early County, thirty-seven candidates vied for five inferior court seats. "But there was no politics in the race," said one county resident. "The candidate just wanted the office to keep him out of the war." M. W. Johnson of Oglethorpe County, a soldier of the Sixth Georgia Regiment, went home on furlough and had himself elected justice of the peace to keep from going back to the front.[25]

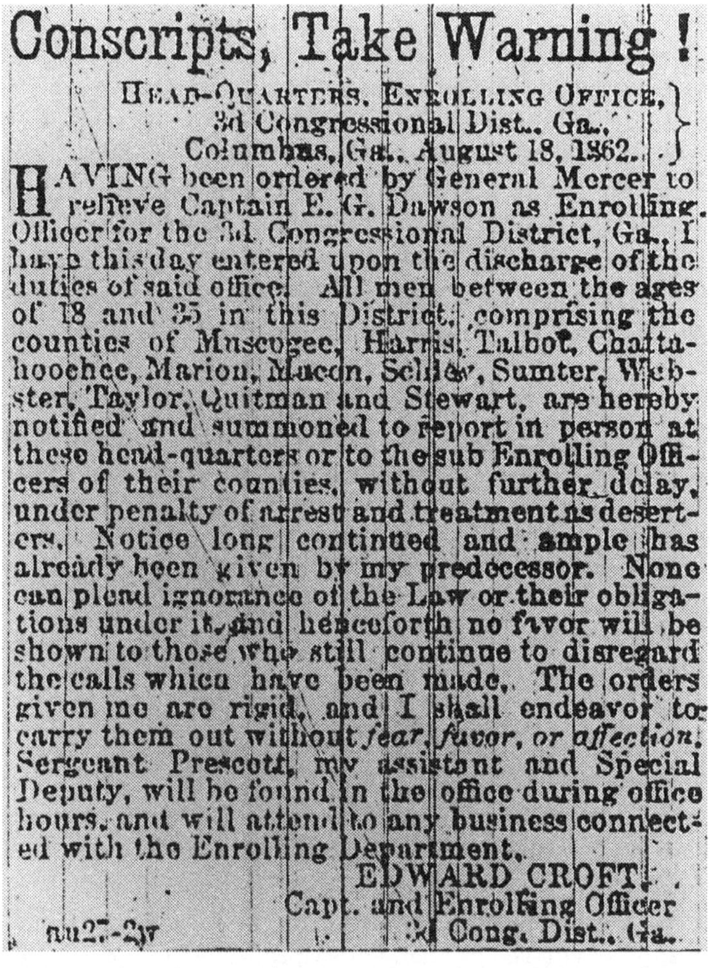

> **Conscripts, Take Warning!**
>
> HEAD-QUARTERS, ENROLLING OFFICE,
> 3d Congressional Dist., Ga.,
> Columbus, Ga., August 18, 1862.
>
> HAVING been ordered by General Mercer to relieve Captain E. G. Dawson as Enrolling Officer for the 3d Congressional District, Ga., I have this day entered upon the discharge of the duties of said office. All men between the ages of 18 and 35 in this District, comprising the counties of Muscogee, Harris, Talbot, Chattahoochee, Marion, Macon, Schley, Sumter, Webster, Taylor, Quitman and Stewart, are hereby notified and summoned to report in person at these head-quarters or to the sub Enrolling Officers of their counties, without further delay, under penalty of arrest and treatment as deserters. Notice long continued and ample has already been given by my predecessor. None can plead ignorance of the Law or their obligations under it, and henceforth no favor will be shown to those who still continue to disregard the calls which have been made. The orders given me are rigid, and I shall endeavor to carry them out without *fear, favor, or affection*. Sergeant Prescott, my assistant and Special Deputy, will be found in the office during office hours, and will attend to any business connected with the Enrolling Department.
>
> EDWARD CROFT,
> Capt. and Enrolling Officer
> 3d Cong. Dist., Ga.
>
> au27-2w

FIGURE 5.3. Drafting men into the army was one thing; convincing them to serve was another. It was not uncommon for draftees to ignore the call to duty, as this notice in the *Columbus Enquirer* of September 2, 1862, makes clear. In Savannah, of 199 men ordered to appear at the April 1862 enrollment, not a single one answered the call.

In December 1862, a Sumter County man noted that many of these officeholders were young men who could be replaced by much older ones exempt from military service. As one man who signed himself the "Reformer" sarcastically wrote: "Young men, burning with a patriotic desire to serve their country, should not be kept at home away from the field of honor and usefulness, to fill these *petty* offices. Turn them loose, to go where glory and fame await them." It was no use. By early 1864, the problem was worse than ever throughout Georgia. In April, General Howell Cobb wrote to Governor Brown of able-bodied young men elected to civil and militia offices "to the exclusion of old men competent to fill the places. . . . This class I fear is large." By November 1864, the head of Georgia's Confederate conscript service reported 8,229 state officials, civil and military, exempt.[26]

Like so many other Georgians, Carroll County men formed a home guard unit in an effort to dodge Confederate and state service. Its members did little more than meet at the courthouse in Carrollton once every few weeks for muster. Such units were supposed to be staffed only by young boys and old men. There was abuse of the home guard system even during the war's early months. In September 1861, Captain James Head of the Georgia state troops complained to Governor Brown that the home guard in Cedar Grove "has tuck over half of my men out of my command . . . ever one of the home gard is stout abel boded men intitled to do militia duty." As enthusiasm for the cause dwindled, more and more of those who wanted to keep out of the war opted for home guard service. The Carroll County home guard went so far as to urge local deserters trying to avoid arrest to sign up. One contemporary reported that "persons wishing to get their friends home from the army write them that they can come home and by joining this command, remain at home."[27]

Increasing sympathy from friends and neighbors encouraged more and more men to desert. As they did, newspapers across the state were filled with long lists of deserters' names as early as the summer of 1862, some offering rewards for their capture and return. A thirty-dollar reward was offered for the return of Fulton County native Thomas Miller. Similar bounties were offered for the return of E. J. Lewis of Hancock County, J. L. Morris of Wilkinson County, and John Burns of Augusta.[28] In July, an Augusta paper ran this notice:

DESERTED

$30 REWARD offered for the apprehension of each of the following. Wm. A Daniel, age 20, Co. A, Banks County Guards. Jere Martin, age 20, Co. D; A. S. King, age 24, Co. F; F. P. Williams, age 20, Co. F; John Huchins, age 26, Co. F. All from the 2nd Regiment of Georgia Volunteers. Reward will be paid on delivery to the jail at Augusta.[29]

Such lists soon took up so much print space that newspaper editors refused to publish them.

By October 1862, over half the soldiers from northeast Georgia had "skedaddled" and were hiding out in the mountains. At least a third of Lumpkin County's "Blue Ridge Rifles" had deserted. Nearly half the county's "Boyd Guards" did the same. The next year, War Department officials reported to Secretary James Seddon that "the condition of things in the mountain districts of North Carolina, South Carolina, Georgia, and Alabama menaces the existence of the Confederacy as fatally as . . . the armies of the United States."[30]

While the problem of desertion was mainly a result of homefront miseries, it was aggravated by the Conscription Act and its enforcer, the conscription officer. These men were among the most detested in the South. According to one account, conscript patrols went "sweeping through the country with little deference either to the law or the regulations designed to temper its unavoidable rigor." William H. Andrews wrote that "conscript officers [are] stationed everywhere I go, watching for some poor devil who is trying to keep out of the army. If he cannot be caught any other way, [the conscript officer] will run him down with Negro dogs, and then take him to the front in chains." Officials in Albany arrested one deserter who had disguised himself as a woman and returned him to his unit still wearing the dress in which he was arrested.[31]

There seemed to be no limits to which some conscript officers would go in quest of recruits. Even a man's physical condition made little difference to them. Men in the poorest of health were sometimes dragged from their homes and forced into service. One young man from Coffee County, "a helpless cripple . . . afflicted with epilepsy," was abandoned in Savannah when it became obvious that he was not capable of military service. His father was fortunate enough to find him.[32]

Men with enough ready cash could usually persuade conscript officers to pass them by. One southwest Georgia editor wrote, "It is strange to us that the Government allows its officers to conscript poor men who have the appearance of *dead men*, while they turn loose rich ones who are *young, hale and hearty*."³³

Very often, cash could purchase a post as conscript officer, coveted for the protection it offered from field duty. Few plain folk could afford such a dodge, so the positions usually went to moneyed men who found it the most convenient way to avoid service. Though most enrolling officials tried to maintain at least a show of adherence to duty, with some it was easy to see through the facade. Samuel D. Knight wrote to Governor Brown from Pine Mount: "if they need men in the army, why don't they take these loafing enrolling officers who is doing the country more harm than that many Yankees could do. . . . poor people has to pay all the tax and do all the fighting, while the gentlemen and their sons are loafing over the country, pretending to hunt conscripts."³⁴

It was not unusual for those who could afford it to buy a secure post to keep them out of harm's way. One Savannah merchant bought a job as night watchman from the city marshal. Others who could wrangle favors often paid nothing at all for such positions. In October 1862, one writer suggested in an open letter that men crippled in battle and now unemployed might make a living as government clerks. But, he complained, most of those jobs were reserved for rich men's sons "to keep them out of the way of Yankee bullets." A Wilkes County conscript suffering from tuberculosis—or consumption, as it was then called—confirmed that observation in a letter to the governor. Medical exemptions were not being enforced, and he urged Brown to ensure that invalids like himself were spared the debilitating life of a soldier: "Our families [are] rendered no assistance. Ourselves looked upon with contempt and scorn. While thousands of healthy and wealthy men are floating in luxury and kept from the hardships of the army by some petit office."³⁵

For those with extra cash, it was not hard to buy a medical exemption whether they were invalids or not. In the spring of 1862, "many persons" in Savannah avoided the draft that way. So did men in Jefferson County, where the medical examiner turned loose "able-bodied *rich* men . . . & put down poor men for the service who are not fit for it." Such obvious class disparity was bound to depress even those most firmly committed to the cause of southern independence. Mrs. James B. Walls, a widow from Twiggs County, wrote Governor Brown: "I am a Southern Lady and I glory in the name. But it is hard to give up my Husband and brothers and then my property taken for tax While others are paying Doctors for exemptions and are making fortunes."[36]

For those with available cash who found themselves drafted into either Confederate or state service, it was still not too late to get out. They could purchase discharges or "certificates of disability" at nearly any time for the right price. Men like John Stephens of the First Georgia Regiment or "Captain Paxton" of Governor Brown's staff were always around, eager to line their pockets by selling phony discharges. In the summer of 1862, a Clyattville man reported that a number of healthy young Lowndes County men were home from the war, all released on questionable disability certificates.[37]

It had been clear to Confederate authorities for some time that the supply of willing recruits was dwindling. To fill the ranks, their First Conscription Act of April 1862 not only drafted civilians but also made existing state forces subject to Confederate service. Governor Brown relented, but he soon recruited two regiments of state troops that might operate in conjunction with, but independently of, Confederate units. In December 1863, Brown further strengthened his independent position with a reorganization of the state militia system.

As a part of this reorganization, each state senatorial district became a military district under the command of a gubernatorial aid-de-camp.[38] Each aid-de-camp was authorized to hire three or more assistants for each county in their district, and it was the assistant's job to enroll every white male between the ages of sixteen and sixty save those subject to Confederate or state reserve duty. One result of this reorganization, however, was that instead of two military departments competing for the same man, there were three—Confederate, state reserve, and militia.[39]

County court records are littered with disputes between the three military organizations, each of which believed it had primary jurisdiction. Colonel Carey W. Styles, aid-de-camp for the Fifth District (Coffee, Ware, and Clinch counties), had to contend with Confederate conscription agents ordered to enlist his militia officers. Styles told his officers to disregard orders to report for Confederate service and to resist, by force if necessary, attempts at kidnapping. "I shall if possible avoid a 'conflict' with these impossible representatives," Styles wrote to Georgia's adjutant general, Henry C. Wayne, who commanded the state militia. In a nod to the social hierarchy, Governor Brown approved Styles's resistance on behalf of his officers; however, he counseled against the actions of Styles's company commanders who had offered the same protection to their enlisted men.[40]

Aggressive conscription officers were hardly unknown to the region. In September 1863, Captain Joseph J. Chaires of the Eleventh Florida Infantry received permission to raise a cavalry company to serve under General Hood and proceeded to organize his new unit at Camp Lamar Cobb in Decatur County.[41] As a part of his enlistment efforts, Chaires ordered Major Thomas W. Arrington of the Brooks County Militia to report for Confederate duty. Arrington, determined that his militia rank should protect him from Confederate duty, forwarded a formal complaint to General Wayne, who authorized Brooks County's home guard unit to "protect [Arrington] by force if necessary, and to send Captain Chaires under guard to [General Wayne's headquarters], if he persists."[42]

Chaires was not acting alone. He and James B. Creech, a Quitman merchant who had once been a member of the Thirteenth Georgia Infantry, collaborated to raise the cavalry company. Following his attempts to enlist Major Arrington, Chaires arrested seven more men from Brooks and Thomas counties, two of whom—Jacob Baum and William G. McKinnon—had already been rejected for military service on medical grounds. Another, Jeremiah J. Williams, was the Confederate sub-enrolling officer for Brooks County. Under threat of arrest, each man was given the opportunity to volunteer in Chaires and Creech's new company.[43]

Criticized as well was Captain James P. Turner's brief trip into southwest Georgia with Company F of the Fourth Georgia Cavalry. Three Thomas County men complained that Turner had arrested them as deserters even though they had never enlisted. When Turner's rapid departure for north Florida in February 1864 left an embarrassed lieutenant to explain the arrests, Judge Augustin H. Hansell released the men.[44]

Enrolling officers could be a deserter's greatest ally or his worst enemy. Greed could make them an invaluable source of falsified discharges, furloughs, and exemptions. Colonel Archibald Thomson MacIntyre, aid-de-camp for the Seventh Military District (Thomas, Colquitt, and Brooks counties), complained that one man he had recently sent forward returned to Thomasville after buying a discharge for three thousand dollars. If enrolling officers would not issue discharges, so-called "drummers" could be found in virtually any town selling forged ones.[45]

Even a casual discussion could be regarded as an enlistment. George W. Ferrell traveled to Tallahassee in May 1863 to discuss joining a Florida company with its captain, but he refused to be mustered in without first

FIGURE 5.4. Hundreds of well-connected Georgians avoided front-line service in the Confederate army by gaining appointments as officers in the state militia. General Howell Cobb wrote to Governor Brown complaining of able-bodied young men—like those shown here at a Georgia Militia camp in 1863—serving as militia officers "to the exclusion of old men competent to fill the places. . . . This class I fear is large." (Courtesy of Missouri Historical Society.)

discussing the matter with his family. He was soon arrested by someone known simply as Cromarty—possibly a conscription broker or bounty hunter—as a deserter from the Florida company and remanded to the Thomas County jail. John R. Jones had discussed joining a local cavalry company but only if he could find a substitute. He, too, was arrested as a deserter.[46]

Patronage and favoritism played major roles in the efforts of some conscript officers. They understood that the war would not last forever and that the way in which they used their authority could seriously impact future social and political standing. Thus, partiality by enrolling officers toward relieving privileged men of society from military duty, regardless of eligibility, was readily practiced and just as readily disavowed.

Perhaps the case that came closest to an admission of partiality on the part of an enrolling officer was the August 1864 conscription of James T. Hall. A mail carrier for Thomas County, Hall was exempt under the conscript laws as long as he was actively engaged in his profession. He was not so engaged. In fact, the person he had hired to perform his job was himself subject to conscription. Under orders from Adjutant General Wayne, Colonel MacIntyre, the local aid-de-camp, ordered Hall to carry the mail himself or risk being sent to the front. Hall refused and MacIntyre promptly arrested him.[47]

Hall petitioned Judge Augustin H. Hansell of the Thomas County superior court for a writ of habeas corpus and produced a letter from Colonel John J. Jones, aid-de-camp to the governor, ordering Hall to resume his mail duties. The court acquiesced, and Hall was released. But Hall was still angry with MacIntyre and accused him of favoritism in allowing millers, police, and physicians to remain at home while he was to be sent to the front. He demanded an apology. In a heavily edited letter that is remarkable for what it almost admitted, MacIntyre offered none:

> I have not only ~~done~~ sought to do my duty but I have sought to do ~~that~~ it in the mildest manner possible, therefore, I have no apology to make. I take occasion to say that I have had no favorites & that all have been treated ~~exactly~~ as near alike ~~as near~~ as the circumstances of these cases would permit. No man has a greater aversion to partiality in office than I have. As to the detail allowed by the Governor for police, millers, & physicians, I had nothing to do with them at all. The Superior Court made them & will doubtless sustain them. I am responsible for any act that I may do, but I am not for the act[s] of others.
>
> I have sought at no time to gratify any feelings of my own (indeed if I have any in this case); a similar case to yours of a mail carrier in Brooks was ordered forwarded (a few days after our first interview, my doubts having been removed) without referring the case to General Wayne—in that you had the advantage.
>
> I have not indulged in recrimination but have simply stated the facts as I believe them to exist—This is the only explanation I have to make. I have sought simply to discharge my duty & if I have ~~not done it in an impartial manner it is because I [illegible]~~ unintentionally treated any man other than my duty required & can be made sensible of it, I will take great pleasure in making reparation at any & all times.

Therefore ~~I have no apologies to make to any man for what I have done.[illegible] becomes my duty to act again I will try & execute [illegible] superior officers [illegible]~~.[48]

In the crossed-out sections of the letter, MacIntyre begins to offer an explanation for his partiality. Such an explanation would have confirmed the existence as well as the practice of favoritism, if not in the case of James Hall, certainly in others. But MacIntyre backed away from such an admission and in subsequent correspondence reiterated his impartiality. "I have no favorites," MacIntyre wrote to Governor Brown. "I have sent forward all without regard to my personal feelings. I sent forward a brother in law of mine, James A. Linton because I thought he was subject [and] incurred his displeasure. . . . Several others have been displeased with me about having to go forward."[49]

Another enrolling officer accused of corruption was Colonel Carey W. Styles. As aid-de-camp for the Fifth District, Styles had one of the more difficult sections of south Georgia from which to draw men. Of primary concern was the lack of competent men to whom he could delegate enrollment duties. He had been forced to draw three or four men from the ranks of the local state guard units only to have them taken back when the state guard was called to Savannah.[50]

Styles was an intelligent, energetic, and ambitious man, but he was also contemptuous of Confederate and state military bureaucracies. In the spring of 1864, that contempt gave way to bitterness and manifested itself in the appearance, if not the actual committing, of conduct unbecoming an officer. Captain David Davidson of Company F, Twenty-sixth Georgia Infantry Regiment, made the first charge. He claimed that between fifty and seventy Ware County men subject to military service were still at home without exemption or discharge. Some had put in substitutes, though none had reported for duty. Others claimed to be state force officers exempt from Confederate service, yet they belonged to no organization. Davidson wrote, "I am informed by the most responsible men of this County, & it is the unanimous belief in the Community at large, that those men have got out by paying money to some person here." W. B. Overstreet from Coffee County complained that Styles was exempting the rich for money while sending the poor to the front. Finally, Major Hilliard, now at home in Waresboro, made his charges.[51]

Hilliard claimed that Daniel E. Knowles and Dr. Daniel Lott—both enrolling officers under Styles's command—were selling exemptions to local conscripts with Styles's knowledge and assistance. As proof, he held a letter written by Knowles offering an exemption for one thousand dollars as well as one of the discharges signed by Styles. What is interesting about this accusation is that Styles, Knowles, Lott, and Hilliard were all fellow Masons in Lodge 217 at Waresboro. All had been acquaintances, and one could assume friends, for a number of years. But Hilliard, apparently enraged that the other three men would attempt to profit from their position by selling exemptions, felt it necessary to write the state adjutant general about the dealings of his companions. The letter was damning evidence.[52]

But these charges were not the first to be leveled against Styles. While struggling to form his partisan rangers in the spring of 1862, Styles was also answering accusations of selling exemptions and medical discharges to wealthy members of the Twenty-sixth. Writing to the *Savannah Republican* from Valdosta in June 1862, "Vox Populi" lamented that "money might buy discharges as well as hire substitutes." While "Vox" wrote that he did not intend to focus attention on the Twenty-sixth in particular, but rather on the problem in general, nonetheless

> Lowndes County was referred to, because the authors knew of such cases in it, "as healthy looking individuals." But we disavow designing to implicate Colonel Styles, or any *true* men or officers of said regiment. We referred to it because most we knew that, "healthy looking individuals" coming home discharged were from that regiment; and most, if not all of them *happened* to be men of means and influence, which looked to us as strange, at least. . . . But one thing we do know, that several healthy looking individuals have come home in Lowndes and Brooks counties, discharged as diseased, mostly if not all from the 26th. . . . Also, one young man, stout and healthy, who has been home since March last on furlough or permits, and only a day or two ago got his furlough extended from the 2nd Lieutenant of a company of said regiment, and certificate that he was a member of the "Bartow Light Infantry," to evade the enrolling officer. And as far as we can judge, there are many *poor men* who have left dependant families, and are compelled to remain at their post, not even being permitted to visit their sick families, who are much more entitled to such liberal furloughs.[53]

Styles identified this criticism as originating with Dr. E. A. Jelks, surgeon of the Twenty-sixth. Jelks had been unappreciative of his efforts to gain Jelks a promotion, Styles wrote, and would lie or bribe to retain his commission. Styles implied that Jelks could be the only source of falsified medical discharges from the regiment and that Jelks was placing the blame on the unit's former commander.[54] Now those charges had resurfaced—brought to light by former members of the Twenty-sixth—and whether they described an extension of Styles's previous illegal activity or a continuance of regimental politics, they needed to be answered.

The state adjutant general's office informed Styles at the end of September 1864 that an official board of enquiry would convene in Savannah, but Styles was never allowed to testify in his own defense. Humiliated, he tendered his resignation, concerned that "my usefulness as an officer in this district has, to some extent been impaired, . . . my official acts must to some degree be embarrassed by suspicion and distrust, . . . my enemies here will throw every obstacle possible in the way of the execution of my orders and retard the business of the district and that I will not be supported by the full confidence of the commander in chief or the . . . officials of the people." The governor, however, rejected his resignation and ordered him to continue his duties "for the present." Styles offered his resignation again in November, and again it was refused.[55]

Despite the adamant denials of conscription officers, plain folk viewed them largely as speculators in human flesh attempting to profit, if not monetarily, at least politically. Loyal Confederates despaired at the corruption. Editorials begged for someone with "Old Hickory Jackson's will, who won't hesitate to put [deserters and layouts] to a tree."[56] Those trying to avoid service realized that they had to use caution in dealing with conscript officers sensitive to criticism. A bribery attempt could sometimes get one hanged. Not offering a large enough bribe could produce the same result. For plain folk, the risks as well as the costs were too great. Most found it wise simply to give their local conscript officer a wide berth.

6

"Distemper of the Time"

The Courts and Planter Privilege

Georgians looking for someone with "Jackson's will" to compel deserters and layouts to perform their duty believed that they could count on the courts to perform that office. In some cases, they were correct. But the application of state and Confederate conscription laws varied from judge to judge, from state to state, and from plaintiff to plaintiff. There were, however, at least a few common veins that ran through court rulings on draft cases. The outcomes generally involved money, status, or politics. Whatever the specific issues, planters nearly always had the advantage over plain folk.

Georgia's legislature controlled the state's judicial appointments, and it based those appointments largely on personal politics and political patronage. Judges usually did not question that arrangement, given that the bench was often a stepping-stone to political office. With planters and planting interests holding sway in southern legislatures, governor's mansions, and polling stations, their influence on judicial elections and appointments is undeniable. That influence was all-important, since it was commonly held that the legal profession not only protected aristocratic interests but was "responsible for conducting the whole operations of society."[1]

When the Confederate Congress passed the first of its three conscription acts and placed political benefactors and their families at risk of forced conscription, only the most nationalistic judges failed to express outrage at the legislation. The Georgia Supreme Court's *Jeffers v. Fair* decision accepting the legality of national conscription only escalated lower state court fears of threats to state and individual rights. In the *Jeffers* decision, Justice Charles Jenkins wrote that "we are told, that the war power, in the extent to which it is exercised by the Congress, better befits absolute despotism. . . . Let us realize, at once, that war is an abnormal condition of society; and that where it obtains, whatever be the form of the Government, the status of the citizen or the subject, is more or less modified to meet its demands," a sentiment that sent shivers through lower courts trying their best to protect planter/politician benefactors.[2]

Such divergent politico-judicial thought often placed lower and appellate courts at odds over interpretation and jurisdiction. Nowhere was this dispute more evident than in judicial actions concerning the Confederate conscription acts. Conscripts sought to have local judges intercede on their behalf to check Confederate, and later state, powers. By having their cases heard in local courts, conscripts could exert locally powerful economic or political influences to manipulate the verdict. But conscription violation was a military matter, not a crime at common law; no civilian court held jurisdiction over it. What, then, was the role of civilian state courts, especially since there was no national Confederate judiciary? Could a state court review Confederate laws such as conscription? Could a Confederate conscript seek redress in a state court, or were civilian courts required to cede all conscript cases to military courts?[3]

Although the Georgia Supreme Court and Confederate attorneys-general offered their interpretations, the nature of the state-Confederate legal relationship was never fully resolved.[4] Most of Georgia's judges held to the theory of concurrent jurisdiction, according to which state and national judicial spheres overlapped in their influence and domain. Chatham County Superior Court Judge William B. Fleming upheld this theory in July 1862, and the Georgia Supreme Court reiterated the concept in 1863, when it ruled that a state civilian court had the right to hear conscript cases as long as the case was initiated in that court.[5] Judge Thomas W. Thomas of Elbert County answered those nationalists who still maintained that states had no right to interfere with national affairs when he wrote that while military courts held sway over soldiers, it was the civilian court's job to decide who became soldiers.[6]

The determination of who was eligible to become a soldier was accomplished through a writ of habeas corpus, a legal inquiry into arrest and

FIGURE 6.1. Unlike the rich, poor men found it difficult to avoid being hauled off to military service by paying an exemption fee, petitioning a friendly judge, or bribing the local conscript officer. The editor of the *Early County News* wrote, "It is strange to us that the government allows its officers to conscript poor men who have the appearance of *dead men*, while they turn loose rich ones who are *young, hale and hearty.*" (Devens, *Pictorial Book of Anecdotes and Incidents*)

detention. While civilian courts technically held neither primary nor direct appellate jurisdiction over conscript cases, they did claim the right of review. Civilian courts could not legally rule on breaches of military law in the execution of the conscription acts, but they insisted that they had authority to ensure that enrolling officers violated no state or local law while pursuing conscription policy.[7] If the court determined that a conscript had been jailed illegally or improperly, or that the arresting officer had no authority over him, then it retained the right to release the conscript from duty under what became known colloquially as "the plea" or "the writ."

The court that issued such a writ varied from county to county. In some counties, both inferior and superior courts issued them. In others, only one or the other did so. In Savannah, the state court heard the majority of writ petitions. The Chatham County Superior Court records show only three writ cases, although there are references to several others in newspaper reports and letters. City courts in larger towns such as Savannah and Atlanta also issued writs. With no set policy, conflicts between these several courts were inevitable. In Savannah, Colonel A. Wilbur complained to Governor Brown that the Chatham Inferior Court and Savannah city court routinely overruled superior court rulings to release conscripts from military service, a reversal of the normal judicial hierarchy. Brown sympathized but pointed out that "the Inferior Courts who make these extraordinary decisions to keep men out of Service" could not be stopped until the habeas corpus laws were changed to dictate an appellate structure and time line.[8]

The majority of conscripts were uneducated, legally naive, or too poor to actively pursue their cases through the court system. They either relented to conscription or disappeared into the countryside. Those with money and connections had other options. The ease with which wealthy conscripts obtained writs from local courts angered the Confederate military from the start of conscription efforts. Assistant Secretary of War J. A. Campbell wrote that

> some judges, apparently catching the distemper of the time to relieve from the burden of the military service that class of men who above all others are interested in carrying through a revolution commenced for the security of their rights and interests, have resorted to the most refined and astute discussions to dispense with [enlistment]. . . . In every State some local judges seem to have bestirred themselves to withdraw from the service all who by any subtlety could be released.[9]

Campbell insisted that the writ of habeas corpus was "a pernicious influence upon the organization of the Army and the measures of the Confederate Government for filling its diminished numbers to a proper standard."[10]

Early in the war, Jefferson Davis argued for presidential authority to suspend the writ. Unlike Lincoln in the North, however, he never attempted such suspensions without congressional approval. While Davis centered his argument on the growing instances of unionist meetings, open disloyalty, and espionage, he was also concerned with the increased use of the writ by local judges to release Confederate conscripts. Leaders in both Confederate congressional houses, who argued that granting such authority to a central government would infringe on state rights, checked Davis's efforts. Fear that such power at the presidential level might encourage military leaders in the field to exercise similar authority prompted Congress to assume a cautious attitude toward granting the power of suspension to one person or office. In the few instances that Congress allowed Davis to suspend the writ, it limited that suspension both in scope and duration.[11]

Even then, public opposition was fierce. When Congress authorized the writ to be suspended in February 1864, one enraged citizen who signed himself "A Georgian" reacted in an open letter to the *Early County News:* "When this war broke out our people thought they had something to fight for, but now they have nothing, but to keep the Yankees checked, so that our own Government may oppress them more." The paper's editor, E. H. Grouby, was in full agreement. "Our freedom is now gone!" he declared. "May the devil get the whole of the old Congress!" Grouby insisted that if only he had the money he would emigrate to Cuba.[12]

Concerned Georgians could point to numerous examples of what they feared. In September 1862, Walter P. Greer, sub-enrolling officer of Warren County, arrested Isadore Rosenfeldt of Augusta as an eligible conscript. When Greer attempted to tie Rosenfeldt's hands, local citizens cut the ropes. When Greer tried to jail his prisoner, Judge Gould of Richmond County Superior Court freed him, ruling that Greer had no authority as a sub-enrolling officer of Warren County to arrest a citizen of Richmond County. Greer responded by saying that he was authorized to declare martial law, suspend the writ of habeas corpus, and arrest whomever he wished. Aid-de-camp Colonel B. B. Hamilton arrested a number of men in the Augusta area to be held for enrollment in the Georgia state troops. All were prominent members of the community who gave their pledge that they would appear for enrollment after getting their affairs in order. Some offered one-thousand-dollar bonds for their appearance. Hamilton refused their terms and remanded all to the county jail.[13]

But local courts usually provided a friendly avenue of redress for such men. With no Confederate supreme court and overlapping spheres of Confederate and state influence, local magistrates and county judges were relatively free to exercise their powers under the writ. Even the Georgia Supreme Court's support of the constitutionality of conscription in *Jeffers v. Fair*—which halted the discharge of all properly enrolled conscripts under the writ—did not prohibit judges from issuing writs to investigate "questionable" enrollments.[14]

Many writs involved underage conscripts, soldiers too young to legally qualify for conscription or enrollment. Young boys—whose romantic notions of military life led them to run away from home, whose poverty led them to think that a soldier's pay could make life easier for their families, or whose patriotism was driven by the rhetoric of wealthy parents—often discovered the error of their ways only after being mustered into the ranks. Courts honored petitions for discharge of underage conscripts, but those who made such petitions usually had money or were connected in some way to wealthy families. Alfred H. Windsor, whose sixteen-year-old son Robert enlisted against his wishes, had an estate valued at nearly thirty-three thousand dollars from which to draw the legal fees of Washington Poe, one of Georgia's most respected attorneys. Gustavus McRea had nearly twenty-six thousand dollars to draw upon to gain the release of his son Hilliard.[15]

Those few parents who had little cash but some knowledge of legal redress cut expenses by paying only for the notary services needed to file the petition and then represented themselves. Some drew upon the kindness of employers for legal assistance. Ira Jennings, a wealthy Bibb County farmer, paid for the legal battle to free Wiley Moncrief, the son of one of his farm laborers, all the way through the Georgia Supreme Court.[16] Others relied on family friends who were literate but had little or no legal training—men such as Rodolphus Tucker, a clerk in a doctor's office, who represented Simon Jay, or William Sloan, a jeweler, who represented Thomas O'Skellie.[17]

Some cases involved resident aliens, people either from the northern states or other countries who tried to avoid Confederate citizenship and military service. Those who found themselves drafted and could afford court access to contest it met with some success, although success in such challenges came more often in the war's latter half. Judicial opinions varied, but early in the war courts generally expected alien residents who availed themselves of the benefits of the local economy to help defend the Confederacy. Bibb County Superior Court Judge Osborn A. Lochrane, himself an Irish immigrant, worked to stir Georgia's Irish population: "We owe it to ourselves—we owe it to our children and to history, that no Irish Tory shall lodge under the Confederate States' flag. . . . A great ancestry inspires us. Liberty calls us. Honor invites us; and let him who falters go back and bequeath meanness and misery to his children."[18] Lochrane had no sympathy for immigrants who shirked what he saw as their duty.

In August 1862, Elias Lovengard claimed exemption from Confederate service because he was a citizen of Württemberg and petitioned

Lochrane for release. The judge issued the writ and, after hearing arguments, remanded Lovengard back into Confederate custody. His decision stemmed from a Georgia law that said that all foreigners residing in the state at the time of secession automatically became citizens of the Confederate States unless they filed papers with the clerk of the court stating their intent not to become a citizen.[19] In the opinion of the court, men of foreign birth in Georgia at the time of secession owed their allegiance to the Confederacy and should not be exempt.[20] Lochrane admonished Lovengard that "he should show his appreciation of this country by acts of courage against its enemies."[21]

In 1863, Lochrane again remanded a foreigner into custody to do military service. This unnamed conscript claimed he was a British citizen and offered consular papers as proof. Lochrane "had little respect for Consular papers at best in behalf of men claiming the protection of this [Confederate] Government." Such protection, he said, was based on a knowledge of the British government and a knowledge of the British consul. Since Britain had not recognized the Confederate States, the court was "not acquainted with Mr. Bull."[22]

But by the winter of 1863–64, Lochrane's stance on the issue had softened. He never fully explained his shift in legal attitude, though increasing economic and political pressures may have played a role. Whatever the case, when Joseph Farrell and William Farrell filed writs claiming British citizenship, Lochrane granted their release. By March 1864, Lochrane was routinely exempting resident aliens from Scotland, England, Germany, and Prussia.[23]

Petitions from overage conscripts were among the most favorably treated. Almost all were discharged at the county level. Those who were not tended to be among the less affluent. Judge Richard Henry Clark of Georgia's Southwest Judicial Circuit ruled in two separate cases that soldiers enrolled under the conscription acts were to remain soldiers for the duration of the war despite their age. The two men Clark ordered back into the ranks, both over the age of fifty, were far from wealthy. One was a middling farmer from Sumter County, the other a shoemaker from Dougherty County. The Supreme Court overruled Clark's opinion, saying that once a soldier reached the age of fifty he was automatically discharged.[24]

A common element in all of these writ cases was their absolutist nature. Either the conscript was too young or he was not; either he was a citizen or he was not; either he was too old or he was not. There was not much middle ground. This was not always the case with medical exemptions, which forced judges to contend with the relative nature of disease, an issue that they were not properly trained to address. Was one person more or less medically fit for duty than the next? To what degree did a disease handicap a soldier in the performance of his duty? Because of the interpretive conflicts inherent in medical determinations, county superior courts and the Georgia Supreme Court shared a reluctance to question the results of a properly charged medical examining board. Some judges put such faith in medical boards that they placed the burden of proof on enrolling officers to show that a conscript was either healed of his wounds or faking an illness. While courts were quick to expose fraudulent medical cases, rarely did a judge remand a conscript into custody who held an authentic medical discharge.[25]

While petition success rates varied depending on the filing times, issues involved, and judges' inclinations, petitioners usually had an advantage going into the case: most were relatively wealthy or well connected. While the financial status of a petitioner did not always determine a judge's decision, it was a factor in a conscript's access to the legal system and his ability to use it. Only those conscripts who had or could get the money to pay notary fees, attorney's fees, and court costs could hope to have their cases heard. Judges typically ordered the conscript, not the government, to pay all court costs regardless of the outcome. Attorneys, acutely aware of their clients' situations and not immune to the speculative nature of the times, made it a practice to delay presenting writ cases in an effort to increase fees. Senator Benjamin H. Hill wrote in 1864 that "some of these [conscripts] employ lawyers (falsely so called,) who, if they do not get the final order as desired, can, at least, delay final action—the fee often being measured by the length of the delay." Pro bono work was nonexistent, and very few conscripts could afford the fees of such legal powers as Washington Poe, William K. deGraffenreid, John Rutherford, George R. Hunter, and Eugenius A. Nisbet.[26]

In the midst of the arguments over writs, Georgia's superior court judges were forced into less than enviable positions. Many had gained their posts through the political patronage of their well-to-do constituents. Yet under existing Confederate laws, which judges were sworn to uphold, they often had to compel those very men to perform unwanted duties. Most judges had been politically and legally weaned on doctrines of state sovereignty and the sanctity of personal property. How did a judge enforce a system of laws with which he did not agree? He generally had four alternatives. He could resign, refuse to enforce the law and risk impeachment, enforce the law knowing that it breached every principle he held dear, or maneuver around the law using technicalities. Most judges used technicalities and semantics to the petitioners' benefit while at the same time holding conscription officers to strict interpretations of law.[27]

Judges were adamant in their insistence on proper enrollment procedure and due respect for the writ. Judge Thomas of Elbert County arrested the enrolling officer of Oglethorpe County in 1862, when he failed to bring Richard S. Fleeman before the court in response to a writ. Joseph M. W. Glenn had arrested Fleeman as a conscript and then removed him from the county by "forcible abduction" once Thomas issued the writ. Glenn swore that he was only following orders, and Thomas gave him the benefit of the doubt. But that did not stop him from throwing Glenn in the county jail until the enrolling officer could somehow convince his superior officer to bring Fleeman back into Oglethorpe County. Referring to *Georgia v. Philpot*, a habeas corpus case from the 1830s involving a free black, Thomas asked: "Is an alleged conscript to be denied the benefit of this writ, and it is to be given to free negroes and to bushmen with tails? Is a conscript a slave?"[28]

Thomas was so concerned about possible repercussions from the Glenn arrest that he wrote to Governor Brown for assistance. Brown, embroiled in state rights arguments with the Davis administration, declined to intervene, although he presumed "the end of the case will be that the proper Department at Richmond will order the body produced before you in obedience to the writ of Habeas Corpus . . . which will be a triumph of the Judiciary over the insolence of a Confederate Officer and a vindication of its proper jurisdiction." Despite his confidence, Brown held troops at the ready should the army attempt to free its officer by force.[29]

In another case, Judge Lochrane ordered the arrest of Lieutenant George R. Hunter for contempt of court. Hunter, who had acted as president of the court martial of Jeremiah McKinney, refused to produce McKinney in response to a writ sued out in Bibb County Superior Court. To prevent the writ's enforcement, Hunter stationed armed Confederate troops around the post prison. Lochrane declined to jail Hunter for contempt, however, swayed by Hunter's argument that he was only acting under orders from his superior officer and that he lacked the necessary intent for a ruling of contempt. It also helped that Hunter was a wealthy attorney. In late 1863, Hunter resigned his commission, returned to his law practice, and successfully argued for the release of underage, overage, and planter conscripts.[30]

Superficial examination might make it appear that judges adhered to law as strictly as they adhered to procedure. The *Augusta Chronicle and Sentinel* wrote that Judge Thomas of Elbert County "has no idea of setting at defiance the late decision of the Supreme Court [upholding conscription], but feels himself bound thereby, as all subordinate tribunals of the State are. The laws of the state require every Judge to observe and decide all cases according to the decisions of the Supreme Court, let his own opinions be what they may."[31]

But few judges, Thomas included, felt entirely bound by the rulings of Georgia's Supreme Court. While the court held great authority over lower circuit courts, those circuits, at least the wealthy and well connected within them, also held great influence over their judges. Protective of their planter patrons and politically tied to planter success, judges molded their legal decisions to suit their leanings and extended their state rights attitudes to county, region, occupational, and class rights, frequently in defiance of judicial precedents and state and Confederate law.

No one benefited more from this set of focused and exclusive rights than state judges themselves. Although members of the judiciary were exempt from conscription—and that exemption had been upheld by the state supreme court—such protection was not always guaranteed.[32] In Elbert County, sub-enrolling officer Horatio Goss presented Judge Thomas with an order from Goss's superior officer instructing Goss to "enroll as conscripts 'constables, bailiffs, deputy clerks of courts, deputy ordinaries, and the members of the council and police officers of the different cities.'" Thomas promptly discharged all judicial employees brought before his court. Jenkins Holmes, a justice of the peace in Burke County, wrote to Governor Brown that the local enrolling officer was "continually harassing me, and insisting that I shall go up to the camp of instruction," despite Holmes's age (he was over thirty-five and ineligible), his profession (a teacher, an exempted position), and his judicial office. In south Georgia, Clinch County Justice of the Peace John Dougherty was threatened with arrest as a deserter despite his exemption as a civil official.[33]

Not all judges shielded members of the judiciary. Judge Edmund H. Worrell of Talbot County remanded Reuban W. Smith to the enrolling officer's custody even though he had been a local bailiff for four years.[34] In

February 1864, Judge Augustin H. Hansell of Thomasville remanded Hillary B. Humphries—the newly, though questionably, elected constable for the 637th Militia District of Thomas County—to the custody of Mirrel Calloway, Confederate sub-enrolling officer for Thomas County.[35] And Governor Brown, who had doggedly fought to protect civil officers, admitted that not all were offered immediate discharge upon election per congressional action.[36]

But cases such as these were exceptions to the rule. Judge Benjamin H. Bigham of Oglethorpe County released a conscript who had been elected justice of the peace *after* being enrolled in the military. He ruled that counties could legally elect to office any citizen, civilian or soldier, and opened the door for the automatic release of any soldier who could gain a judicial post.[37]

Judge Richard Henry Clark also released conscripts who claimed to be members of the judiciary. Unlike Thomas, however, he never questioned the legitimacy of the claims. He discharged Joseph E. Sellars from the Fifty-first Georgia Infantry in February 1865 because Sellars had been elected constable of Albany. He released David Meads from the Fifty-first Georgia Infantry when Meads was elected a justice of the peace. And he refused to uphold the arrest of three judges in Sumter County. Clark's initial order to release the three men was ignored by the arresting officer, Captain Asbury A. Adams of the First Regiment Georgia Reserves. Clark ordered their release again a month later, and the men were promptly rearrested under direct orders from Governor Brown.[38]

Local courts protected nonjudicial officeholders just as vigorously, and the arguments supporting their protection followed the same lines as those protecting the judiciary. With civic personnel, however, came the recognition at both state judicial levels that just as Confederate officials could not impede the operation of state governments, state governments could not impede the operation of the Confederate government. If the Confederacy could not conscript state personnel, then state reserves and militia could not conscript Confederate officials. That admission had not been made in relation to the judiciary, although the seemingly one-sided nature of the argument probably stemmed from the low number of Confederate judicial members and not from a complete denial of their rights.[39]

Protection was not strictly limited to civic and judicial personnel. It also encompassed judicial powers—powers judges had worked hard to develop and worked even harder to maintain. Even though the Georgia

Supreme Court had decided that, in theory, civil law must occasionally be subordinate to military duty, judges were reluctant to relinquish their authority. In Muscogee County, Judge Benjamin H. Bigham threatened to hold two soldiers in contempt when they tried to arrest a juror out of the jury box. The juror had been absent from his post for several days to attend court. Only the soldiers' confession of misunderstanding and the sympathy expressed by attorneys present saved the men from a fine and jail time.[40]

Worth County's inferior court ordered J.M.C. Holaman, a soldier arrested as a suspected murderer, released on bail and refused to return him to his unit. The court held that in posting bond the suspect was exempted from military duty until his guilt or innocence could be determined. Colonel Jones, aid-de-camp for that district, was so angered by the Holaman decision that he took the matter to Governor Brown, who was visiting in Macon. Brown shared Jones's contempt: "The conduct of the Inferior Court in ruling that a murderer who slays his fellow being in cold blood . . . and gives bail . . . and is at large, is on that account and for that reason exempt from military service, and entitled to remain at home . . . is so outrageous as to shock the moral sense of every good man, and I think all will agree that the Justices of the court that would so far abuse its powers . . . deserve to take the place of the murderer screened by them." Jones, understanding Brown's comment to be an order, delivered the message to the Worth County Inferior Court. Unless they changed their order within one week, the justices would be ordered to the front to take the alleged murderer's place regardless of their judicial exemptions.[41]

Reaction against the governor's order was severe. The Worth County Inferior Court voted to ignore the threat as "an assumption of power" and an "indignity." The *Milledgeville Confederate Union* decried the governor's attempts to blackmail the state's courts. "And this is the man who is shocked at the usurpation of power by the President, and who aspires to be the champion of State and Judicial rights," its editor wrote. "The army will hardly thank Governor Brown for making its ranks the receptacle of murderers and dishonest Judges."[42]

At times, advocacy of judicial discretion exceeded locally acceptable limits. In 1863, Webster, Terrell, and Stewart county citizens—already concerned over the rapidly depreciating Confederate currency—were incensed when it became apparent that courts were beginning to support refusal of paper money as payment for outstanding debts. Columbus Judge Grigsby E. Thomas instructed Stewart County's sheriff not to accept Confederate currency in payment of certain fieri facias.[43] Lucius Mansfield of Lumpkin refused to accept paper money as payment in a court settlement he had recently won, and Judge James T. Clarke of Atlanta refused Confederate currency as payment on notes he held against citizens of Stewart County. Grand jurors empaneled in Webster County denounced the judge's stance and refused to sit before his court. Terrell County grand jurors were expected to follow suit.[44]

Even though citizens passed a resolution condemning such actions, the Columbus newspapers initially refused to print it. Wielding what influence he held in the region, Judge Clarke convinced the papers' editors that the resolution had been passed by a very vocal minority and in no way reflected the facts of the situation. Still, others insisted that it had been the largest meeting Stewart County had seen in years, and that the resolution had passed with only four dissenting votes.[45]

Community leaders called a second meeting and unanimously passed the resolution a second time. Local pressure was building. Mansfield backed away from his earlier position; he agreed to accept Confederate currency, and his name was stricken from the resolution. But Judge Clarke stood firm, saying that it was perfectly legal to refuse Confederate currency for debts incurred before the start of the war.[46] However, such distinction in debts was not the issue. The notes being paid were those held by wealthy planters against smaller, poorer farmers. Planters were well aware of the devalued state of Confederate currency. It was, at least in part, the planters' cotton production that had caused currency devaluation in the first place. Unless rampant speculation could be checked, the value of the Confederate dollar would only drop more. In the meantime, the planters, backed by the courts, would happily take what little the poor farm families had, including their land, in lieu of currency.

Lower-class debtors were equally aware of the currency devaluation. They were faced daily with the fact that what one Confederate dollar purchased the day before might cost two or three dollars the day after. Many had saved their few remaining prewar dollars in United States notes, scrip, or specie and did not wish to part with them. This left many farmers in a predicament. The only other source of income for debt repayment was the liquidation of their land, their crops, their livestock, or their home. If plain folk were having difficulties feeding their families with the devalued currency, how difficult would it be with no home and no farm?

The district's dispute offered no solace to plain folk. By the next sched-

FIGURE 6.2. Judge Richard Henry Clark—author David Carlson's great-great-great-uncle—regularly defied enrollment authorities and higher courts in protecting Georgia planters from military conscription. Said one contemporary of Clark, "It sometimes required all his amiability and gentleness of disposition to keep him from breaking into open insubordination and treating the [Georgia Supreme] court with official discourtesy." (From the collection of David Carlson.)

uled court date in Webster County, Judge James Clarke had empaneled his own handpicked grand jury. It published fawning praise of Clarke as a "prophet receiving 'honor even in his own land and his own country.'" The "rumors" concerning Webster's jurors were false, it claimed. There had been some recalcitrant jurors, but they had been fined "to the limit of the law," and court had proceeded as usual. But Confederate currency still had no value in this judge's courtroom.[47]

More than civil officers and judicial powers, planters benefited from the protection of the local judges. From the beginning of conscription efforts, planters and their overseers had received the majority of the available exemptions from service. Planters with twenty slaves or more were automatically exempted. Those with too few slaves could simply pay an exemption fee. Overseers in control of a sufficient number of slaves over the age of sixteen were also automatically exempted. Although their exemption contained the qualification that they remain home to grow corn and other food crops, cotton was too often their prime staple.

As the fighting wore on and the army called for more men, those exemptions began to be threatened. Confederate exemption did not necessarily mean state militia exemption or even Confederate reserve exemption. To correct what they saw as an inconvenient oversight, the affluent turned to local courts. One of the first deserter cases to gain prominence in Georgia—and one of the best examples of the judicial mind-set when dealing with planters—was *Patterson v. Camfield*, brought before Judge Richard Henry Clark in 1863. Captain Caleb H. Camfield arrested William Patterson, a Decatur County overseer, and ordered him to report to General Howell Cobb at Quincy, Florida. Patterson, insisting that his arrest was illegal, petitioned Judge Clark for a writ of habeas corpus, claiming that he was exempt from military duty as an overseer. Camfield argued that Patterson had accepted his position as overseer on December 1, 1862, *after* the passage of the April 1862 conscription act. At the time of the law's passage, Patterson worked in Bainbridge as a merchant, a nonexempted profession. Because Patterson was in a nonexempted profession at the time of the act's passage, he was eligible for conscription regardless of his subsequent employment and any exemptions attached to that position.

Patterson argued that he had never been ordered to report for duty, had never been enrolled, and thus could not be considered a deserter. Judge Clark agreed and released Patterson because

> it was not designed by Congress that without enrollment and without notice, (which should consist in an order to report for duty at a certain time and place), that a citizen should be arrested on the highway—at the Court ground—at a place of business, put under a guard and hurried off to a camp of instruction.... [I]t appears to have been the practice of conscript officers of the Government to recognize this employment [overseers], though entered into subsequent to the

date of the conscript Acts, and before enrollment, as a good cause of exemption.[48]

The Georgia Supreme Court—in keeping with its support of Confederate conscription—overturned the decision. But Clark's ruling highlights two important points: first, local judges were answerable to local political and economic pressures that frequently influenced their decisions; and, second, the conscript officer's power to arrest alleged deserters and layouts was held by some local judges to be restricted. Conscription's opponents could point to this ruling as protection against unduly harsh or abrupt arrest procedures. Clark's opinions may also have been at least partially shaped by a fear shared by many of his contemporaries: that the conscription act was the first step in the eventual subjugation of the state to the national government.[49]

Such apprehension was not uncommon. The core of Governor Brown's argument against conscription was that it contained the power to strip the state of every means of self-government, leaving its citizens subject to the whims of the Confederacy. Judge Clark's initial reaction to conscription had been that it was constitutional under the powers granted the government to raise armies for the national defense, although it was an "outrageous exercise of power if it was meant to be fully executed." But the state rights arguments of Governor Brown and local political realities led Clark to reconsider his position. "I had not examined the question," he admitted in a July 1862 letter to Brown. "I have [since] carefully read the controversy between yourself, and the President, and I was made fully satisfied it was unconstitutional."[50]

Clark soon became one of the state's most vigorous supporters of planter interests and made a habit of releasing slaveholders and overseers from military service. In one case, he upheld the exemptions of Nathaniel Mercer, Isaac Brinson, and William Warren of Dougherty County, all of whom were overseers and exempt from service under the Second Conscription Act. Nevertheless, Colonel Edwin T. Jones, aid-de-camp for the Tenth District (Dougherty, Worth, and Lee counties), held that the exemptions did not extend to state service and arrested the men as deserters from the Georgia militia. Mercer, Brinson, and Warren argued that if they owed military service at all, they owed it to the Confederacy, not to the state. They were within legal conscription age and were it not for their overseer exemptions, they would be in the Confederate army. That eligibility for Confederate service—even though it was suspended by the exemption policies of the conscription acts, they insisted—rendered them ineligible for state duty.[51]

Judge Clark agreed. A soldier could be exempted in one of two ways under irrevocable exemptions enacted by the Confederate Congress or under various revocable exemptions ordered by the secretary of war. Clark held that the overseer exemption was one granted under an act of Congress and could not be denied by a court of law. If the Confederate army, acting under these congressional acts, determined that Mercer, Brinson, and Warren could best perform military service as overseers, that decision could not be rescinded. Just because they did not hold a weapon did not mean they were not serving in the military. Their duty was not to fire a weapon but to raise crops for the Confederacy.[52]

The equation of planting crops with military service did not sit well with the small farm families whose menfolk were in the army and could not get furloughs to plant their own crops. That pill was doubly hard to swallow when these exempt overseers claimed to be growing corn at a time when food was scarce, prices were inflated, and cotton was still in the fields. State force officers fumed as Clark's ruling effectively reduced the number of men available to rebuild Georgia's last line of defense when Sherman's forces were marching across the state. Colonel Jones appealed Clark's decision to the Georgia Supreme Court in November 1864, and the court heard the three cases, combined with two from Bibb County, as *Barber v. Irwin*. Justice Charles Jenkins, writing for the court, ruled that Confederate exempts were eligible for state militia and reserve duty.[53]

Despite the high court's ruling, Clark upheld two more exemptions based on his original reasoning. John Cutliff and Francis Billingslea held Confederate exemptions not as overseers for other planters, but as planters themselves. As with the earlier cases, Colonel Jones arrested the two as militia deserters only to have Judge Clark release them. Again the Georgia Supreme Court overturned the lower court's ruling and remanded the two men to Jones's custody. While the release of the two planters raised questions about Clark's impartiality, he was not alone in his advocacy of the planter class. Brooks County's inferior court released a planter from militia duty when it ruled that James King's exemption as a planter was the same as a detail to the Confederate commissary department.[54]

The military exemption of planters granted by Congress and upheld—and at times expanded—by the courts, proved increasingly disconcerting to the mass of Georgia's plain folk, who bore the brunt of military service. In increasing numbers, they wrote to political and military leaders about the inequities inherent in the conscription acts. Politicians began to worry about the rising discontent surrounding the exemption laws and gradually took steps to either limit them or do away with them completely. What had started as a fairly wide range of exemptions with broadly defined qualifications was gradually amended to restrict their application to a more select population.

Substitution, for example, was gradually phased out. Moneyed men had seen its end coming for some time as criticism of speculation in substitutes grew. They had attempted to postpone the inevitable by tempting the Confederacy with profits it could make by assuming control of the selection and payment of substitutes. Supporters of the plan pointed out that by taking control of the substitute system, the government could collect the substitution fees, use a portion of the proceeds as a bounty payment to the substitute, and keep the remainder as a finder's fee. Elites were hardly sincere when they expressed hope that the government would not "undertake the business to make money out of it" and fall into managing substitute speculation. They knew full well that profit was the bait by which they hoped to salvage the dying system.[55]

Planters were, above all else, businessmen, and their complaints and suggestions concerning the war, conscription, and exemption were informed by that perspective. So when the Confederate Congress amended substitution in September 1862 and then eliminated it altogether in December 1863, planters changed the vernacular of the argument and accused the government of one of the greatest taboos of the business world: breach of contract.[56] After all, had not nearly every state politician and judge been defending contracts all along in their state rights arguments? Was not the Confederate government, from its inception, born of a contract with the people? Politicians and judges were, after all, planters and businessmen themselves, and if planters could establish that the Confederate government had violated its contract with the people, not only would that argument prove the despotic nature of a centralized government and reinforce their state rights position, it might save them from any form of compulsory military service.

Hints at the judicial acceptance of this contract theory had been made as early as Judge Thomas's first rulings in early 1863, soon after the first amendments to the substitution laws. Thomas ruled in numerous cases that enrolling officers could neither attempt to enroll a conscript more than once nor reenroll a discharged soldier without a new act of Congress. His argument went something like this: Congress established a framework for military service and set the terms of a contract within which every citizen who qualified was required to offer his service. The government's acceptance of that offer established a contract for service that, once completed, could not be renewed, altered, amended, or impaired without just cause. Government rejection of that offer—whether for medical disability, age, or employment—voided the contract, and the Confederacy could not revive it without the establishment of a new framework. Thus, the army had one chance to conscript someone. Once rejected for medical or other reasons, the conscript could not be reexamined for any reason without a new conscription act. Once a soldier had been discharged, the military could not reactivate that veteran without a new conscription law.[57]

It is apparent that judges had their own agendas when dealing with writs of habeas corpus, agendas dictated either by geography or by personal and professional biases. Judge Lochrane heard more underage and medical writs by virtue of his court's proximity to Camp Oglethorpe in Macon, and his Irish heritage may have given him a special affinity for Irish conscripts. Judge Clark showed preference to local planters and overseers because of close political and economic ties to the planter elite of southwest Georgia. Judges in the Columbus and Atlanta regions proved reluctant to honor Confederate currency in their courts for fear of the losses planters might incur while collecting their outstanding debts. Judge Thomas's strong state rights beliefs led him to declare the entire conscription system unconstitutional and to free every conscript who appeared in Elbert County's superior court.

Economic and political realities of the legal system worked against the plain folk. While the writ was available to all who could petition the court, the cost of doing so remained well above what most conscripts could pay. The majority of plaintiffs in Georgia's writ cases were from the moderate to high end of the economic spectrum. The few middling to poor soldiers who appear in county court records are mainly those who were able to tap familial or employment relationships for the necessary funds. Those kinds of allies were hard to find.

7

"Very Improper Conduct"

Slaves and Plain Folk

Plain folk who sought to avoid Confederate entanglements did have at least one ally—the slave. Because poor whites sometimes shared the fields with enslaved blacks, a complex relationship developed between them, often based upon their mutual subjugation to a planter elite. While this relationship may have begun as a cautious acquaintance, it developed, in some cases, into one of trade and mutual support. And it was frequently a source of worry for planters.[1] Certainly those plain folk deserters hidden in the southern backwoods came into contact with escaped blacks. Sometimes slaves gave shelter to deserters right on the plantations. William McDonald, a McIntosh County slaveholder, was killed by a deserter when he discovered the man hiding in his slave quarters. And there were some plain folk like Willis Bone of Irwin County who hid both deserters and fugitives from slavery.[2]

Planters of the late antebellum era frowned on close contact between plain folk and slaves, even though many looked on common whites with less regard than chattel. In the planters' view, both plain folk and slaves were bound by nature to their respective socioeconomic positions, and separation had to be maintained to avoid any possibility of a biracial alliance that might threaten planter control. While separation along racial lines had never been absolute, it became even more of an imperative for slaveholders during the war. They saw the possibility that deserter bands roaming the countryside could tap into slave discontent to form small armies that could raid Confederate supply depots for food or seek revenge against wealthy planters.

Planter fears of lower-class cooperation across racial lines had been on the rise throughout the late antebellum era. Those fears became more acute in late 1860 during the presidential campaign and resulting secession crisis. In August came reports of a thwarted slave insurrection in Floyd County. The *Rome Courier* noted that white men were probably involved, "as there are several suspicious individuals prowling about in the county." The *Upson Pilot* editor wrote in September, "We have heard a great deal lately of worthless white men attempting at various places, to excite slaves to insurrection, arson, and murder." He felt such rumors were exaggerated but added that there were "many strolling white vagabonds throughout the South capable of just such attempts." One such "vagabond" was driven out of Thomasville that fall for "carrying incendiary publications." He turned up a few months later in Quincy, Florida, where a copy of Hinton Rowan Helper's *Impending Crisis* reportedly was found concealed in his clothing. A local "Vigilance Committee" shaved one side of his head and ran him out of town. "It appears," said one report, "the fellow had been trying to sell his trumpery to negroes."[3]

Not all interracial threats to slavery came from whites who were passing through. Most came, in fact, from local men. In October 1860, three Burke County residents—Peterson B. Cochrane, John Hart, Sr., and John Hart, Jr.—were ordered out of the county "for very improper conduct in connection with the negroes in the neighborhood."[4] A few weeks later, Mrs. Phillip Martin of Habersham County overheard several slaves and a free black discussing a plot to throw her into a well. Implicated in the affair was a local white gardener, John K. Wilson, who had for some time been "reading incendiary doctrines to them." By the time confessions had been beaten out of the conspirators, Wilson was nowhere to be found.[5]

On November 9, two days after Lincoln's election, the *Macon Telegraph* reported a slave insurrection in neighboring Crawford County. More than twenty slaves—perhaps many more—near Hickory Grove had gone on a rampage but were subdued before they could do any major damage. Playing on racist "miscegenation" fears, a man wrote from Fort Valley that "their intentions were, on Tuesday [election day], while the men were gone to the polls, to kill all the married [white] women and children, but to keep the young women for their wives . . . and kill the men on their return home." Perhaps most disturbingly, the insurrection had been instigated by two local white men: Cullen Davidson and a Hickory Grove merchant named Grier. Of the slaves arrested, according to the *Milledgeville Recorder*, "some will be burnt, others hung." The paper did not mention what fate might have awaited Grier and Davidson.[6]

Though the motives of whites involved with such plots were not always clear, a close eye had to be kept on expressions of unionism or abolitionism. A hint was dangerous; advocation could be deadly. That fall in Macon County, an "abolitionist" was whipped "for manifesting too great a solicitude for the welfare of the negro population in that vicinity. A gentle admonition, amounting to one hundred and seventy-five lashes on his naked back with a buggy trace, was administered to him." A well digger named Parker in Quitman County apparently took pity on a slave belonging to a Mr. Robinson. According to news accounts, he advised the woman, who had been roughly treated by an overseer, to set fire to Robinson's house and then make a run for freedom. Parker promised to help get her out of Quitman County and to some free state up North. Worst of all, in the eyes of local slaveholders, he had told her "that she was as good as the white folks." Mrs. Robinson had overheard the conversation. When Parker found that his plan had been uncovered, he tried to get out of the county. He was chased down with bloodhounds, tried in a mock proceeding, and hanged.[7]

Most wartime antislavery activity, black and white, probably went unreported. Allowing one's antislavery actions to be discovered was deadly, as men like Parker found. Besides, such activity was an acknowledgment of social ills that Georgia's elites were reluctant to recognize. Newspaper editors who expounded on the hardships of plain folk might hesitate when it came to publishing anything that challenged racist preconceptions. The possibility that slaves might be more than chattel, that they might rebel, and that some whites might help them was a prospect slaveholders found uncomfortable. But it was also too dangerous to ignore. That so many nonslaveholding voters had opposed secession was taken as a sign that there was cause for concern. W. A. Campbell of Fannin County wrote a frantic letter to Governor Brown in February 1861, only a few weeks after Georgia left the Union. He was sure that "the results of the late election for delegates in the mountains does not only indicate the Union sentiment, but more and worse, anti nigger slavery!"[8] Though such concerns were certainly exaggerated, fears that they might be true were real enough.

In April 1861, news reached the governor from southwest Georgia's Calhoun County that "there is some reason to suspect that there are low white men in the county who have communicated with the negroes." The next month in Monroe County—squarely in the heart of Georgia's cotton belt—Chappell Levy Robinson was found "trifling with negroes." He was forced to leave the state or face prosecution. In June, a citizen in middle Georgia's Johnson County wrote that there was in the area "a certain class of persons who are not disposed to enter the service of their country and whom it would not be safe to trust with the black population." One local white man had been heard to say that "he and the Negroes would have fine times with the wives of the volunteers after they, the volunteers, left for the service!" Later that month, Governor Brown got word that a man named Harris in Effingham County, just northwest of Savannah, had tried to talk two slaves into poisoning their owner.[9]

In July, the *Columbus Sun* reported that the vigilance committee of southwest Georgia's Mitchell County had uncovered plans for a slave uprising to be led by several local whites. James Patillo, William McLendon, Samuel Edwards, Romulus Weeks, Stephen G. W. Wood, John C. Morgan, and Ephraim McLeod were all implicated in the scheme. According to the *Sun*, Patillo was to supply the slaves "with as much ammunition as he possibly could to butcher the good citizens of the county." Patillo, McLendon, Weeks, Morgan, and McLeod all received the lash for their crime and were expelled from the county. Edwards and Wood escaped a whipping but were ordered never to set foot in Mitchell County again "under the penalty of death."[10]

December 1861 brought word to Governor Brown from north Georgia's Gordon County of local unionists holding secret meetings and organizing a military force to protect themselves from Confederate authorities. They swore both to resist attempts to draft them into the Confederate army and to aid the Yankees should they reach that far south. Most troubling was the writer's insistence that the unionists "say in case of an insurrection they will help the Negroes."[11]

In the spring of 1862, three Calhoun County men tried to do just that. Mindful of the previous year's failed attempt in nearby Mitchell County, Harvell Scaggs, William Scaggs, and Giles Shoots—all citizens of Calhoun County—brought the Federals in on the venture. Traveling down to the Gulf Coast under the pretense of making salt, the trio contacted Union blockaders. Soon they were running "superior new guns" to the slaves in Calhoun County. The plot came to light in June, and the three men were sentenced "to receive a sound whipping, to be tarred all over, and then ordered to quit the State." Some thought the punishment much too light. One southwest Georgia editor asked, "is it safe to the community to suffer such inhuman wretches, such dangerous animals, to go at large?" He suggested changing the sentence to perpetual imprisonment or death.[12]

Compounding such fears were the attitudes and actions of the slaves. Slaveholders had worried for some time, though they rarely admitted it, that slaves might draw strength from discontented plain folk. The slaves' discontent became obvious enough early on. "The idea seems to have gotten out extensively among [the slaves] that they are soon all to be free," wrote William Harrison of Calhoun County in April 1861, and "that Mr. Lincoln & his army are coming to set them free."[13]

Despite efforts to conceal the war's implications from them, slaves and free blacks were adept at sorting out the relationship of slavery to the war. Reverend Garrison Frazier, a black Savannah preacher, expressed that relationship in these terms: "The object of the war was not, at first, to give the slaves their freedom, but the sole object of the war was, at first, to bring the rebellious States back into the Union. . . . Afterward, knowing the value that was set on the slaves by the rebels, the President thought that his [emancipation] proclamation would stimulate them to lay down their arms, . . . and their not doing so has now made the freedom of the slaves a part of the war." Not all southern blacks were this aware of the war's finer points, but they were increasingly aware that a northern victory would mean their freedom. When a white minister preached that slavery was a divine institution and prayed aloud for the Lord to drive the Yankees back, one Georgia slave prayed silently to herself, "Oh, Lord, please send the Yankees on."[14]

Slaves had many ways of learning about the war and what it meant for them. Years after the war, former slave Hattie Nettles remembered climbing a fence as a young girl to watch Confederate soldiers marching past. She did not know at the time why they were on the move, but it was not long before she heard rumors of war. Mary Gladdy of Columbus recalled "the whisperings among the slaves—their talking of the possibility of freedom." On a nearby plantation, Louis Meadows and his fellow slaves knew that as long as Jefferson Davis was in power they would never be free. "That was why," Meadows said, "everybody hoped Master Lincoln would conquer."[15]

Georgia slaves frequently met in secret during the war to hold prayer meetings for freedom. According to Mary Gladdy, Muscogee County slaves gathered in their cabins two or three nights a week for such meetings. According to one report, they placed large pots against the doors to keep their voices muffled. "Then," she said, "the slaves would sing, pray, and relate experiences all night long. Their great, soul-hungering desire was freedom." Those few slaves who could read kept up with events through stolen newspapers and spread the word to their neighbors. As news of Confederate reversals became more frequent, excitement among the slaves grew. Young Ella Hawkins of Muscogee County heard older slaves on her plantation whispering among themselves: "Us is gonna be free! Jes as sho's anything. God has heard our prayers; us is gonna be free!"[16]

As the war went on, slaves assembled more openly. The Albany newspaper warned about slaves in town who "congregate together contrary to law, *exhibit their weapons,* and no doubt devise their secret, but destructive plans."[17] A Worth County grand jury was also concerned about rebellious slaves and warned against a sudden influx of small arms. It suggested that the state legislature make it a capital offense "to sell to, buy or procure for a slave, any gun, pistol, dirk, or Bowie knife, or any other instrument."[18]

Tales of imminent Yankee invasion only made the slaves more eager for their freedom and the slaveholders more frightened. Rumors spread early in the war of federal ships ready to raid the Georgia ports of St. Marys and Brunswick "to carry out this new Yankee idea of incendiarism, murder, arson, robbery, insurrection, libertinism, Republicanism (Black) under the holy banner of liberty." Newspapers reported that James Redpath, a northern abolitionist, along with a son of the famous John Brown, had landed on Cumberland Island and were planning to transport rescued slaves to Cuba. Former Congressman Eli Thayer's 1863 Cooper Union proposal to colonize Florida with freedmen and women, followed by assaults at Jacksonville and Fernandina by black Union troops, reinforced fears among slaveholders.[19]

The most common response to such fears was a call for stricter enforcement of the laws, especially the patrol laws. From the beginning of the war, some whites feared that individual acts of insubordination might ultimately lead to a general slave uprising. That fear had a devastating impact on the Confederate war effort. While southern armies were constantly outnumbered by their northern counterparts, up to two hundred thousand southern men were kept at home to guard against the possibility of slave rebellion. For state and local officials, it seemed worth the cost. A Baker County grand jury deemed patrol laws so important that their enforcement would "conduce as much to our safety as 'men and arms.'"[20]

Patrols were, nevertheless, often left to men who were incompetent to handle them. In some cases, slaveholders left the duty of patrolling to poor whites who had little stake in the job. The result was that patrol laws were half-heartedly enforced or completely ignored. So badly was the job handled in Sumter County that some urged the local patrol commission to "appoint men to execute such duty as they know will do it in a proper manner." Lowndes County leaders, "aggrieved that the patrol law has been so much neglected," issued repeated calls for stricter enforcement. "We recommend," they wrote, "that the patrol laws be strictly enforced in fact we deem it indispensable to the protection of property in various sections of our county." Thomas County leaders complained that the county's slaves "under the present want of discipline are an absolute evil" and ordered that every plantation supply the captain of the patrol commission with a listing of all slaves.[21]

One explanation for lax enforcement was that some planters found these laws an impediment to the profitability of slaves and crops. Some farmers, planters, and shopkeepers—in violation of state laws and local ordinances—allowed their slaves to travel and to sell their owner's goods at local markets. Strict patrolling might curtail such activities. In the summer of 1863, Sumter County's grand jury heard a special presentment against William Parker for giving his slave August permission "to travel, barter, trade, and contract for himself." Clay County officials ordered all slaves and free blacks hiring themselves out arrested and remanded to the custody of a white owner or guardian. Thomas County warned against slave-run shops as "the general resorts of negroes where they meet and conceal schemes of mischief." The Dougherty County Superior Court decried the practice of allowing slaves to sell fruit, cake, and beer from stands along Albany's streets. Despite such concerns, few slaveholders were called to task for allowing slaves such freedoms.[22]

Slaveholders could hardly have prevented slaves from taking on new liberties in any case. The more excited slaves became at their anticipated freedom, the more difficult they were to control. Passage of the First Conscription Act in 1862 intensified the difficulty. With many white males drafted into military service, officials increasingly tightened local and state laws governing slaves. A Lowndes County grand jury suggested that "Negroes from the county [should] not be allowed to assemble in town at any time nor under any circumstance except on Sunday to attend preaching at the usual hour of morning service and then upon the condition only that they disperse immediately after service." Private patrols were formed that allowed the "aged and infirm" to supplement slave management systems. Petitioners in Stewart County asked for a special military exemption for James T. Gordy because he had a good pack of "negro dogs" that he could use to oversee that county's slaves and round up deserters. Thomas County slaveholders convinced President Jefferson Davis to temporarily suspend the conscription of local overseers.[23]

As refugees from captured or threatened parts of the state fled to south Georgia, the region's population, both black and white, grew dramatically. Food, already in short supply from Confederate impressment, became more scarce, and slaves competed with whites for dwindling local resources. Hunger was the driving force behind much theft by slaves, just as it was for similar theft among whites. Colonel A. T. MacIntyre wrote that the slaves in Brooks and Thomas counties, desperately underfed, "will plunder the adjoining plantations & families of soldiers unless strongly policed." Slaves, searching for meat, had already raided small farms in sections of Lowndes County, causing "serious loss to families of limited circumstances."[24]

In areas of the black belt from which many of the white males had gone off to war, slaves were particularly defiant. In August 1862, slaveholder Laura Comer wrote in her diary: "The servants are so indolent and obstinate it is a trial to have anything to do with them." Slaves feigned ignorance or illness, sabotaged equipment, and roamed freely in defiance of laws requiring them to carry a pass. Roving slaves became so common that some slaveholders tried, apparently with little success, to lock them up at night. What work slaves did, they did grudgingly. Some refused to work at all. A Georgia mistress wrote concerning one of her slaves: "Nancy has been very impertinent. . . . She said she would not be hired out by the month, neither would she go out to get work." Another woman wrote to her husband, "We are doing as best we know, or as good as we can get the Servants to do; they learn to feel very independent."[25]

As early as 1861, a Georgia overseer complained to his absentee employer that the slaves would not submit to physical punishment. One slave walked away when the overseer told him he was about to be whipped. "I wish you would . . . come down and let the matter be settle," the overseer wrote, "as I do not feel wiling to be runover by him." Another Georgia slave drew a knife on an overseer who tried to whip him. His owner locked him up and put him on a bread and water diet, but it did little to subdue him. Such actions tended only to make slaves more rebellious. "I am satisfied that his imprisonment has only tended to harden him," one overseer wrote soon after releasing an unruly slave. "I dont think he will ever reform."[26]

Besides being terribly painful, whipping was for slaves a key symbol of their lowly status. It is hardly surprising then that resistance to whipping became one of the main ways slaves sought to achieve some measure of independence. Such resistance could, of course, be dangerous. One Troup County planter was noted for turning his dogs on slaves who refused to be whipped. A slave on the Hines Holt plantation near Columbus was shot for it. He had beaten off six men who had tried to hold him down.[27]

Despite such dangers, slaves continued to resist. According to former Troup County slave Celestia Avery, Peter Heard whipped his slaves "unmercifully." One day while hoeing the fields, Celestia's grandmother Sylvia was told by an overseer to remove her clothes when she got to the end of a fence row. She was going to be whipped for not working fast enough. When the overseer reached for her, she grabbed a wooden rail and broke it across the man's arms.[28]

To avoid punishment for anything from "insolence" to murder, slaves often fled to nearby woods and swamps temporarily or for the war's duration. Charlie Pye of Columbus said that his mother would hide out in the woods for months at a time rather than be whipped. But she always returned "when the strain of staying away from her family became too great."[29] Celestia Avery told an especially harrowing story of her grandmother Sylvia's sadistic treatment at the hands of her master, Peter Heard.

> Every morning my grandmother would pray, and old man Heard despised to hear anyone pray saying they were only doing so that they might become free niggers. Just as sure as the sun would rise, she would get a whipping; but this did not stop her prayers every morning before day. This particular time grandmother Sylvia was in [the] "family way" and that morning she began to pray as usual. The master heard her and became so angry he came to her cabin, seized and pulled her clothes from her body and tied her to a young sapling.

He whipped her so brutally that her body was raw all over. When darkness fell her husband cut her down from the tree. During the day he was afraid to go near her. Rather than go back to the cabin she crawled on her knees to the woods and her husband brought grease for her to grease her raw body. For two weeks the master hunted but could not find her; however, when he finally did, she had given birth to twins. The only thing that saved her was the fact that she was a mid-wife and always carried a small pin knife which she used to cut the naval cord of the babies. After doing this she tore her petticoat into two pieces and wrapped each baby.[30]

After his own severe beating, another Troup County slave named William escaped and dug out a large cave near the Chattahoochee River. Several nights later, under the cover of darkness, he moved his wife and two children to the cave where they lived for the rest of the war.[31]

Thousands of slaves deserted their masters in what historian W.E.B. Du Bois referred to as a general strike against the Confederacy. Every slave taken to the front by Clarke County's Troup Artillery fled to Union lines. Eleven slaves held at the saltworks near St. Joseph's Bay, Florida, which supplied salt for much of Georgia, sought refuge with the Union blockading fleet. One southwest Georgia slave was hanged for attempting to organize a mass exodus of local blacks to the Federals on the Florida coast. Slaves ran off individually as well as in groups. A slave who escaped from Conecuh County in southern Alabama made it all the way to Troup County, Georgia, before being captured and taken to the local jail. Other fugitive slaves stayed much closer to home. A slave named Bill who escaped from a West Point, Georgia, slave dealer remained in the area for three years before he was finally caught.[32]

Whites sometimes assisted these escapees. In December 1862, Robert Bezley of Atlanta was arrested for writing out fraudulent passes to help slaves reach Yankee lines. For those who could not make it that far, whites such as Willis Bone of Irwin County, William F. Huskey of Clay County, Lindsey H. Durham of Lee County, and John Anderson of Lumpkin County were willing to give them safe haven.[33]

Like deserters and draft evaders, runaway slaves often gathered in small, isolated communities. Frequently these settlements were multiracial. So numerous were such communities in south Georgia's wiregrass country that one source called it "the common retreat of deserters from our army, tories, and runaway negroes." A number of escaped slaves hid

FIGURE 7.1. A young Confederate patriot tries to "redeem" deserters and escaped slaves hiding out in south Georgia's Okefenokee Swamp in this illustration from Louis Pendleton's postwar novel *In the Okefenokee*, one of many period literary works that idealized the Lost Cause.

out with Jeff Anderson's deserter band in the mountains around Dahlonega. Like their white counterparts, groups of runaway slaves sustained themselves by making raids on local towns and plantations. S. S. Massey of Chattahoochee County complained to Governor Brown that local slaves were "killing up the stock and stealing every thing they can put their hands on." The *Early County News* reported in April 1864 that "*stealing*, and *rascality generally*," was going on in Blakely and Early County. Although the newspaper reported that "negroes are doing a great deal of this stealing," it also added that "there certainly are some *mean white men* connected with the negroes." The editor told of blacks selling stolen goods to "*mean, trifling, low-down white persons* . . . who bought them in the *dead hour of night.*"[34]

Interracial trading had been common for decades, and its pace quickened with the outbreak of war. As early as April 1861, the *Albany Patriot* warned of it. In Effingham County, Brad Jones was hanged for it. A small shop owner in Springfield, Jones had been accused in the summer of 1861 of purchasing from local slaves items that he knew to have been stolen. In March 1862, there was so much crime in Columbus that the *Sun* called the city "a den of thieves." Some said blacks were responsible; others said it was whites. Still others were sure there was a partnership of both. "The latter opinion," wrote the *Sun* editor, "we are inclined to believe, is nearest the mark."[35]

Trying to stem the rising tide of crime and rebelliousness among slaves, the Georgia General Assembly made several additions to the state penal code. In December 1861, it stipulated that any black person found guilty of arson would be put to death. It also forbade owners to let slaves hire themselves out and required slaves to reside on their owner's premises. In 1862, the assembly reinforced laws forbidding slaves to travel without passes and canceled all exemptions from patrol duty.[36]

In the summer of 1864, Governor Brown and state Adjutant General Henry C. Wayne instituted a new exempted police patrol to supplement existing slave patrols. It consisted of one white male—selected by the county inferior court from those men not eligible for conscription—for every five hundred slaves in the county. Its stated duty was to see that slaves left on plantations without overseers were kept subjugated and that planter property was protected. Brown also noted that one of the patrol's most important duties would be to protect "negros from the corrupting influence of bad men, who as deserters from the army, or skulkers from duty, are at home attempting to mislead and use the negros for their own wicked purposes."[37]

Some city and county governments considered the danger so great that they went further. Officials in Blakely hired extra police for every district in Early County. The editor of the *Early County News* called it "the duty of all good citizens to go out nightly on patrol." Cuthbert's city council divided the town into three wards and tried to put all available white males between the ages of sixteen and sixty on patrol duty. Each ward was to be patrolled by at least two men every night.[38]

Along with the general crackdown on slaves, controls tightened on free blacks as well. Some were literate, and whites viewed them as potential leaders of slave insurrections. Insisting that "idle negroes are public curses," a Columbus resident suggested that all free blacks be pressed into government service as laborers. He added that they should, of course, be closely watched by white supervisors. Some free blacks already worked in government factories, but Georgia did impress free blacks to help construct fortifications.[39]

In November 1863, the Georgia Assembly considered an act to sell all free blacks into slavery. The proposal never got out of committee. But the assembly did require free blacks to register at their county courthouse and to list a white guardian who would be responsible for their actions. Those who had no guardian were subject to being sold into slavery by the state. Randolph County imposed a registration fee of twenty-five dollars, and there were severe penalties—including nominal enslavement—for those who failed to register. In some towns, free blacks, like slaves, had to have a pass from their guardian or employer if they wanted to leave their homes after dark.[40]

By 1864, the patrols clearly inspired little fear among slaves. The slaves had long since begun to anticipate their coming freedom, even taking it for themselves, and were more and more ignoring the patrols. One slave boy who outran the patrollers made fun of them after he was safely behind his owner's fence. Some slaves fought back. They often tied ropes or vines neck-high across a dark stretch of road just before the patrollers rode by. According to a former slave, these traps were guaranteed to unhorse at least one rider. When patrollers raided a prayer meeting near Columbus, one slave stuck a shovel in the fireplace and threw hot coals all over them. Instantly the room "filled with smoke and the smell of burning clothes and white flesh." In the confusion, every slave got away.[41]

Despite their inability to control slaves, slave patrols filled what for some was an important need. As with local military details, the slave patrols were a haven for otherwise eligible conscripts, and frequently the patrols were such in name only. Complaints of fraud were almost universal, and the state inspector general's office called into question a number of appointments in various Georgia counties, including Dooly, Early, Lowndes, and Decatur. Among the most controversial were the patrol appointments in Brooks County.[42]

In July 1864, the five justices of the Brooks County Inferior Court appointed seventeen men to serve as the county's exempted patrol. Twelve were eligible conscripts evading military service. Members of the local militia signed a petition accusing the justices of "arrogat[ing] to themselves the power of exempting twelve men" in violation of the order creating the patrols. That order specified that only men not otherwise eligible for military service would be detailed for patrol duty. Based on age limits set by the third and most recent Confederate conscription act, patrol membership would be limited to men under age sixteen and over age fifty-five. While there were plenty of men in the county over fifty-five years old, the court had selected the majority of the men from those under fifty-five. While the local aid-de-camp refused to issue state certificates of exemption for the men selected, that refusal did not stop the justices. They confirmed their selections and named the seventeen as the new police force. Adjutant General Wayne's office refused to intervene, telling the justices only that if they had "acted in conformity to [the Governor's] rule, your action is approved—if otherwise, it is annulled." The county would have to deal with the controversy as best it could.[43]

Sixty percent of the militia members can be found in the 1860 census. Over two-thirds of these identifiable men were planters. While planters would most likely have backed the appointment of a fellow planter to the police patrol, they might have contested the appointment of a man of draft age from the ranks of the plain folk: someone, perhaps, like John Vickery.

Little is known of Vickery. He was born about 1827, the son of one of two Vickery brothers—Jesse or Elias. Both were illiterate nonslaveholders who frequently moved in search of work. By the mid-1840s, the Vickery brothers packed their belongings to leave their Lowndes County homes. Jesse Vickery and his wife, Mary, along with their son Benjamin's family, moved to Baker County. Elias Vickery took his wife and three youngest daughters into Irwin County, where he became a shoemaker.

The teenaged John Vickery was left behind to apprentice with Henry J. Holliday, a local blacksmith. John Vickery, it appears, was not destined to follow his father's migratory lifestyle.[44]

What happened to Holliday and Vickery during the early years of the war is not known. Neither is listed in the 1860 Brooks County census, even though their homes had been incorporated into that county at its creation in 1858. Vickery is listed in Brooks County Inferior and Superior Court records of 1863 but not in lists compiled at the reorganization of Georgia's militia that year. If Vickery served in the Confederate army, it was not from the state of Georgia, although he was within conscription age.[45]

Vickery next appears on August 23, 1864, at the end of a hangman's rope on Quitman's courthouse square. Details of the events leading to his death vary according to the sources, but all agree that Vickery, with the assistance of local slaves, organized a small insurrectionary force that intended to murder some of the wealthier plantation owners and their families in Brooks County—Judge James O. Morton; Robert A. Durham; Captain Bufort Elliot; Mitchell Jones; and Jones's father-in-law, James W. Spain. "They have held their meetings," wrote Mrs. Mitchell Jones, one apparently intended victim, "and have organized their company and were soon to begin their horrid work of murdering our men, women and children."[46]

After killing their owners and stealing whatever weapons they could find, they planned to set Quitman afire and seize the local depot of the Savannah and Gulf Railroad. From there they planned to head toward Madison, Florida, and to seize and then burn that town. Hoping to be reinforced by deserters and Union troops from the Gulf Coast, the men would return to Quitman from where they could control the region. Planters learned of the plot from a slave arrested for theft on the eve of the planned uprising. After more interrogations, the Brooks County police patrol arrested Vickery and four slave coconspirators.[47]

The motivation behind Vickery's planned uprising is unclear. If he had somehow managed to gain a place on the Brooks County police patrol and then had lost or had been threatened with losing that position due to the militia's complaints, that might provide one of two motives for the Vickery slave conspiracy of 1864.[48] All of the named targets were connected with either the militia, the planter class, or the Brooks County Inferior Court. James O. Morton was a former inferior court justice and a prominent planter in Brooks County.[49] Spain and Jones—the primary targets of the plot—had both signed the militia's petition contesting the inferior court's patrol appointments. Together they owned over one hundred slaves and estates valued at almost two hundred thousand dollars.[50] If Vickery—either out of desperation to retain his patrol assignment or in revenge for losing it—was to make a point about the need for a *youthful* police patrol, these two men provided an excellent opportunity.

A second hypothesis involves Buford Eliott. A member of the local militia, Eliott was also a merchant from South Carolina exempted from Confederate service because of disability. In fact, several "disabled" South Carolina merchants were in Brooks County in late 1864, possibly to purchase items for speculation in their home state. It could be suggested that Vickery's motivation was a sense of outrage that the planters of the county were conspiring to export food from Quitman not for the troops but for speculation in South Carolina.[51]

Aggravating the social and economic disparities in Brooks County was a severe shortage of food, a shortage made all the more aggravating by the existence of Confederate food stores at depots along the rail lines of north Florida and south Georgia. By the time of the planned insurrection, the only line of defense between the Gulf of Mexico and southwest Georgia was a single line of Confederate troops assigned to protect the Pensacola and Georgia Railroad. At stations along the route—Quincy, Tallahassee, Madison, and Monticello—Confederate officials had stored ten days' ration of meat and breadstuffs for twelve thousand troops in west and central Florida.[52]

These depots were tempting targets for both invading Union troops and hungry southerners. By the time of the Vickery conspiracy, deserter bands in Taylor, Lafayette, Levy, and other Florida counties—cooperating with escaped slaves—had already attacked the depots at Tallahassee and Madison. Vickery and other citizens of Brooks County surely knew of these depots, since cattle drovers from central Florida made frequent trips to Thomasville and Quitman and brought war news from Florida. Vickery's promise of freedom and food would have proved an effective tool in prompting Brooks County's slaves to join the plot. After seizing what food was stored in Quitman, there would be an even larger bounty in Florida.[53]

It is hardly surprising that Vickery's plan involved Union troops. As early as January 1863, General Howell Cobb had received reports that Deadman's Bay—at the mouth of the Steinhatchee River on the Gulf coast of Florida—should be considered a prime target for a Union invasion. It was in Taylor County, Florida, a center of unionist and deserter activity, that northern troops could gain assistance. The ground was firm, no natural obstructions blocked the roads between the bay and the interior of the state, and there was a direct route from the bay to Madison, Florida. Just such a landing occurred one week prior to the planned Vickery uprising. Eight hundred men landed at the mouth of the Aucilla River with another five hundred landing at Deadman's Bay. It is possible these were the men that Vickery and his men were to meet at Madison and lead back into south Georgia.[54]

Following Vickery's arrest by the county police patrol, the Brooks County Militia took steps to use the conspirators as warning examples against further such plots. A special court session convened to try the case, although it was improperly seated. Governor Brown had specified that either the county inferior court or the district aid-de-camp would try all cases resulting from police patrol arrests. Brooks County's inferior court, which by this point had lost most of its credibility, did not preside over Vickery's trial. Neither did the aid-de-camp, Colonel A. T. MacIntyre, a surprising absence given that MacIntyre was in the midst of responding to accusations of neglecting his duties. Instead, Brooks County, for that day at least, was controlled by the militia, and the Vickery conspirators received a military trial. Of the five inferior court justices, only two were involved in the trial, Robert A. Hardee and David Creech, both members of the Brooks County Militia, as was every other presiding official and special committee member. Given the circumstances, Vickery and the three slave coconspirators stood little chance of acquittal.[55]

At ten o'clock on the morning of August 23, 1864, the citizens of Brooks County gathered to hear charges read against the accused conspirators. While the militia had arrested several other slaves the day before and men still scoured the countryside searching for two white men—suspected deserters from Florida—everyone seemed sure that the leaders had been captured. There would certainly be a hanging. Captain C. S. Gaulden, planter and sometime minister, took the chair as presiding officer for the trial and read a summary of the events. Captain James L. Moseley, a member of the Brooks County Militia and a planter exempted from Confederate service due to a "disease of the eyes," moved that Gaulden appoint a committee of twelve to "decide on confession and evidence as to their guilt; and also the punishment to be inflicted." The court unanimously approved the motion, formed its committee, and recessed until that afternoon.[56]

Court reconvened at three o'clock, and the committee of twelve presented its findings. John Vickery—guilty of arson, inciting slaves to insurrection, and aiding slaves to flee to the Yankees; the slave Sam—guilty of insurrection and inducing slaves to insurrection; the slave Nelson—guilty of insurrection; the slave George—guilty of insurrection. The committee recommended hanging for them all. Its members could not reach a verdict on the slave Warren, property of Buford Elliot, and recommended that he be committed to the local jail until further evidence of his guilt could be gathered. Dr. H. M. Farrensides moved that the committee's findings be adopted and carried out. It was seconded by Thomas Folsom and unanimously passed.[57]

Captain Lane offered a motion that a committee of five be named to decide on a place and time for the executions. That motion also passed. The selected committee—Captain Marion J. Culpepper, "disabled" planter; Captain Robert A. Hardee, wounded Confederate veteran and justice of the inferior court; David Creech, justice of the inferior court; Joseph W. Stalnaker, South Carolina merchant; and J. T. Crawford—retired for ten minutes before reporting that the executions would take place in one hour.[58]

The scaffold was prepared, and at six o'clock Vickery and the three slaves walked out of the jail. One can imagine the clink and shuffle of shackled feet as the condemned were led under heavy guard before the crowd. Old men, planters, women, and children strained for a better view as Inferior Court Justice Reverend O. L. Smith read scriptural comforts and the four men were positioned under the scaffold. All were asked if they had anything to say, undoubtedly in the hope they would publicly confess. The slave Sam reportedly admitted his guilt and accepted his "richly deserved . . . punishment." But Vickery launched into a vitriolic tirade, proclaiming his innocence. His speech rang hollow, however, when the hood was secured over his head and he shouted, "God have mercy on me for my lies!" as he dropped to his death.[59]

The chief purpose of such public trials and executions was to discourage further such conspiracies. Though the public was called to the initial meeting, the examination of evidence and the passing of judgment were left to a select few members of the militia and planter class. And evidence

FIGURE 7.2. Vigilante "justice" was common in the Civil War South. White men such as John Vickery—accused of involvement with a slave conspiracy—could quickly find themselves at the wrong end of a rope. (Courtesy of Hargrett Rare Book and Manuscript Library, University of Georgia.)

was limited to "decid[ing] on confession[s]" either already given or to be obtained. Guilt had already been decided, and everyone knew it.[60]

Relief at the Vickery executions reached as far north as the Rappahannock River in Virginia. Bryant Folsom, writing to his wife from camp near Brucetown, "was glad two hear of Vickery and them three negroes being hung as they undertaken what they did. I am truly glad two hear of them being put to death."[61] Folsom had good reason to be concerned. His wife and children lived just two houses away from Mitchell Jones and James Spain, two of the intended victims. Whether Vickery was motivated by anger, hunger, revenge, or anti-Confederate sentiment may never be known. Perhaps a disputed police appointment, the suspected presence of South Carolina speculators, or both prompted him to action.

Vickery's attempted uprising pointed out a weakness in the solidarity of the South that many were reluctant to admit. Plain folk—saddled with a struggle against planter-dictated social expectations, hunger, poverty, and disillusionment with the Confederacy—tapped into and exploited slave discontent. If neither state nor Confederate officials could find a remedy, the Confederacy was doomed to self-destruct.

8

"We Are Fighting Each Other Harder Than We Ever Fought the Enemy"

Georgia's Inner Civil War

The reluctance of many white southerners to serve in the armies of the Confederacy—and the willingness of some to join slaves in working against it—reflected a broad discontent. From its beginnings, many plain folk had seen the conflict as a rich man's war. That view became more widely held as the months dragged by. In a September 1863 letter to the *Savannah Morning News*, one outraged Georgian asked: "What class has most interest in the war and has made the most money by it, *and sacrificed the least to maintain it?* . . . It is the class known as the planters."[1]

Planters had been largely responsible for bringing the Confederacy into existence but would not grow enough food to feed its soldiers or their families. Speculators were driving prices of even basic necessities far beyond the reach of most southerners. The burdens of taxation and impressment fell heaviest on the small farmers, and it was they and other plain folk who bore the brunt of conscription. For those who could afford to, it was easy enough to avoid the draft. An anonymous letter to Governor Brown from Catoosa County expressed that familiar complaint. The writer pointed to class inequity between two men named Stuart and Lee: "Old Mr. Stuart has five sons in the army, one sent home dead. Stuart is a poor man. Lee is rich and his sons are all at home. And it is so with other familiys. They want other people [to] do all the fighting and let them ly at home." One southwest Georgia man who signed himself "An Old Soldier" wrote that one way to get rich at the life insurance business would be to take "only those applicants who are shouting for their fellow citizens to go to 'the front.'"[2]

Such attitudes produced a class-based political consciousness among plain folk that made itself felt in the 1863 elections. As campaigning heated up that summer, many loyal Confederates worried about the impact the coming elections would have on the war effort. The editor of Augusta's *Chronicle and Sentinel* noted that the South contained "a large number of persons who not only sympathize with the Federals, but who are doing all in their power to injure us in every possible manner." The summer of 1863 found some Georgia citizens, such as D. H. Johnson, editor of Griffin's *Southern Union*, publicly calling for an end to the war and a reconstruction of the old Union. In north Georgia, several candidates for the General Assembly from Gilmer and surrounding counties ran on the "Union" ticket. Southern voters ousted over half their congressional representatives that fall.[3]

Not all of those who voted against incumbents were anti-Confederate, nor did they all do so for class-related reasons. But for many plain folk, class resentment certainly swayed their votes. Citizens in southeast Georgia made that clear when, in an open letter to the *Savannah Morning News*, they called on two of the region's assemblymen to make public their positions on a recent state tax: "There was a tax act passed at the last session for the support of indigent widows and orphans of deceased soldiers, *from which the planters were specially exempted.* Did you, or either of you, vote *for that exemption*, or oppose it? And how did you manifest your opposition to that gross and palpable injustice?" The writers signed themselves "Many Voters Who are not Planters."[4]

Planters and their allies became so worried that their political control might be slipping away that calls came from their ranks to restrict the vote along class lines. Some called for an increased poll tax. Others supported property qualifications for voting and office holding. In May 1863, the Reverend H. W. Hilliard, a former member of Congress, spoke out publicly for restricted suffrage. When word of Hilliard's remarks reached Athens, one local paper bitterly commented that "the most unfeeling, unjust and cruel wrong we have ever witnessed, is this effort of designing politicians and juggling priests who are lying about home doing nothing, and worse than nothing, to disfranchise the brave and noble poor men who are fighting the battles of the country."[5]

Most elites were more discreet than Hilliard in their opposition to universal white male suffrage, expressing their opinions only to members of their own class. In a private letter to a friend, Godfrey Barnsley accused Joe Brown, because of his opposition to Confederate conscription, of trying to "make himself popular among the lower classes to get re-elected." Barnsley held England's restricted franchise to be an example the Confederacy should follow.[6]

Disaffected as most plain folk had become by fall 1863, the October 7 election results could hardly have surprised any careful observer. Milledgeville's *Confederate Union* reported of the General Assembly, "but few of the old members have been returned." The news was even worse for Georgia's congressional incumbents. Voters sent nine new representatives to Congress, eight of whom were elected on platforms opposing the Davis administration. Julian Hartridge of southeast Georgia's First District was the only member of the state's ten-member House delegation to retain his seat. This 90 percent freshman rate was the highest of any Confederate state. Little wonder that the new members were much more attuned to the concerns of plain folk than were their predecessors. Most Georgia delegates to the First Confederate Congress had supported both conscription and impressment. In the Second Congress, only three backed conscription, and only one supported impressment.[7]

Plain folk had an impact on local elections as well. In Columbus they offered their own slate of candidates for city office on the "Mechanics' and Working Men's Ticket." According to the *Enquirer*, the new party "prevailed by a very large majority." Its success sent shock waves through the ranks of the city's political establishment.[8]

The *Enquirer*'s editor voiced upper-class fears just two days after the vote when he chastised plain folk for their "antagonistic" attitude and condemned the "causeless divisions of our citizens into classes." The *Enquirer* conceded that because of their numbers the city's plain folk could control any election in which they were united. But he insisted that this fact alone was among the strongest reasons why they should not unite. "Nothing can be more mischievous in any society," he warned, "than antagonistic organizations of its classes. Such divisions are more bitter in their alienations than any other political parties, and are far more apt to produce hurtful collisions."[9]

Reaction to the *Enquirer*'s criticism was swift and direct. On October 13, a competing city paper, the *Daily Sun*, ran a letter it received from a local man signing himself "Mechanic." He argued that mischief had already been done by the elite. Common folk were trying only to protect themselves from further harm.

Voting by Classes

Editor Daily Sun:—I notice in the Enquirer, of Friday evining, an article complaining bitterly of the people voting by classes, in which both classes are accused of clannishness, but the burden of his complaint seems to rest on mechanics and working men. He says, "there is certainly no ground for any antagonism in the city." In this the Enquirer is mistaken; for any man, woman or child can see that the people are dividing into two classes, just as fast as the pressure of the times can force them on. As for example: class No. 1, in their thirst for gain, in their worship of Mammon, and in their mighty efforts to appropriate every dollar on earth to their own account, have lost sight of every principle of humanity, patriotism, and virtue itself, and seem to have forgotten that the very treasures they are now heaping up are the price of blood, and unless this mania ceases, will be the price of liberty itself; for we know something of the feeling which now exits in the army, as well as in our work-shops at home. The men know well enough that their helpless families are not cared for, as they were promised at the beginning of the war.... They know, too, that every day they remain from home, reduces them more and more in circumstances, and that by the close of the war a large majority of the soldiery will be unable to live; in fact, many of them are ruined now, as many of their homes and other effects are passing into the hands of speculators and extortioners, for subsistence to their families. Thus you see, that all the capital, both in money and property, in the South, is passing into the hands of class No. 1, while class No. 2 are traveling down, soon to take their station among the descendants of Ham. You can easily see who are class No. 2. The soldiery, the mechanics, and the workingmen, not only of Columbus, but of all the Confederate States. In view of these things, is it not time that our class should awake to a sense of their danger, and in the mildest possible manner begin the work of self-defense, and endeavor to escape a bondage more servile than that imposed by the aristocracy of England on their poor peasantry? Then we claim the right, as the first alternative, to try and avert the great calamity, by electing such men to the councils of the nation as we think will best represent our interests. If this should fail, we must then try more potent remedies.

Efforts to find "more potent remedies" had already given rise to the South's most widespread antiwar organization, the Peace Society, generally dedicated to ending the conflict with or without southern independence. The Peace Society was one of perhaps half a dozen secret or semisecret organizations that sprang up across the South to oppose the war. Little is known of the Society's early days. It probably formed in northern Alabama or eastern Tennessee during the spring of 1862 and later spread to Georgia. Though it was composed mostly of those who wanted nothing more than an end to the fighting, unionists were at the heart of the organization and remained its principal advocates throughout the war.

FIGURE 8.1. The Peace Society was among the most active of the secret or semisecret organizations that sprang up across the South to oppose the war. Composed mostly of those who wanted nothing more than an end to the fighting, unionists were at the heart of the organization and remained its driving force throughout the war. (*Harper's Weekly*)

Though its membership numbered in the thousands and it counted many more as sympathizers, the Peace Society was only loosely organized. One contemporary wrote that it had "no regular times or places of meeting, and has no organized 'lodges' or 'communities.' Men who have studied the obligations, signs, &c., and who can communicate them well are styled 'eminent,' and pass through the country giving the 'degree' to all whom they regard as fit subjects." Those inducted into the society promised always to aid other members and their families. They also promised never to "cut, carve, mark, scratch, show, &c., upon anything, movable or immovable, under the whole canopy of heaven, whereby any of the secrets of this order might become legible or intelligible." Finally, the inductee concluded with this statement: "I bind myself under no less penalty than that of having my head cut open, my brains taken from thence and strewn over the ground, my body cast to the beasts of the field or to the vultures of the air should I be so vile as to reveal any of the secrets of this order."[10]

Members recognized each other by a variety of complicated signs. One of the most complex was the society's handshake. It was, according to one report, "given by taking hold of the hand as usual in shaking hands, only the thumb is turned with the side instead of the ball to the back of the hand." The following dialogue, which each member committed to memory, would then commence:

> What is that?
> A grip.
> A grip of what?
> A constitutional peace grip.
> Has it a name?
> It has.
> Will you give it to me?
> I did not so receive it, neither can I so impart it.
> How will you impart it?
> I will letter it to you.
> Letter it and begin.
> Begin you.
> No, you begin.
> Begin you.

Then, starting with any letter but the first, they spelled the word *peace* by calling out letters alternately to each other.[11]

Other signs of recognition included a salute with the right hand closed and the thumb pointed backward over the shoulder; throwing a stick to the right using both hands; and tapping on the toe of the right foot three times with a stick or switch, then waving it to the right. In a crowd, a society member made himself known by three slaps on the right leg. One might also use the phrase "I dreamed that the boys are all coming home." A distress signal was given by using the expression "Oh! Washington!" or "by extending the right hand horizontally and then bringing it down by three distinct motions." Repeating the word *Washington* four times could get a member of the Peace Society released from jail within twenty-four hours if his guard happened to be a brother member.[12]

The society's activities included spreading dissent among soldiers as well as civilians. Apparently the organization met with considerable success. James Longstreet, Lee's senior corps commander, said that "the large and increasing number of desertions, particularly amongst the Georgia troops, induces me to believe that some such outside influence must be operating upon our men." In October 1863, a Savannah man wrote that troops in southeast Georgia were demanding peace and would soon turn to mutiny or desertion if they did not get it. A few months later, an insurrection plot was discovered among troops at the Rose Dew Island batteries south of Savannah. Encouraged by local citizens connected with the Peace Society, the soldiers took an oath never to fight the Yankees, to desert at the earliest opportunity, and to encourage others to do the same. The Peace Society even claimed credit for Confederate defeats at Vicksburg and Missionary Ridge.[13]

From the war's outset, unionism had considerable strength in the South. About three hundred thousand southern whites served in the Union armies, not counting those in irregular units who numbered many more.[14] Thomas A. Watson of Fannin County, William Fife of Harris County, Cornelius Dawson of Clinch County, and Andrew T. Harris of Murray County—all Confederate deserters—were among more than 2,500 white Georgians who joined federal units.[15]

Baldwin County native David R. Snelling had deeply personal reasons for his Union stand. David's father, William, a man of modest means, died of fever when David was five. His mother, Elizabeth Lester Snelling, whose family had never approved of her marriage, was forced onto a small plot of land adjoining the Baldwin County plantations her brothers owned. When Elizabeth died a few years later, young David was taken in as a farmhand by his uncle, David Lester. While his cousins were sent

FIGURE 8.2. Thomas A. Watson of Fannin County—a poor farm laborer before the war—deserted from the Sixty-fifth Georgia Infantry Regiment at Kingston, Tennessee, on June 12, 1863, and joined the Union army. He is pictured here in his federal uniform. (Courtesy of Georgia Department of Archives and History.)

away to school, David was put to work in the fields along with Lester's slaves. Treated much as a slave himself, David came to detest slavery and to hold an abiding compassion for the enslaved. In May 1862, he joined the Confederate army, deserted that summer, and signed up with the Federals. Two years later, as a lieutenant in Sherman's cavalry escort during the March to the Sea, David went out of his way to lead a raid against his rich uncle's plantation a few miles from Milledgeville. His troops seized provisions and livestock and burned the gin house.[16]

Unionism found its greatest strength among whites in areas with few slaves such as the mountains of north Georgia and the pine barrens of the southeast. But even in black belt regions, where slaves sometimes made up over half the population, there were anti-Confederates. In March 1862, John O'Connor of Fort Gaines in southwest Georgia's cotton country warned Governor Brown of "spies and traitors" operating all along the lower Chattahoochee River. General Howell Cobb was so concerned about Union sentiment in southwest Georgia that he began censoring the mail service later that year.[17]

Antiwar feeling across Georgia was so strong by 1863 that state and Confederate officials could do little against it. Popular support and innumerable hiding places made it nearly impossible to track down deserters and draft dodgers. The Bureau of Conscription's superintendent admitted that public opinion made it difficult to enforce the draft act. There was, he lamented, no disgrace attached to desertion or draft evasion. One band of deserters quietly set up camp on an island in the Chattahoochee

FIGURE 8.3. Raised a poor farmhand in Baldwin County, David Snelling was a lieutenant in the Union army when he led a raid against his uncle's plantation during Sherman's march through Georgia. (Courtesy of Ina Dillard Russell Library, Georgia College and State University.)

River. Despite the risk of imprisonment for harboring deserters, family and friends kept them supplied with food and other necessities until the war was over. Some deserters were more defiant. In Stewart County, several men of the Third Georgia Regiment openly declared that they had no intention of returning to the army.[18]

For those few deserters and draft dodgers who were captured, there was no guarantee of punishment. When a conscript company in Franklin County captured several deserters, the local jailer would not lodge them. In White County, twenty-two men broke into the jail to release a draft dodger. So strong was antiwar feeling in some counties that judges could not hold court on draft evaders without a military escort. Even when trials were held, convictions were rare. Juries consistently refused to return guilty verdicts against those who opposed the war. Howell Cobb conceded in August of 1863 that to drag antiwar men into court was "simply to provide for a farcical trial." He was right. Later that year, two Lumpkin County men, John Woody and John A. Wimpy, were tried on charges of treason. In the face of strong evidence against them, and after Woody confessed his refusal to fight, a jury acquitted both men.[19]

Antiwar feeling could be found in the state militia itself. Indeed, many had joined militia units to avoid front-line service. When Joe Brown reorganized the state militia in December 1863, John Oliver of Effingham County declared himself a unionist and ran on that platform for captain of his local unit. "He lives in a section of the County," wrote one local man to Governor Brown, "that is generally poor people and where it has been with great difficulty to inforce the Conscript act."[20]

From Richmond County, Colonel A. C. Walker wrote to the governor that "most of the militia officers in the counties around here are young & robust men, and without exception obtained these offices from the most sordid motives. As far as I know them I heartly believe they would take the oath of alligence to Lincoln tomorrow." A month later, Samuel D. Knight of southwest Georgia wrote to Brown that there was widespread disapproval of his militia act. After three months of "mingling freely with the common people," Knight had found that "among that class generally there is a strong Union feeling existing. . . . the same feeling exists among the soldiers in the field to an alarming extent."[21]

The main source of disaffection among soldiers was summed up by J. F. Morton of Chattooga County in a December 1863 letter to Governor Brown. Morton had often heard the question asked, "What is the Confederacy worth to a man when it has taken all he has, brought himself and family to poverty and want, his posterity together with himself burdened with a debt that will enslave them for generations to come?" Throughout the war, concern for the well-being of their families remained the dominant influence in the soldiers' decision to either desert the ranks or evade the draft. Enlistments had left many women home with small children and little help to tend the fields. William J. Evers of Thomas County was so concerned about his family's survival that he wrote from the battlefield for his wife to "write mee how my crops did turn out. I want to know what prospect you have for something to eat. I want to know how my hogs done. They was so little that I was doubtful that they would not make meat anuff for my famaly. I want to know how you are fairing about sault to save your meat."[22]

In February 1862, Private M. N. Cody asked for a furlough to make arrangements to have his crops planted and cultivated. Without it, he said, "my family will suffer for provisions." The request was approved by his captain and colonel. But as the war entered its second year, furloughs were increasingly difficult to get. For many, especially in the enlisted ranks, they were impossible to come by. As early as January 1862, Private James Atkins of Calhoun County wrote in his diary that "all my efforts to get a furlough are unavailing—What shall I do?" In April, Atkins deserted. So did John Sheffield of Miller County later that year. According to his friend, Milo Grow, Sheffield "cursed the government and everything connected with it." Grow was himself "fully sick of the manner in which the government is administered."[23]

Their own difficulties were hard enough to endure, but despondent letters from home were more than many Johnny Rebs could stand. Desperate to help their families, soldiers did what they felt they had to do. A young soldier from Columbus wrote home to a friend: "If it is the best our government can do, I am willing to live on dry bread for our cause; but I don't want mother to suffer for anything as long as I live. I am willing for her to work and I know she will do it; but when I hear she is in want of provisions and cant get them, I am going home.... The last two letters I received from her don't suit me." R. H. Brooks of the Fifty-first Georgia Infantry Regiment wrote to his wife, "tell Charles Sirmons if he ever gets home to stay there. . . . if ever I get home I will stay as long as I can." Lee Dupont's feelings on the difficulty of soldiers getting furloughs were apparent. When it came to begging for a furlough, he insisted that he "did not belong to that breed of dogs who could so humble themselves, that if it became an imperative duty to visit my family I should do it without leave and risk the consequences."[24]

The consequences could be severe indeed. Unauthorized leaves could and often did result in execution. One Georgia soldier in Robert E. Lee's Army of Northern Virginia wrote that it was "an everyday occurrence for men to get letters from home stating that their families are on the point of starvation. Many a poor soldier has deserted and gone home in answer to that appeal, to be brought back and shot for desertion." Some were never returned for execution. Samuel Henderson Frier of Irwin County, like the rest of his family, had opposed secession. Too poor to hire a substitute, he joined the army under threat of conscription in May 1862. Frier deserted later that year in Virginia and made his way back home. In October 1863, he was shot and killed by Confederate forces sent to arrest him. Frier's widow, two young children, and other family and friends laid him to rest in the Brushy Creek Primitive Baptist cemetery. Regardless of such risks, soldiers continued to abandon their ranks by the thousands. Aiming their rifles at anyone who dared challenge them, they made their way over hundreds of rugged miles to help their starving families.[25]

For soldiers to leave their posts was nothing unusual in 1863. By the end of that year, with 278,000 men present for duty out of nearly 500,000, close to half the Confederate army was absent with or without leave. Promising amnesty for those who returned voluntarily, Jefferson Davis assured his reluctant countrymen in August 1863 that if all those subject to military service would simply do their duty, the war could quickly be won: "Victory is within your reach. You need but stretch forth your hands and grasp it." Davis's plea did little to draw dispirited plain folk to the front lines. The next month, in a letter to the *Savannah Republican,* one citizen pointed out what by then was obvious: "A large portion of our army are sick and tired of war, and those who have been for months hiding from ... the conscription officers had as soon become gally slaves as to be mustered into our army."[26]

The Confederacy's recruitment difficulties only worsened over the following months. In February 1864, Howell Cobb wrote that "there are men enough at home able to be in the field to make another army." Later that year, President Davis publicly admitted that "two-thirds of our men are absent ... most of them without leave."[27]

Despite their growing numbers and empathy from local residents, life for deserters could be precarious. They were harassed by state patrols, and sympathizers had little food to give them. Some became so desperate that they sought refuge with the Yankees, and there were local residents who helped them on their way. Austin Mason of Union County helped organize a chain of safe houses to shelter prisoners and deserters as they fled north through the Georgia mountains.[28]

Men like Mason were not unusual in the region. The peace movement in north Georgia established an extensive network of safe houses, guides, and secret signals to aid refugees, deserters, draft dodgers, and escaped Federal prisoners in making their way to Union lines. Those requiring the services of Georgia's mountain unionists were most grateful. A Wisconsin colonel trying to reach Sherman's army in Chattanooga later wrote that they were "generous, hospitable, brave, and Union men to the core; men who would suffer privations, and death itself, rather than array themselves in strife against the Stars and Stripes, the emblem of the country they loved. . . . under their homespun jackets beat hearts pure as gold, and stout as oaks."[29]

While Sherman was still at Chattanooga, hundreds of Georgia deserters and their families entered Union lines. In February 1864, word reached the governor's office from Dawsonville of "a grate many citizens or unionists moving to the enemy." When the Yankees set out for Atlanta in the spring, more unionists greeted the invaders. After Sherman captured Atlanta in September, hundreds of soldiers and civilians remained in the city and aided the federal army. Later that year during Sherman's famous March to the Sea, Confederate deserters and draft dodgers from Liberty and Tattnall counties sent him a letter insisting that they opposed secession and offered him their services in whatever capacity he saw fit. Some went further than that. One gang of Georgia ex-Confederates led by Alonzo Rogers and Porter Southworth formed themselves into a battalion and called it the "Volunteer Force of the United States Army from Georgia."[30]

In southwest Georgia, deserters sometimes turned to the Union blockade fleet on the Gulf Coast for help. In early 1863, John Harvey, representing a group of five hundred Wiregrass deserters and draft dodgers, met with Lieutenant George Welch of the USS *Amanda* at Apalachicola, Florida, to discuss placing the men under protection of federal authorities. Armed only with shotguns, they had been skirmishing with conscript companies for months, and their ammunition was running low. They preferred to be taken into protective custody either as prisoners or refugees but, according to Welch, added "that they would follow me or any other leader to any peril they are ordered to rather than leave their families and go north." Welch was sympathetic but declined, saying he did not have enough manpower to guarantee safe passage for that many men from that deep in enemy territory. However, as Confederate strength along the Apalachicola declined, the Federals did begin running ammunition and other supplies upriver to anti-Confederate partisans.[31]

As their ranks grew, some of these deserters formed guerrilla bands, described by one historian as "no longer committed to the Confederacy, not quite committed to the Union that supplied them arms and supplies, but fully committed to survival." They raided plantations, attacked army supply depots, and drove off impressment and conscript officers. Some regions were so hostile to the Confederacy that army patrols dared not enter them. The pine barrens tract of southeast Georgia was a favorite hideout for those trying to avoid Confederate entanglements. Soldier Camp Island in the region's Okefenokee Swamp was home to as many as one thousand deserters. To the west, a Fort Gaines man begged Governor Brown to send a company of cavalry for protection against deserters and layout gangs. So did pro-Confederates in northwest Georgia's Dade and Walker Counties. All across Georgia—from the mountains to the Piedmont to the Wiregrass—there raged an inner civil war. So violent was this struggle by 1863 that the editor of Milledgeville's *Confederate Union* wrote: "We are fighting each other harder than we ever fought the enemy."[32]

As early as September 1862, forty men in west Georgia's Marion County "secured and provisioned a house and arranged it in the manner of a military castle." Well armed and well provisioned, they swore not only to prevent their own capture but to protect other Georgians who sought sanctuary in their makeshift fortress. While Confederate and state military officials attempted to drive them out, military assaults had little impact on men who held a "determination to resist to the last extremity."[33]

The situation was just as dangerous in the northern part of the state. From Gilmer County came news in July 1862 of "tories and traitors who have taken up their abode in the mountains." The mountains provided an ideal haven for such men. The terrain made it difficult to send troops in after them, and so did the attitudes of the mountain people. That same month, a letter arrived on the governor's desk from Fannin County, just north of Gilmer, warning that "a very large majority of the people now here perhaps two thirds are disloyal." A few months later, anti-Confeder-

FIGURE 8.4. Confederate and state troops sent to round up deserters and draft evaders encountered stiff resistance. So violent did Georgia's inner civil war become by late 1863 that one Milledgeville newspaper editor wrote, "We are fighting each other harder than we ever fought the enemy." (Ellis, *Thrilling Adventures*)

ate resistance became so aggressive in Fannin that one man called it a "general uprising among our Torys of this County." Most of northeast Georgia's tory bands wanted nothing more than to sit out the war. Others, especially those with no family ties in the region, were more prone to violence. September 1862 found Lumpkin County being overrun by unionists and deserters who were robbing local citizens of guns, money, clothes, and provisions. One Confederate sympathizer wrote that "the Union men—Tories—are very abusive indeed and says they will do as they please." The *Dahlonega Signal* estimated that one of Lumpkin County's tory bands, led by "the notorious Jeff Anderson," numbered between one and two hundred.[34]

One of the earliest formed and most active bands of Union men in northeast Georgia was led by Horatio Hennion. A northerner by birth, Hennion had moved to White County's Mossy Creek community in his early twenties and married a local girl. The other men in his band of at least two dozen were born in Georgia and the Carolinas. All were nonslaveholders, and some were tenants or day laborers who owned no land.

Those who did own land held no more than a few hundred dollars worth of real estate and personal property.

Hennion worked as a wagon maker in Gainesville during the secession crisis and made his support for the Union clear. Even after war broke out, Hennion remained openly anti-Confederate even as other local unionists were falling silent. Threats to his life forced him and his family back to Mossy Creek, where he hoped to live in peace until local pro-Confederates tried to kill him. In August 1861, he fled to North Carolina, but he returned a year later and organized a band of anti-Confederates that included men from White County and neighboring Hall County. They fought running battles with Confederate conscript companies, rescuing one of their members from the White County jail after his arrest by a conscript officer. Hennion's band became even more effective when he and his men signed "an agreement of mutual protection" with deserters hiding out in the region.[35]

Soon after he got word of events in the mountains, Governor Brown issued a proclamation aimed at the "very considerable number of deserters and stragglers" and those who aided them. Brown knew "that numbers of these deserters, encouraged by disloyal citizens in the mountains of Northeastern Georgia, have associated themselves together with arms in their hands and are now in rebellion against the authority of this State and the Confederate States." He issued a proclamation "commanding all persons . . . to return to their respective commands immediately." Brown also warned "all disloyal citizens to cease to harbor deserters or encourage desertion . . . as the law against treason will be strictly enforced against all who subject themselves to its penalties."[36]

Brown's warning had little effect, and in late January 1863 he took action. Brown sent a mounted force under Colonel George Washington Lee, commandant of Atlanta, and Captain E. M. Galt to Dahlonega with orders to "secure the arrest of deserters and restore the public tranquility." By early February, around six hundred deserters had been rounded up and marched back to the army. Fifty-three civilian unionists had been arrested and sent to Atlanta, among them the tory leader Jeff Anderson. Only a month later, Confederate loyalists in Lumpkin County were begging Governor Brown for more troops. In June, the *Athens Southern Watchman* reported that "some of those who were forced into the army by the cavalry last winter have returned with Government arms and ammunition in their hands and are creating serious apprehensions of future troubles." Already anti-Confederates led by a Hall County man calling himself Major Finger had attacked a small ironwork in White County. They burned the coal, stole the tools, and broke the forge hammer. In Fannin County, tories had attacked a group of Confederates sent to arrest deserters, killing one man and wounding several others.[37]

Fannin County was hit again in August when tories led by Soloman Bryan disarmed all the pro-Confederates. According to one pro-Confederate, they "robbed our people of every single gun and all the ammunition." Similar confrontations took place all over northeast Georgia. A Union County man informed the governor that the "mountains are filling with deserters and disloyal men" and begged him to send arms and ammunition. Brown sought help from the Richmond government, telling Jefferson Davis in an August 25 letter that "tories and deserters in North Eastern Georgia are now disarming the loyal people and committing many outrages." Brown got no response, and the outrages continued. He finally sent another expedition to northeast Georgia in October 1863. It arrested "quite a number of deserters, stragglers, marauders" but had little effect on the general state of affairs.[38]

In early November, White County Confederates went after the tories themselves. They hid along a wooded roadside, posted a sentinel up the way, and waited for his signal. When it came, the men sprang from the woods and ordered their adversaries to halt. The tories responded with a hail of gunfire, wheeled their horses, and rode off, with their pursuers firing after them. One Confederate loyalist, Lewis Pitchford, died in the exchange. A few weeks later, pro-Confederate vigilantes apprehended Jake Wofford, believed to have fired the shot that killed Pitchford. The mob stood Wofford on a plank with a rope around his neck hoping to force a confession. But the condemned man refused to say a word. Someone in the crowd finally jerked the plank away from Wofford's feet and sent him, with whatever secrets he knew, to his death.[39]

Brown ordered yet another detail to northeast Georgia in early 1864, but that force fared even worse than its predecessors. One Gilmer County Confederate wrote that "the Tories with their squirrel rifles, pick off our men from behind rocks and trees and all manner of hiding places. In this way they have killed six or eight of our soldiers." J. J. Findley of Dahlonega reported that "the District is overrun with Deserters, Tories, and Rogues . . . and that the condition of things is worse in that region than ever."[40]

Conditions were just as bad in northwest Georgia and had been for some time. As early as October 1862, deserters led by a man named

Crawford terrorized the citizens of Marietta and Cobb County. Early the next spring in Walker County, tories threatened to destroy the crops of any man who sided with the Confederacy. In March, a group of Confederate loyalists wrote to Governor Brown begging him for assistance. One pro-Confederate had already been shot at, and another's house had been robbed. Violence broke out in neighboring Dade County as well.[41]

Brown sent a company of state troops to quell the tory uprising and asked for Confederate troops to help. In a letter to General Joseph E. Johnston, who commanded the Confederacy's western armies, Georgia's adjutant general Henry C. Wayne stressed the urgency of the problem but suggested a delicate handling. Both he and Brown knew that popular support for the Confederacy was unsteady to begin with. A heavy-handed invasion by Confederate troops might turn inactive layouts into active partisans. "As these misguided people are our own citizens, His Excellency [Governor Brown] desires that . . . you will deal with them as gently as the heinousness of their offense will permit. It is thought that some of the insurgents are deserters from your armies." Gentle response or not, military efforts did little but make matters worse for loyal Confederates. Most had been driven out of LaFayette in Walker County by the spring of 1864.[42]

In neighboring Floyd County, the town of Rome and its environs were almost entirely controlled by plundering outlaw gangs that professed loyalty to neither the Confederacy nor the Union. The most notorious of these was a band of deserters under Captain Jack Colquitt. He and his men invaded Rome soon after the Yankees left in the fall of 1864 and terrorized local citizens, pro- and anti-Confederate alike. The very evening they arrived, Colquitt's gang robbed at least three men, nearly killing two of them. One of Rome's erstwhile Rebels found herself longing for Sherman's men to return, "since we can't get a Confederate force to protect us." Colquitt was finally caught in a drunken stupor and gunned down by two brothers, John and James Prior, who went on to kill seven more of Colquitt's gang. A grateful community never brought the Priors to trial.[43]

In the state's southern half, newspapers warned communities throughout Georgia's piney woods region to beware of deserters and other suspicious individuals. They suggested offering rewards to slaves who turned in the names of anyone discussing unionism or desertion. The *Albany Patriot* advertised a $250 reward for the apprehension of George Martin, dead or alive, for issuing "treasonable sentiments against the Confederacy" and for the attempted murder of a lieutenant who had tried to arrest him. Doctor A. Blasdell, a Wilkinson County dentist, was ridden out of town on a rail for displaying Yankee sympathies and was suspected of still being in the area.[44]

Much of south central and southeast Georgia was especially popular country for those evading military service. South of the Ocmulgee and Altamaha rivers, the swamps, bottomlands, and pine barrens provided ample cover from Confederate and state enlistment officers. Unlike the fertile, rolling hills of cotton-producing southwest Georgia, piney woods and marshy lowlands dominated to the east. The land was less fertile, and the people were generally poorer. The farms were small and isolated, and the inhabitants clannish in the Celtic traditions of their ancestors. Cattle supplanted cotton, and slaveholding dropped off dramatically. In some southeast Georgia counties, slaves accounted for only ten percent of the population.[45]

Travel was difficult for those unfamiliar with the territory, making searches for deserters challenging for military officials sent into the region. Bridges were in a constant state of disrepair. Roads were scarce, "mere trails . . . a person not accustomed to them [could] scarcely follow them." The swamps and cypress hammocks dotting the region allowed draft evaders to "run from swamp to swamp & from one locality to another so quickly & easily that it is almost impossible to catch [them]."[46]

While the draft evaders in the north Georgia mountains were both Union and Confederate, south Georgia's were predominately Confederate. Many succeeded in hiding when the enlistment officer appeared, as one Wilcox County slave remembered his owner doing in 1863. Others did not. Lee County officials arrested a deserter found masquerading as his own widow. The man had faked his death by throwing his hat and outer garments on the banks of Kinchafoonee Creek, making it appear as if he had drowned. For three months he wore women's clothing and masked his face with a three-foot long scoop bonnet.[47]

Some deserters formed mounted units and rode the Wiregrass plains, pine barrens, and cypress swamps posing as impressment officers. One outraged editor wrote: "These scoundrels seek the fairest, fattest and most quiet portion of our territory for the theatre of their depredations. They pounce suddenly upon the prosperous plantations, and sweep them of their best laboring stock, and such stores of meat, grain and forage as they can carry off, under pretense of a legal impressment."[48]

Some sought only to lie low, building camps in the pine barrens of

FIGURE 8.5. Some layout gangs went on the offensive, attacking government supply wagons, raiding local plantations, and harassing impressment and conscript officials. They virtually eliminated Confederate authority in large parts of Georgia. (*Frank Leslie's Illustrated Newspaper*)

southeast Georgia where "no unfriendly soljier is perusin around and axin for papers. Here the melanckoly mind is soothed. Here the loanly runagee can kontemplate the sandy roads, the wiregrass woods, and the million of majestik pines." Still others turned farmhouses into armored fortifications—such as those in Marion and Coffee counties—or hid at safe havens established on the lands of sympathetic neighbors.[49]

One such haven was operated by George M. Kierce, a sixty-year-old farmer in the Isabella district of Worth County. Kierce frequently allowed deserters and layouts to hide out on his property. In November 1862, Kierce and his thirteen-year-old son, John, disappeared. Some said they had moved to the North; others insisted they were in Florida. Most were sure they had been murdered. According to Worth County court records, Justice of the Peace Hudson Tabor had issued warrants against George and John Kierce the day before they vanished. Deputy Sheriff Lewis Simmons had arrested Kierce and his son and was escorting them to Judge Tabor's home when they were stopped by George Green, the local conscription officer, and thirteen other men. Green took custody of the Kierces, then directed his men to "continue their search for said deserters as it would be a more easy matter now to take them." That was the last time anyone admitted to seeing Kierce and his boy alive. Weeks later, a family member finally discovered their bodies sunken in nearby Abram's Creek. Their throats had been cut, John's almost to the point of decapitation, and their clothes had been knotted and filled with gravel to weight them down.[50]

Losing Kierce's aid may have had an impact on the surge of deserters and layouts moving into a region just south of the Ocmulgee River in the spring of 1863. While Kierce's Worth County safe haven was one of several refuges hidden in the region, the disappearance of the Kierces destroyed a secure refuge for some of the region's draft evaders.[51] Where could draft evaders go instead? To the west lay Albany, site of a Confederate muster station for conscripts and volunteers; to the north lay the Flint River, and across that, the heart of the plantation belt, a dangerous region for draft evaders on the run. To the south, roads led to Thomasville and Valdosta, only slightly better than Albany, as troops frequently passed through those two railroad towns. To the east was some degree of safety in Irwin and Coffee counties, and it was to these counties that many deserters and draft dodgers fled. But that safety was, at the time, relative at best.

Although Colonel Duncan L. Clinch and his Fourth Georgia Cavalry patrolled the Georgia coast primarily to fend off Union attacks, Clinch sometimes sent detachments into the swamps and piney woods. The first such expedition set out on May 19, 1863. Clinch ordered most of Company A to march from Saville on the Altamaha River, just upstream from Darien, westward into Irwin County to search for deserters. The troopers spent a month in the Irwin County area, but their only recorded success came on May 22, the day they arrived, when they arrested twenty-two men and sent them to Savannah for enlistment or prosecution. They made no other known arrests. Perhaps they lost the benefit of surprise, and the draft evaders were better able to hide. In July, Clinch sent a small detachment of four men—under the command of Corporal George Brown—into Charlton and Camden counties to "arrest and bring to these Hd Qrs all deserters at all hazzard." Brown also had permission to go into Florida, if necessary, in pursuit of deserters. A month later he escorted only six deserters back to Camp Lee. Clinch himself led a detachment of troops from Companies B, F, and K in early September 1863.[52]

Clinch's efforts to track down deserters may have done more harm than good. Many of his own troops deserted and moved inland toward the Okefenokee Swamp, joining deserters already living there. Blackjack Island, one of the larger and more isolated islands in the swamp, held most of the resident deserters. Richard Hunter's survey of the swamp in 1857 characterized Blackjack as a low pine island almost identical to the pine and palmetto flatlands surrounding the swamp—a familiar and easily worked hiding place for men on the run. Living in fortified encampments—some of which were still standing almost two decades later—they lived on deer, fish, alligator, and wildcat as well as cattle stolen from farms on the edges of the swamp.[53]

Those troops who did not desert were doing little to apprehend those who did. Reports reached the War Department that mounted Confederates stationed below the Altamaha River, presumably the Fourth Georgia Cavalry, were calling for an early peace and spreading dissatisfaction along the Georgia coast.[54] Given the unit's lackluster performance in arresting deserters, Confederate leaders needed to try something else.

In November 1863, Colonel George Washington Lee, who earlier that year had headed the Dahlonega expedition, took a battalion of state troops into south Georgia looking for deserters. His search took him through Houston, Wilcox, Ware, and Coffee counties before settling him in Clinch County. There he met Captain Thomas Wylly, commander of Company H, Fourth Georgia Cavalry, who had led his company to the area a few weeks before. Both held the opinion that the reports of deserters, Yankees, and slaves hiding in the swamps were highly exaggerated. Wylly estimated that there were no more than fifty men hiding in the Okefenokee. Lee placed the number at one hundred. Both agreed that there were no escaped slaves and no Yankee deserters.[55]

Earlier estimates placed the number of draft evaders in the swamp at between 1,000 and 1,500, roughly equal to the entire population of Echols County. Those numbers may have been exaggerated, or Lee and Wylly may have purposely underestimated them to account for the few arrests they made. During the four months that Lee's men were in south Georgia, they captured only twenty deserters and killed three more in a "sharp skirmish."[56]

Whatever the numbers, Colonel Lee's expedition highlighted one of the most effective tools the draft evader held—the corrupt enrolling official. Critics charged that the number of deserters roaming the countryside could be reduced if only enlistment officers would be more diligent in the performance of their duties. Lee appeared to support such criticism with his assertion that many of the men he arrested were deserters who had returned home with furlough extensions and medical discharges issued by enlistment officers and local physicians not authorized to grant them. Colonel Archibald Thomson MacIntyre, state aid-de-camp for the Seventh Military District (Thomas, Colquitt, and Brooks Counties), complained that one man he had recently sent to the army returned to Thomasville after bribing army officers for discharge.[57]

In August 1864, General Henry Wayne, responding to accusations of lax enrollment procedures and corruption, began a campaign to stop profiteering by enrollment officers and step up arrests of draft evaders. In a carefully worded letter sent to all of the state's aides-de-camp, Wayne all but accused enrollment officers of shirking their duty for personal gain and allowing otherwise eligible recruits to remain at home. "Officers in the rear," the letter read, "are not sent home to attend to their *private business*. . . . let no pretext of private interests shield a man from being sent forward at once." Colonel MacIntyre of the Seventh District received one of these letters, as did Colonel Edwin T. Jones, aid-de-camp of the Tenth District (Dougherty, Worth, and Lee Counties).[58]

Jones vehemently denied the accusations: "I mean no disrespect by the tone of this letter but that I am compelled to write plainly or fail to meet the charges contained in your [letter]." He admitted that there were a few men in Dougherty County who had not reported due to illness but vowed that if ordered, "I will send these men up [to Macon] on litters." The Worth County Inferior Court had released several men from his custody and, while he had requested assistance from the adjutant general's office, he did not know how to proceed with the matter. The only exemptions in his district were those issued through the adjutant general's office. "No pretext of private interest shielded me or any other man as I am aware of in this dist from going to the front," he wrote.[59]

Wayne's letter had its effect. Jones redoubled his efforts, and in October 1864, he contested eight writs of habeas corpus in the Dougherty County Superior Court. Colonel Milton A. Smith, aid-de-camp of the Twelfth Military District (Quitman, Stewart, and Webster Counties), was "no little surprised & mystified at the information" and swore that General Wayne's informant was either "ignorant of the facts or maliciously false in his statements." But by week's end, Smith visited Stewart County, where he sent armed men out to arrest deserters. He attributed much of that county's problem to Sheriff Duncan McKinnon's refusal to arrest deserters. Smith wanted him replaced. Colonel Carey Styles, still trying to reclaim the respect he felt he had lost in the accusations of selling discharges in Ware County, also renewed his efforts to arrest all men liable to service. Despite his pledge that all deserters would be "sent, shot, or driven to the swamp," Styles's efforts did not last. These bursts of energy did little to combat draft dodging.[60]

On top of his letter-writing campaign to curb rogue enlistment officials, Wayne took further steps to block draft evaders from forging alliances with slaves. In the summer of 1864, he and Brown ordered an expansion of the slave patrols. Though partially intended to keep draft evaders in check, the new slave patrols often became a haven for them. Complaints of fraud in the selection of the patrol members were almost universal, and the state inspector general's office questioned the legality of appointments in Dooly, Early, Lowndes, Brooks, and Decatur counties.[61] Controversy over police appointments and the impact they had on draft evaders may have been the catalyst in John Vickery's planned Brooks County slave uprising of August 1864.

Confederate and state cavalry detachments as well as local defense forces stepped up efforts, but they too had little effect. Captain Caleb H. Camfield of Company D, Cobb's Legion, was stationed at Bainbridge with a detachment of a dozen cavalrymen to search southwest Georgia for conscripts and deserters. But by early 1865, while in command of a 150-man detachment from the Twenty-ninth Battalion Georgia Cavalry, Camfield was forced to withdraw his troops in south Georgia and north Florida after fierce battles with local deserter gangs.[62]

Captain Winburn J. Lawton led a Dougherty County home guard cavalry company into Irwin, Berrien, Echols, and Coffee counties in August 1864. Lawton, a Confederate combat veteran, had resigned as the colonel of the Second Georgia Cavalry in October 1862 and returned to Albany to oversee his plantation. Conscription, he said, had taken all of his overseers and left "200 negroes in rather an insubordinate condition where my wife & two little daughters reside without a relative within a hundred mile radius." In 1863, concerned over the number of deserters scattered throughout southwest Georgia, Lawton volunteered his services as the commander of a state cavalry brigade.[63]

But by early 1865, "the few loyal citizens of these parts" questioned whether anything could be done to stop the deserter bands. Mollie Dunlap of White Sulphur Springs wrote to her brother that "there are deserters traveling about all through the whole country and they are stealing

FIGURE 8.6. On July 20, 1864, Macon's *Georgia Journal and Messenger* reported that "guerrilla warfare has been going on with fierce fatality. . . . Not a few have been found in secluded by-ways, dangling their pitiful carcasses from swinging limbs." (Ellis, *Thrilling Adventures*)

horses and doing every thing else that is mean.... Four deserters met Jack Wilson in the road the other day and stopped him and scratched him and took two hundred dollars and gave him an old shot gun." Worth County citizens petitioned Governor Brown to grant Deputy Sheriff J. J. Williams an extended furlough to protect them from deserters and layout gangs. They reported that "the lawless villains are prowling over the county stealing and committing depredations of various kinds." Elizabeth Fields wrote Brown from Colquitt County that she feared "the deserters will steal nearly all there is in the country. I am here in the midst of them, and, because I will not be a friend to them, they are mad and has threatened to burn my house."[64]

In Coffee County, Ben Pearson accused a layout gang headed by "Old Man" Bill Wall of stealing his produce and livestock. Trouble had been brewing between Pearson's and Wall's men for some time. At one point, Pearson found a grave dug outside his front door. He finally issued a public demand, apparently offering a reward and amnesty for Wall himself, that the "Old Man" come forward and turn his men in to local authorities. Something of a poor man's poet, Wall could not resist poking fun at Pearson's assumption that he might do such a thing:

> If it is my choice to stay at home,
> and the woods in beauty roam;
> Pluck the flowers in early spring,
> and hear the little songsters sing!
>
> Why, then, should I, for the sake of gain,
> leave my conscience with a stain.
> A traitor! who could hear the name
> with no respect for age or fame;
>
> Who, for the sake of a little gold,
> would have his friends in bondage sold?
> I would rather take the lash
> than betray them for Confederate trash.
>
> You say they kill your sheep and cows,
> You say they take your hoss and your plows,
> You say they took your potatoes away,
> You say they dug your grave one day.
> All this may be true;
> It makes me sorry for you.

Yet, sir, if I, these men betray
and they were all taken away,
And they did not in the battlefield fall,
They would then come back and kill
"Old Man Bill Wall"[65]

By late 1864, every effort to reduce draft evasion in south Georgia had failed. District sub-enrolling officers and captains of police patrols were resigning their positions for fear of assassination.[66] Deserters raided Blackshear seven times in February 1865, ransacking local stores. A Confederate inspector in Ware County wrote that south of the Altamaha River there were more deserters than ever, all swearing to fight efforts to arrest them. To make matters worse for Confederate officials, Clinch's Fourth Georgia Cavalry and the Twenty-ninth Georgia Battalion (cavalry), patrolling that same area, were out of control, vowing to ignore orders that required them to leave the area. They were certainly well equipped to resist Confederate authority. Clinch had resupplied his men from the Macon Arsenal in the fall of 1864 with new clothing, rifles, revolvers, sabers, ammunition, tents, spurs, saddles, and other gear.[67]

Even hardened veterans were turning their backs on the Confederacy. Captain Robert A. Hardee, a wounded Confederate veteran, served as Brooks County's Confederate enlistment officer. By the war's last year, he was writing to members of his old company and encouraging them to desert. Almost the entire company did just that. Hardee, who also commanded the local police patrol, refused to arrest members of the militia who would not report for duty.[68] Hardee was hardly alone in his disdain for Confederate authority. In ever-increasing numbers, Georgians were questioning support for a government that seemed to ignore their interests.

9

"Don't Think There Is Much Regret for the Loss"

The rise of anti-Confederate guerrilla bands was only the most blatant reflection of widespread discontent with the Confederacy and the war. That discontent was so widespread that, as the war entered its final year, few expected the Confederacy to survive for very long. In a March 1864 *Early County News* editorial, E. H. Grouby wrote: "We cannot help thinking this is the last year of the war. . . . we have now entirely too many little jackass upstarts filling positions in our government." As Grouby's comment suggests, many Georgians were so disgusted with the Confederacy, its policies, and its agents that they looked forward to its fall. In October, Grouby wrote that the only people who still backed the Confederacy were those who held "fat Government contracts" and corrupt officials who were "not yet done fleecing the Government." "Their voice," he said, "is still for war, war, war!"[1]

The voice of plain folk was expressed by their increasing refusal to support the war effort. Even when the state was directly threatened, Georgia men were reluctant to leave home. In January 1864, with the Yankee army in Chattanooga preparing to invade the state, General Joseph E. Johnston, commanding Confederate forces in north Georgia, wrote, "Many persons in Georgia . . . are recruiting for cavalry, ostensibly under authority of the War department." But, he noted, they "never complete their companies—having no other object than to keep themselves and few friends out of service."[2]

Among Johnston's own men, desertion was up by that spring, and it became worse as the Yankees pushed them south. Backed up to the city of Atlanta, one Georgia soldier wrote to his wife: "The men is all out of heart and say that Georgia will soon have to go under and they are going to the Yankees by the tens and twentys and hundreds most every night. Johnston's army is very much demoralized as much so as a army ever gets. ... I see that the Officers is down in the mouth and their faces looks very long and some of them say that they are fearful that all their men will go to the Yankees."[3]

With William T. Sherman's troops bearing down on Atlanta and Confederate forces drained too weak by desertion to stop them, Governor Brown issued a proclamation ordering home guards, state and local officials, and even bonded planters to rally at the city and hurl the Yankees back. Few answered the governor's call. Some avoided duty by claiming protection from the central government, saying they had been "mustered into Confederate Service for local defense." In a desperate letter to the secretary of war, Brown protested that "the thousands who have such details cannot be permitted to hide behind them when the State is being overrun."[4]

Others claimed exemption as county officeholders. D. A. Johnson, a bailiff in Berrien County, was one of many who refused to go. A more patriotic neighbor, who anonymously signed his letter "Over Fifty," wrote to Governor Brown that Johnson was "a Tory, and ought to be in front of some good man." Hall County Justice of the Peace William O'Kelley had two brothers who had already deserted from the Georgia Militia. Hardly a Brown supporter to begin with, O'Kelley refused to take up arms. An acquaintance wrote to Brown of O'Kelley, "I have heard him say myself that he had rather shoot you than a deer."[5]

Soon after Brown's proclamation, one Georgia farmer published a Shakespearean-like expression of his dilemma in the *Milledgeville Confederate Union*.[6] It gave voice to many plain folk who faced the same question.

To go, or not to go.

To go or not to go, that is the question:
Whether it pays best to suffer pestering
By idle girls and garrulous old women,
Or to take up arms against a host of Yankees,
And by opposing get killed—To die, to sleep,
(Git eout) and in this sleep to say we "sink

To rest by all our Country's wishes blest"
And live forever—(that's a consummation
Just what I'm after). To march, to fight—
To fight! perchance to die, aye there's the rub!
For while I'm sleep, who'll take care Mary
and the babes—when Billy's in the low ground,
Who'll feed 'em, hey! There's the respect
I have for *them* that makes life sweet;
For who would bear the bag to mill,
Plough Dobbin,[7] cut the wheat, dig taters,
Kill hogs, and do all sorts of drudgery
If I am fool enough to get a Yankee
Bullet on my brain! Who'll cry for me!
Would patriotism pay my debts, when dead?
But oh! The dread of something after death—
That undiscovered fellow who'll court Mary,
And do my huggin—that's agony,
And makes me want to stay home,
Specially as I aint mad with nobody.
Shells and bullets make cowards of us all,
And blam'd my skin if snortin steeds,
And pomp and circumstance of War
Are to be compared with feather beds,
And Mary by my side.

If most Georgians were unwilling to help Brown, some were willing to help Sherman. When Brown issued his call, several Dawsonville citizens wrote that their county surveyor, Elias Darnel, "instead of obeying your proclamation went about organizing a federal home guard to assist the enemy." Mary Gordon of Walker County and Carrie King of Columbus assisted the enemy too; both were recruited as spies for the Union army. James George Brown of Murray County led a network of native pro-Union spies who operated throughout northeast Georgia. James C. McBurney of Macon, who had previously guided a federal raid through Alabama and Georgia, provided Sherman with information on Georgia's resources and railroads. In Gordon County, a group of local unionists captured nine Confederate soldiers and turned them over to the Yankees. One hundred twenty-five Pickens County men formed a Union home guard to protect themselves from the local militia, raid pro-Confederate plantations, and assist the advancing Federals. One Yankee officer was sure that several hundred more men in neighboring counties could be called to arms.[8]

In August 1864, the Federals did just that. Hoping to form not simply a home guard but a regular fighting force, they recruited about three hundred Northeast Georgia men. Some were sent directly to the Fifth Tennessee Mounted Infantry. Others formed an independent company operating in Fannin County attached to the Fifth Tennessee. The rest were enrolled as the First Georgia State Troops Volunteer Battalion. Though well armed, the First Georgia was ill trained and never much use to the Federals in regular combat. But driven by a desire to protect their families from, and to take revenge against, Confederate home guards and the state militia, the men of the First Georgia fought a guerrilla war that kept Confederate loyalists busy who might otherwise have been put into battle against the Yankees.[9]

On September 1, 1864, Sherman's men entered Atlanta, and there they stayed into November. All the while, Governor Brown begged for Georgia men to come together and help drive out the invaders. His pleading

FIGURE 9.1. Despite Sherman's efforts to discourage them, thousands of slaves abandoned Georgia plantations during the Union army's March to the Sea. Several fugitives from slavery are shown in this rare image, reported to have been taken in Georgia. (Courtesy of United States Army Military History Institute.)

was in vain. Among those already gathered, many were giving up and going home. From Camp Stephens, one of the militia's assembly points, William Dickey wrote that there was "great disatisfaction" in the ranks, especially among those who thought they were exempt. Some were of the opinion that Brown had no legal right to hold them. By the time of Dickey's letter on October 26, two hundred had deserted Camp Stephens alone.[10]

Dickey was among the few Confederate loyalists still left and was disgusted at the lack of Rebel patriotism he witnessed among his fellow Georgians. Hardly anyone was willing to fight for the Confederacy. "I wish," wrote Dickey," they would get every man that is able to carry a gun out at once irrespective of exemptions, details, or anything else. Bring them all out at once and I don't think they would be needed long." If only they would come, said Dickey, Atlanta could be surrounded, laid siege, and taken without firing a shot.[11] But they would not come. During its March to the Sea later that year, Sherman's army—followed by thousands of escaping slaves—passed through Georgia largely unmolested by state troops.[12] It spoke volumes about how most Georgians, black and white, viewed the conflict.

With much of the state under federal control, Governor Brown received letter after letter begging him to get Georgia out of the war. One was especially poignant. J. T. Smith of Bibb County had sacrificed as much as anyone for the Confederacy. One son had been killed in battle, and another maimed for life. Three more were still in the army, and all his property was gone. He encouraged Brown to "leave the sinking ship." He warned that southern newspapers "all state falsehoods when they say that the armies are anxious still to fight. It is not true. The officers with high [salaries] and easy situations . . . get up meetings and pass resolutions to that effect without the knowledge and consent of nine tenths of the privates in the army. . . . They are going home as fast as they can get there. The country is full of deserters and almost every man in the community will feed them and keep them from being arrested. Stop it, my friend, stop it. All the enlightened world is against us, and God himself is against us!"[13]

Smith knew what he was talking about. It was easy enough for deserters and draft dodgers to find local support, and it had been for some time. In 1863, John Woody of Lumpkin County was hauled into court for harboring deserters on his farm. Despite Woody's admission of anti-Confederate sentiments, the jury refused to convict him. People like Woody and the men he befriended were frequently protected by friends and family, all the more so as the war dragged on. Some Georgians assisted anyone, Yankees included, who was trying to avoid Confederate entanglements. Late in 1864, J. B. Norman, Sr., of Colquitt County was visited by two Union escapees from Andersonville prison. Norman fed the men and allowed them to stay the night. Next day, he gave them a helping of steak before they went on their way.[14]

Like Norman, Willis J. Bone of Irwin County aided escaping Union prisoners. And like George Kierce of Worth County, Bone operated a safe haven for deserters and draft dodgers. He even harbored runaway slaves. Originally from South Carolina, Bone immigrated to Georgia in the 1850s and settled at Bone Pond (now Crystal Lake) in Irwin County's Third District. A staunch unionist, Bone was exempt from Confederate service because he owned a small gristmill and rendered to his community what was defined by law as an essential service. Shielded himself, Bone turned his attention to protecting other Georgians from Confederate authority.

Bone was little different from most people of his community. Irwin was south Georgia's third-least-populated county and one of the poorest. The district in which the Bone family lived had just fourteen families, all of whom raised cattle, sheep, and hogs, and grew subsistence crops of corn, peas, oats, and sugar cane. There were only nine slaves spread among four white families in the district. Bone owned no slaves. What land he held was mostly undeveloped, aside from his steam-powered gristmill. He grew corn, sweet potatoes, and a little cotton. He owned one horse, one mule, one ox, eighteen hogs, eight head of cattle, and nineteen head of sheep. Most of his meager earnings came from the mill. He was hardly any better or worse off than his neighbors. Neither was he a social or political outcast, in spite of his political views. Bone was regularly seated as a petit juror beside his neighbors and gristmill customers. Either Bone was very good at hiding his unionism, which is unlikely, or most of his contemporaries were tolerant, even accepting, of it.[15]

Bone's reputation spread regionwide and probably peaked in February 1865, when he—along with other local unionists "and a large number of deserters"—convened an antiwar meeting in Irwinville. They adopted a number of resolutions, including one calling for the Confederacy's surrender. When a militia lieutenant tried to break up the meeting, Bone knocked the officer down with his musket and led three cheers for Abraham Lincoln. The assembly then drove the lieutenant, and every other pro-Confederate, out of town.[16]

By the time of the Irwin County meeting, Sherman had completed his March to the Sea and was heading back north through the Carolinas. Some of his troops were left behind to hold Savannah, and other Federals occupied the rest of Georgia's coast. Most of what the Yankees did not control in Georgia, unionists and deserters did. Confederate authority in the mountains of the north and the pine barrens of the south had been shaky for some time. It collapsed entirely during the winter of 1864–65. In southeast Georgia's first congressional district, the largest by area in the state, Lieutenant Alfred Prescott reported that "all law, both civil and Military seems to be overthrown." The region was, he said, "to a greater or lesser extent, disloyal. . . . No officer of the C. S. Army who is a stranger to the people can travel through these counties with safety." In an open letter, "the few loyal citizens" of Irwin, Berrien, Echols, and Coffee counties begged for help from the commanding general of the district. Deserters had stolen supplies from the government's storehouses at Blackshear and Homerville and had run conscript officers out of Berrien and Irwin counties. The district enrolling officer, Duncan Clinch, wrote General Cobb that "not only the deserters, but almost the entire population of Appling County, as well as Coffee, Pierce, Berrien, Clinch, Ware, Wayne and adjacent countys," were resisting Confederate authority. And, he wrote, they were determined to drive him off.[17]

In north Georgia, the conscript officer of Paulding County had to protect himself with posted guards. Further to the northeast, one Confederate loyalist wrote that the mountain region was in a "deplorable condition—desertions from the army, straggling to an incredible degree, and all kinds of irregularity." These irregularities were, he wrote, "not only tolerated, but I must say connived at by those whose duty it is to rectify these evils." Even those who did not support the tories usually turned a blind eye to their activities. Some state militia units, like the command at Dahlonega headed by Colonel James J. Findley, hardly bothered with an occasional muster. When General A. W. Reynolds went to investigate, he found Findley's men "scattered over the country, as if quartered at home." In January 1865, Richmond sent a detachment to the region under General W. T. Wofford with orders to arrest all stragglers and deserters. Findley warned that it would do little good. He knew his men could keep themselves well hidden in the hills; it would be impossible for Wofford's force to track them all down. Reynolds agreed that it was a wasted effort. Even if they could be captured and returned to the army, Reynolds knew they would simply go home again or desert to the Federals.[18]

Things were nearly as difficult for Confederate officials in the cotton belt. In December 1864, B. J. Fry reported to General Cobb from Augusta that "the whole country from here to the Ocmulgee [a stretch covering the eastern half the state] appears to be full of stragglers.... Complaints are made here almost daily from the surrounding counties of their depredations." In Walton County, bands of armed deserters and unionists controlled the countryside. The same was true in Morgan County. In the west Georgia counties of Marion and Chattahoochee, bands of deserters fought running battles with what Confederate authorities remained. Some state militia officers suggested abolishing conscription as a means of appeasing the disaffected. Enforcement efforts had become useless anyway. In March 1865, Georgia assemblymen adopted a resolution calling on Congress to repeal the Conscription Act.[19] It was a useless gesture. Time and tide were turning too quickly against the Confederacy.

During the winter of 1864–65, citizens held antiwar meetings in every part of the state and demanded an end to the war. A Hart County assembly, attended by "a large number," asked Governor Brown to call a state convention to arrange "a speedy peace." Citizens in Lumpkin County did the same. "All most to a man," wrote James Findley, they were eager for peace. When Jackson County men tried to hold an antiwar meeting, Confederate cavalry broke it up. Undeterred, the men met again a short time later to draw up resolutions urging an end to the "bloody and destructive war." They sent a list of their demands to Governor Brown and the *Athens Southern Watchman*. The *Watchman*'s editor published their demands and called the cavalry's action "an assumption of power unparalleled in any professedly free Government."[20]

Such demands were common in central Georgia's cotton belt as well. Asserting their "inalienable right of popular assemblage," Jasper County folk met at the courthouse to insist on an end to "the great sufferings of our people." Upson County citizens met at Thomaston and voted "to stop the war on any terms." According to one attendee, "some of the citizens go so far as to say that they will be glad to see Lincoln in possession of the state." One assembly in a rural district of Bibb County was especially aggressive in its demands. A crowd of about sixty voters, all but four of them antiwar men, met to elect local justices. After the balloting, one of the newly elected justices threatened to drive every government official out of Macon and "pledged himself to raise 300 men in twenty-four hours for that purpose if required."[21]

In south Georgia, Echols County's citizens called for a state convention so that a "free discussion may be had relative to the situation of our bleeding country." Thomas County's peace meeting turned violent when the assembly was forced to beat back an assault of pro-Confederates. An antiwar gathering in Wilcox County urged Governor Brown "to settle this Bloody conflict at once by negotiations before the whole white male population is butchered up." So did citizens in Berrien and Pierce counties. Residents of Tattnall and Liberty counties insisted that they would rejoin the Union whether Georgia did or not. Already under Union occupation, Savannah formally severed its ties to the Confederacy.[22]

There was at least one prowar meeting in Georgia that winter. In February 1865, the *Augusta Chronicle and Sentinel* editor sarcastically wrote of "the 'great' war meeting—with a slim attendance, recently held in Coweta County." The soldier who reported the story noted that only five of those present had ever been in the army. The rest were exempts "occupying profitable bomb-proof positions—and of course wanted the war to go on." The editor hardly found that surprising. "They want our difficulties settled? Not a bit of it! . . . they would be obliged to come down to the level of common people. . . . This kind of patriotism," complained the editor, "is altogether too prevalent." The editor of the *Columbus Sun* agreed. It seemed to him that those most likely to advocate "fighting it out" were among the least likely to do so: "We know men of this stamp in Columbus."[23]

As they began to realize the inevitability of Confederate defeat, many prominent secessionists became outspoken friends of the Union. Among those at the Thomas County meeting urging a restoration of the old Union were Judge Peter E. Love and Congressman James L. Seward. Both had held strong secessionist views before the war. Fifteen years earlier, Love had disrupted a "Friends of the Union" meeting in Thomasville held to support the Compromise of 1850. Seward had been a driving force for secession in the Thomas County Democratic Party. But, as one Georgia editor made clear, times had changed and attitudes with them: "These men, and such as they, are the ones who have plunged this country into war. Upon their hands is the blood of slain thousands. Once, none were so blood-thirsty, and ferocious as they. To hear them talk, you would think they could swallow the universal yankee nation at one mouthful. It was this class who were ready to drink all the blood shed in this revolu-

FIGURE 9.2. While poor families with absent husbands and fathers faced the threat of starvation every day, many wealthy Georgians enjoyed a lifestyle hardly touched by the war. As late as March 1865—only weeks before the war's end—one lady wrote of a meal at the Cook House in Columbus where the table was so heavy with fine foods that it *"actually groaned."* (*Frank Leslie's Illustrated Newspaper*)

tion. Seward was a noted fire-eater. . . . And yet, now, you find him leading a Union meeting in Thomasville."[24]

Though southern nationalism was subsiding among elite Georgians, friction between them and the plain folk was not. With the Confederacy crumbling around them, the social barriers that had contributed to its fall remained firmly in place. So did the planters' insistence on growing cotton. Though production was down, cotton still dominated much of Georgia's landscape. In September 1864 alone, at least 440 bales were shipped out of Griffin. Other black belt towns reported similar receipts through that fall and into the winter. Sherman's men found about 25,000 cotton bales stockpiled in Savannah after they captured the city in December. When Columbus fell to Yankee troops the next April, there were 125,000 bales packed in warehouses and lining the wharves.[25]

While planters devoted prime farmland to cotton, thousands went hungry. In March 1865, a commissary agent wrote from Atlanta that "the suffering for [lack of] food is absolutely heart rending." Knowing that poor women would break in and take what they wanted in any case, he had long since opened his doors to them. His office was, he said, "almost constantly thronged with women and children begging for bread. They do not ask for meat, but are satisfied with bread alone. During the late freezing weather, females walked as far as sixteen miles in the mud and ice, for the purpose of getting meal, which they would carry home upon their sholders." It was a pitiful sight, he wrote, to see them come in from the cold with their bonnets and shawls crusted with ice.[26]

Not all Georgians were struggling so in the war's closing months. Finer foods were still available for those who could afford them. Blockade runners had long since given up importing basic necessities, preferring to smuggle in items they knew would bring top dollar from people of wealth. In December 1864, T. J. MacGare, owner of Augusta's Morgan Restaurant, put an ad in local papers aimed at "lovers of good living and drinking." The *Chronicle and Sentinel* editor, who had visited the establishment, praised its "delicacies and luxuries" as well as its "excellent assortment of the finest kind of liquors." As late as March 1865, only weeks before the war's end, one lady wrote of a meal at the Cook House, a posh Columbus inn, where the table was so heavy with food it *"actually groaned."* There were sausages, roast pork, cold turkey, biscuits, hot rolls, cornbread, and cake. The next morning at breakfast there was real coffee—not the more common substitutes—with milk and sugar.[27]

Such inequities were a sure formula for continued and at times violent class antagonism. As a symbol of class inequity, cotton was sometimes the target of that violence. In December 1864, a band of captured deserters broke out of their Albany barracks and set fire to several buildings containing at least five hundred bales of cotton. The next February, a fire of mysterious origin broke out in Valdosta. "A considerable amount of cotton" was destroyed, most of it belonging to local planter L. D. Rountree. An Early County resident clearly expressed the ongoing class-conscious frustration of plain folk throughout the cotton belt when he wrote in April 1865 that there were planters who would not give a starving man a morsel of bread or meat even to save a life. The man sarcastically asked: "Ain't it a pity but what the Yankees would take every thing such men have, and leave them without a single mouthful of anything? We hope to live to see the day."[28]

With Confederate defeat assured and class divisions as sharp as ever, desertion continued to plague the army. Even among those who did not desert, few had much enthusiasm for the war. Most simply wanted to go home. Requests for discharges and extended furloughs flooded Confederate and state offices. From Randolph County came a petition to have Private B. F. Brooks relieved of duty. His wife, Julia, headed a list of twenty-six names pleading on his behalf. Already at home on leave, Daniel Chessy of Steam Mill in Decatur County asked for an indefinite extension of his furlough. West Sheffield of neighboring Miller County did the same.[29] Most never bothered to ask. They simply abandoned their posts and never went back.

So many soldiers left the ranks that the Confederacy's remaining supporters began to consider seriously what until then had been, for most of them, unthinkable—arming the slaves and setting them free. As early as 1863, high-ranking Confederate officials had begun to advocate such a policy. As enthusism for the cause waned and prospects for Confederate victory became ever more dim, support for arming slaves began to grow. By late 1864, Jefferson Davis himself favored the idea.

On January 5, 1865, William Scruggs, editor of the *Columbus Sun*, published a strongly worded editorial in which he attacked Vice President Alexander Stephens's view of slavery as the Confederacy's cornerstone. Scruggs called it a shortsighted policy and suggested that freeing the slaves "would excite the sympathy and secure the aid of the Christian world." By March, Scruggs had become more direct in his editorials. The Confederacy's fate, he said, was entirely in the hands of the slaves: "It is now evident that the negro slave is to be a sort of balance power in this contest, and that the side which succeeds in enlisting the feelings and in securing the active operation and services of the four millions of blacks, must ultimately triumph."[30]

The Confederacy's most venerated general, Robert E. Lee, agreed. In January 1865, he wrote to a friend that although he considered "the relation of master and slave . . . the best that can exist between the white and black races while intermingled as at present in this country," slaves had already been freed and used by Lincoln to crush the Confederacy. Why should the Confederacy not use them in its own defense? He advised Congress to authorize slave enlistment immediately and adopt a plan for "gradual and general emancipation" following the war.[31]

The *Albany Patriot* editor suggested making slaves a better offer. The Union had already promised them freedom, forty acres, and a mule. Why not freedom and fifty acres? The editor was sure that slaves would never fight without such an incentive: "Let those who fight truly, after the war, be owners of their own homes and fifty acres. Let the army negroes know that they are fighting for their own lands."[32]

Most slaveholders stubbornly resisted suggestions that slaves be placed in the military. They feared not only the loss of their "property" but also what slave conscription would mean for the future of the Confederacy and slavery itself. Howell Cobb summed up such concerns when he insisted that "you cannot make soldiers of slaves. . . . The day you make soldiers of them is the beginning of the end of the revolution. If slaves will make good soldiers our whole theory of slavery is wrong."[33]

Slaveholders found strong support in the Georgia statehouse. In a February 1865 message to the Georgia Assembly, Governor Brown warned that arming slaves would be "a great error." As Brown asked, the assembly rejected every resolution put forward for arming blacks. Proponents of slavery's status quo found supporters in the press as well. The *Athens Southern Watchman* saw promising freedom to the slaves as "a base surrender—the most abject *submission* to the enemy! . . . the country was assured at the outset that the object was to prevent the abolition of slavery by the Lincoln party. If we abolish it now, have we not yielded all that our leaders in 1860–'61 said they demanded?" E. H. Grouby of the *Early County News* felt even more strongly about the matter. He called on his friends and neighbors to lynch anyone who dared "preach abolitionism."[34]

Aside from threats to the Confederacy's cornerstone institution, there was the question of whether giving guns to slaves would make them Confederates. It was an unlikely assumption. To *Columbus Times* editor J. W. Warren, the idea seemed ridiculous. He was certain that slaves would never fight for the Confederacy even if they were freed. Warren's great fear was that blacks would join the Yankees as soon as they reached the front lines. If the slaves were armed, he warned, "we will ourselves, take the best in the country, drill and train them, and then hand them over—ready made warriors—to the enemy."[35]

Despite such fears, on March 13, 1865, at the urging of President Davis and General Lee, Congress finally passed legislation authorizing the recruitment of up to three hundred thousand blacks. There was, however, no promise of freedom for those who agreed to serve. Congress insisted that both the states and individual slaveholders must agree to any alterations in the legal standing of slave-soldiers. In his General Order No. 14, which implemented the new recruitment program, Davis went a step further, stating that "no slave will be accepted as a recruit unless with his own consent and with the approbation of his master by a written instrument conferring . . . the rights of a freedman."[36]

Reaction in Georgia was predictably mixed. Most slaveholders raised "a devil of a howl," denouncing the legislation as a direct threat to their property rights. But the *Columbus Enquirer* praised Congress and the president for their action and urged slaveholders to offer one-fourth of their adult male bondsmen as soldiers to the Confederate army. T. E. Speight, who had replaced E. H. Grouby as editor of the *Early County News*, condemned the "starch-shirt gentry" who supported military service for everyone but themselves and their slaves. Since they would not fight, Speight was glad to see that their slaves might have to.[37] It hardly mattered one way or the other. By then it was too late.

In April 1865, the last major Confederate armies surrendered. On May 10, Yankee troopers captured Jefferson Davis near Irwinville, Georgia, as he fled south in a vain effort to get out of the country and establish a Confederate government-in-exile. Other Rebel officials were soon in custody, and the Confederate nation ceased to be.

In a way, though, the Confederacy as a nation had never really existed at all. Eminent Georgia historian E. Merton Coulter, enamored as he was with the Lost Cause, could still admit that the Confederacy never was an "emotional reality" to most of its people until long after the war was over.[38] From its beginnings, the cause of southern independence lacked support from a majority of southerners themselves. That was the main reason it was lost. Less than half of white southerners had favored immediate secession in the first place. A majority of Georgians had opposed it. Black southerners could hardly have felt much enthusiasm for a government that considered slavery their "natural and normal condition."[39] What support the Confederacy did have began to erode as the passions of 1861 died away.

In spring of 1862, conscription only accelerated the decline of support for the war. Most devastating to the war effort were the attitudes of the planters and the privileges granted them by the government. Not only were planters exempt from the draft, but they continued to grow too much cotton while their poorer neighbors and Confederate soldiers went hungry. By putting their personal interests before the welfare of their neighbors, the planters earned the resentment and mistrust of the plain folk, many of whom became convinced that the Confederacy was a rich man's cause, unworthy of their allegiance and sacrifice.

Hunger in the army and hunger at home contributed to a desertion rate that crippled the war effort early on. Robert E. Lee wrote in the fall of 1862 that desertion and straggling were the main reasons for his army's defeat at Sharpsburg.[40] That loss had a far-reaching effect. It spurred Lin-

FIGURE 9.3. A four-year veteran of the Army of Northern Virginia, Sergeant William Andrews of Clay County wrote in May 1865: "While it is a bitter pill to have to come back into the Union, don't think there is much regret for the loss of the Confederacy. The treatment the soldiers have received from the government in various ways put them against it." (Courtesy of Mark Reynolds, Tucker, Ga.)

coln to announce the Emancipation Proclamation, which enticed nearly two hundred thousand African Americans—three-fourths of them southerners—into the Union ranks. In declaring emancipation a Union war aim, the Emancipation Proclamation also made diplomatic recognition of the Confederacy by Britain or France impossible. And it gave the Union a moral cause without which Lincoln—who was having his own problems with popular support in the North—may not have been able to sustain his war effort.

The Union's victory is frequently attributed to greater northern industry and population. Though it is true that the North had more factories and people than the South, to assume that these were the reasons for Confederate defeat ignores more decisive realities of the battlefield and homefront. So successful was the Confederacy's munitions program that never did its forces lose a major battle for lack of war materiel. What they constantly lacked was food. Cotton overproduction was largely responsible for that. It was equally responsible for homefront food shortages that contributed to inflation, speculation, women rioting, and ultimately to soldiers deserting. Had it not been for the two-thirds of soldiers who by 1864 were, as Jefferson Davis put it, "absent . . . most of them without leave," the Confederacy might well have been able to offset the North's population advantage. As it was, Union armies nearly always held the numerical edge—an edge made even greater by the nearly half-million southerners who fought for the Union.[41]

For southerners who had not already grasped the war's base reality, it became increasingly clear with the First Conscription Act of 1862 that the struggle was little more than a rich man's war. Active support for the war among plain folk inevitably declined once that realization set in. Thousands refused to serve, and thousands more already in the service abandoned their ranks. Ultimately, as historian Paul Escott put it, "the decision which common soldiers made with their feet sealed the fate of the Confederacy." Some went so far as to take up arms against it. Many voiced their displeasure at the polls in 1863 and would surely have done so even more strongly in 1865 had the war not ended when it did. Frank Lawrence Owsley, Sr., the leading authority of his generation on the Old South's plain folk, believed that "the Confederacy, even had it not suffered military defeat at the hands of the North in 1865, would have been defeated in the next state and congressional elections, which would have disintegrated its armies and brought peace."[42]

But the Confederacy did not last that long. By the winter of 1864–65, social and economic disparities among southerners had taken their toll just as had the Union armies. Speculation, cotton overproduction, and government corruption—all in the face of suffering among the plain folk—made the war's outcome a matter of indifference to most southerners. Whether the government was seated in Richmond or Washington, it would be one of wealthy men serving their own interests. Evidence for that seemed clear enough as the war was winding down. In February 1865, one Georgian chastised the rich for their continued hypocrisy and callousness:

> That is right. Pile up wealth—no matter whether bread be drawn from the mouth of the soldier's orphan or the one-armed, one limbed hero who hungry walks your streets—take every dollar you

can, pay out as little as possible deprive your noble warriors of every comfort and luxury, increase in every way the necesaries of life, make everybody but yourself and non-producers bear the taxes of the war; but be very careful to parade everything you give before the public—talk boldly on the street corners of your love of country, be a grand home general—and, when the war is over, point to your princely palace and its magnificent surroundings and exclaim with pompous swell, "These are the results of my patriotism."[43]

Patriotism, at least for the Confederacy, was a sentiment long since abandoned by most Georgians. Even among those who served to the end, some did so with waning resolve. What loyalty they still felt was more for their commanders and comrades than for the Richmond government. Sergeant William Andrews of the First Georgia Volunteers had joined the army in February 1861 and remained through the entire war. Few could match his service to the cause of southern independence. Still, only a few weeks after his surrender with Robert E. Lee at Appomattox, Andrews wrote: "While it is a bitter pill to have to come back into the Union, don't think there is much regret for the loss of the Confederacy. The treatment the soldiers have received from the government in various ways put them against it."[44] That was true of the civilian population not only in Georgia but throughout the Confederacy. Such attitudes among southern plain folk, spawned by class resentment, were a major cause of Confederate defeat.

Notes

The many quotations in this volume from Civil War–era sources reproduce the spelling, punctuation, and grammar of the original letters. Emphasis shown in these quotations is also present in the original sources.

Introduction: "A Rich Man's War"

1. Although Georgia Lee Tatum hinted at class disparity in her 1934 book, *Disloyalty in the Confederacy*, it was Roger W. Shugg who, five years later, became the first to directly address the influence of wartime class issues in his *Origins of Class Struggle in Louisiana*. Bell Wiley followed in 1943 with *The Plain People of the Confederacy*, in which he briefly addressed class discord and how it affected southern morale. Almost twenty years later, Stephen Ambrose wrote of "Yeoman Discontent in the Confederacy." In 1978, Paul Escott presented more evidence for general class-based disunity in *After Secession: Jefferson Davis and the Failure of Confederate Nationalism*.

Several state and local studies have appeared in the last twenty years that—while chiefly focused on pre- or postwar class-related issues—touch on wartime class antagonism: Steven Hahn, *The Roots of Southern Populism: Yeoman Farmers and the Transformation of the Georgia Upcountry, 1850–1890*; J. William Harris, *Plain Folk and Gentry in a Slave Society: White Liberty and Black Slavery in Augusta's Hinterlands*; Paul Escott, *Many Excellent People: Power and Privilege in North Carolina, 1850–1900*; Bill Cecil-Fronsman, *Common Whites: Class and Culture in Antebellum North Carolina*; Victoria Bynum, *Unruly Women: The Politics of Social and Sexual Control in the Old South*, which looks at three North Carolina counties; Robin E. Baker, "Class Conflict and Political Upheaval: The Transformation of North Carolina Politics during the Civil War"; Carl H. Moneyhon, "Disloyalty and Class

Consciousness in Southwestern Arkansas, 1852–1865"; and Charles C. Bolton, *Poor Whites of the Antebellum South: Tenants and Laborers in Central North Carolina and Northeast Mississippi.*

Precious few books devote themselves to an exploration of class issues in the Civil War South. There are still fewer than half a dozen, including the current study. The group includes Fred A. Bailey, *Class and Tennessee's Confederate Generation*; Wayne K. Durrill, *War of Another Kind: A Southern Community in the Great Rebellion*, which highlights a coastal North Carolina county; David Williams, *Johnny Reb's War: Battlefield and Homefront*, focusing on the common soldiers' experience during the Sharpsburg campaign and troubles of soldiers and their families on the Georgia homefront; and David Williams, *Rich Man's War: Class, Caste, and Confederate Defeat in the Lower Chattahoochee Valley*, which examines a fifteen-county region of southeast Alabama and southwest Georgia. These works all stress wartime class issues and their impact, but Williams goes further than the others in laying a major part of the blame for Confederate defeat on the South's internal divisions, especially those involving class.

While acknowledging some degree of class conflict, William Blair, in *Virginia's Private War: Feeding Body and Soul in the Confederacy*, argues that it was not a significant factor in the Confederacy's downfall. Blair notes that Confederate policy changes addressing concerns of the plain folk moderated the impact of class divisiveness, at least in Virginia. Daniel Sutherland finds much the same in his essay "The Absence of Violence: Confederates and Unionists in Culpeper County, Virginia." Such differing conclusions suggest that class conflict may have been more intractable in the Deep South. Perhaps Virginia's plain folk, as near the front lines as they were, felt less threatened by local elites than by invading Yankees. Farther from the battlefront, plain folk in Georgia—particularly women left to fend for themselves—tended to view speculators, impressment officials, conscript officers, and planters who grew too much cotton as the more immediate threats.

2. Planters are usually defined by their ownership of twenty or more slaves. The term *yeoman* refers to small farmers and herdsmen ranging from those who owned at least three acres of land and no slaves to those who held up to four slaves. Tenants, sharecroppers, and farm laborers—generally referred to (along with unskilled urban workers) as "poor whites"—worked land owned by someone else. The designation *plain folk* as used in this study generally refers to yeomen and poor whites, although most often it includes small merchants and skilled artisans (or "mechanics") as well.

Classification of such groups as yeomen, poor whites, and plain folk varies from one source to another. Steven Hahn, in *Roots of Southern Populism*, tends to view nonslaveholders as a group, as does Grady McWhiney in *Cracker Culture: Celtic Ways in the Old South*. Bill Cecil-Fronsman, in *Common Whites: Class and Culture in Antebellum North Carolina*, treats nonslaveholders and small slaveholders as a group because of their nonelite self-image. In *Masters of Small Worlds*, Stephanie McCurry locates the dividing line between yeomen and planters at ownership of eleven to twelve slaves, the number usually needed to remove a slaveholder from field labor, at least in her South Carolina study region.

Beyond those already mentioned, some of the most insightful works available on the antebellum South's socioeconomic types and their interrelationships are *Plain Folk of the Old South*, by Frank L. Owsley, Sr.; *Southerners All*, by F. N. Boney; and *Slavery and Freedom*, by James Oakes.

3. Georgia Lee Tatum first tried to draw distinctions between disloyalty, disaffection, and unionism in *Disloyalty in the Confederacy*, xxiv. For collections of recent essays on the varieties of southern opposition to the Confederacy, see John C. Inscoe and Robert C. Kenzer, *Enemies of the Country*, and Daniel E. Sutherland, *Guerrillas, Unionists, and Violence on the Confederate Home Front*. Inscoe's and Sutherland's introductions to their respective edited volumes are both particularly valuable sketches of southern anti-Confederate sentiment and recent scholarship dealing with the topic. The most in-depth study of local unionism and conflicting loyalties in urban Georgia—a study centered around the northern-born Cyrena Stone—is Thomas Dyer's *Secret Yankees: The Union Circle in Confederate Atlanta*.

4. In his seminal study of the secession crisis, David M. Potter looked at the vote on secession throughout the South and concluded: "At no time during the winter of 1860–1861 was secession desired by a majority of the people of the slave states. . . . Furthermore, secession was not basically desired even by a majority in the lower South, and the secessionists succeeded less because of the intrinsic popularity of their program than because of the extreme skill with which they utilized an emergency psychology, the promptness with which they invoked unilateral action by individual states, and the firmness with which they refused to submit the question of secession to popular referenda" (Potter, *Lincoln and His Party in the Secession Crisis*, 208). Potter's conclusions are supported by Paul Escott's more recent study, *After Secession: Jefferson Davis and the Failure of Confederate Nationalism*, 23–28, 42–44.

5. Escott, "Southern Yeomen and the Confederacy," 157; Kibler, "Unionist Sentiment in South Carolina," 358.

6. Tatum, *Disloyalty in the Confederacy*, 38.

7. Anonymous to Brown, August 7, 1863, Cuyler Collection.

8. Watkins, *Co. Aytch*, 69; Bynum, *Mississippi's Longest Civil War*, 103; Bynum, "Telling and Retelling the Legend of the 'Free State of Jones,'" 24; Lonn, *Desertion during the Civil War*, 226.

9. Samuel L. Holt to Governor Zebulon Vance, May 24, 1863, Gienapp, *Civil War and Reconstruction*, 198; Mrs. H. A. Briant to M. C. Briant, January 26, 1865, Briant Papers.

10. *Richmond Examiner*, August 22, 1862; Wiley, "Confederate Letters of John W. Hagan," 196.

11. Lebergott, "Through the Blockade," 883.

12. Frederick Burtz to Brown, March 29, 1862, Governor's Incoming Correspondence; J. H. Jones and D. Dudley to Brown, March 5, 1862, ibid.

13. Though there has been recent scholarly interest in the role of southern women during the Civil War, the plight of women of the plain folk has hardly been at center stage. Most attention has focused on women of the slaveholding class and enslaved African Americans. Historian Catherine Clinton explored the lives of both black and white women in the slave system in *The Plantation Mistress: Woman's World in the Old South* and *Tara Revisited: Women, War, and the Plantation Legend*. Elizabeth Fox-Genovese discussed the relationships between plantation women in *Within the Plantation Household: Black and White Women of the Old South*. One of the most remarkable insights on women in the 1860s came with C. Vann Woodward's editing of *Mary Chesnut's Civil War*, a 1982 Pulitzer Prize winner in history. Chesnut's diary offered readers a glimpse into the life and wartime experiences of a highly placed government official's wife. George Rable expanded the scope of study to women generally in his *Civil Wars: Women and the Crisis of Southern Nationalism*. LeeAnn Whites, in chapter 3 of *The Civil War as a Crisis in Gender: Augusta, Georgia, 1860–1890*, discussed the difficulties women had cooperating across class lines and the ultimate failure of public and private relief efforts for the destitute. Drew Gilpin Faust reinforced Whites's findings in *Mothers of Invention: Women of the Slaveholding South in the American Civil War*.

Most recently, in her sweeping work *Scarlett Doesn't Live Here Anymore: Southern Women in the Civil War Era*, Laura F. Edwards argues that women of the plain folk ultimately determined that the survival of their families was much more important than the survival of the Confederacy. Through robberies, riots, and defiant letters to government officials, lower-class women challenged Confederate authority and undermined the war effort.

Still, the popular image of women in the Old South continues to be dominated by films like *Gone with the Wind*, based on the novel by Margaret Mitchell. More representative of most women's lives was Caroline Miller's 1933 Pulitzer Prize–winning novel, *Lamb in His Bosom*. This story of Cean Carver Smith and her nonslaveholding family living in South Georgia's piney woods was well received, but the book was quickly overshadowed by *Gone with the Wind*. See S. Walker, "Living on the Southern Frontier: Georgia Novelist Caroline Miller's View of One Woman's Life in the Other Old South."

14. *Savannah Morning News*, September 4, 1863; Blakey, Lainhart, and Bryant, *Rose Cottage Chronicles*, 307.

15. *Athens Southern Watchman*, September 28, 1864; Riley, "Desertion and Disloyalty," 106–7.

16. Fleming, *Civil War and Reconstruction in Alabama*, 138; Degler, *The Other South*, 169.

17. *Milledgeville Confederate Union*, November 24, 1863; Samuel D. Knight to Brown, February 22, 1864, Governor's Incoming Correspondence.

18. Bynum, *Mississippi's Longest Civil War*, 98.

19. Degler, *The Other South*, 154–56; D. Williams, *Rich Man's War*, 142, 145.

20. McPherson, "American Victory, American Defeat"; McPherson, *Drawn*

with the Sword; W. Davis, *Cause Lost;* Gallagher, *Confederate War.* For a brief summary of these historians' arguments and a response to them see David Williams, *Rich Man's War,* 210–11. See also Paul Escott's introduction to the University of South Carolina's reprint of Bell Wiley's *Plain People of the Confederacy.*

The issue of the extent to which internal dissent contributed to Confederate defeat is a source of continuing controversy among Civil War historians. In 1997, Gary W. Gallagher argued in his *Confederate War* that internal divisions had little to do with the Confederacy's failure. Gallagher's book was a direct response to *Why the South Lost the Civil War,* in which Richard Beringer, Herman Hattaway, Archer Jones, and William Still argued that various internal weakness ultimately made the Confederacy's survival impossible. William Freehling lends support to the view of Beringer et al. in his most recent work, *The South vs. the South,* which focuses on anti-Confederate activities among border state whites and southern blacks.

21. Rutledge, "Stephen W. Rutledge," 108; Hill, *Senator Benjamin H. Hill of Georgia,* 238–50; *Atlanta Southern Confederacy,* October 25, 1862.

Chapter 1. "This Fuss Was All for the Benefit of the Wealthy": Secession and Dissent

1. U.S. Bureau of the Census, *Population Schedule, 1860.*

2. In *Poor Whites of the Antebellum South,* Charles Bolton argues that although many poor whites immigrated west in search of cheap land, few found any significant degree of upward mobility. Victoria Bynum, in her review of Bolton's work, comments that "most poor whites' geographic mobility grew out of class immobility rather than frontier opportunities.... Many moved time and again in search of elusive prosperity" (602).

3. Oakes, *Slavery and Freedom,* 118; Bartley, *Creation of Modern Georgia,* 21; Wright, *Political Economy of the Cotton South,* 34.

4. Freehling, *Road to Disunion,* 46–47.

5. DeBats, *Elites and Masses,* 260.

6. Ibid.

7. Harris, *Plain Folk and Gentry,* 67.

8. Fitzhugh, *Sociology for the South,* 162–63, 225. For a detailed examination of Fitzhugh's thoughts, see Genovese, "The Logical Outcome of the Slaveholder's Philosophy," in *The World the Slaveholders Made.*

9. Barney, *Road to Secession,* 38; Harris, *Plain Folk and Gentry,* 64, 91. Although Michelle Gillespie, in her *Free Labor in an Unfree World: White Artisans in Slaveholding Georgia* (156–61), agrees that white artisans feared skilled black labor, free and slave, she argues that white criticism was primarily aimed at the influence of skilled black labor on the slave population as a whole and that fear of competition was a secondary issue.

10. Barney, *Secessionist Impulse,* 42; *Charleston Mercury,* October 11, 1860; Barney, *Secessionist Impulse,* 48–49.

11. Rawick, *American Slave,* supplement, ser. 1, vol. 1, p. 255.

12. Anthony Carey, in his *Parties, Slavery, and the Union in Antebellum Georgia*, generally takes exception to this view. "To argue," he writes, "that Georgia seceded primarily because immediate secessionists feared other white Georgians seems to me a drastic overstatement contradicted by far more voluminous evidence" (323, n. 60). That evidence, however, consists mainly of public pronouncements that Carey appears far too willing to take at face value. He too readily discounts less abundant, though more revealing and meaningful, evidence from private communications that leading secessionists exchanged between themselves. These communications clearly address fears of internal dissent generally and of its threat to slavery in particular. Carey's argument that those fears were largely unfounded may be justified, but the fears were nonetheless very real and had a profound influence on the secession movement.

Carey's comments were made in response to Michael Johnson, who most fully explored this issue in his *Toward a Patriarchal Republic: The Secession of Georgia*. Johnson argues that most Georgia slaveholders, like those in other Deep South states, saw secession mainly as an opportunity to revise the state constitution in such a way that popular influence would be minimized and Georgia would become more of a "patriarchal republic" than it already was. Viewed in this light, the entire Confederate experience can be seen as essentially an antidemocratic revolution. Certainly many southern plain folk of the period saw it that way, as is made clear by their widespread attitude that this was a "rich man's war."

13. Phillips, *Correspondence of Toombs, Stephens, and Cobb*, 527; Freehling and Simpson, *Secession Debated*, 82.

14. Those who ran in opposition to secession adopted the label *cooperationists* to indicate their belief that any southern response to Lincoln's election should be made in cooperation with the slave states as a whole. Beyond that, however, the cooperationists' position was uncertain and ill defined. Their rhetoric may well have represented an attempt to thwart secession by garnering the undecided vote. For a discussion of the "confused and ambiguous" nature of the cooperationist position, see Johnson, *Toward a Patriarchal Republic*, 26.

15. *Augusta Chronicle and Sentinel*, November 27 and 30, 1860; *Thomaston Upson Pilot*, November 10 and December 8, 1860; *Rome Tri-Weekly Courier*, January 1, 1861; *Griffin American Union*, December 14, 1860; *Augusta Chronicle and Sentinel*, December 11, 1860.

16. *Harris County Enterprise*, November 29, 1860; *Co-Operation Meeting of the Citizens of Stewart County*, December 18, 1860; Phillips, *Correspondence of Toombs, Stephens, and Cobb*, 524; *Milledgeville Southern Recorder* in *Augusta Chronicle and Sentinel*, December 18, 1860.

17. *Athens Southern Watchman*, January 9, 1861; *Atlanta Gate City Guardian*, February 23, 1861; Johnson, *Toward a Patriarchal Republic*, 5–6, 63, 73; Carey, *Parties, Slavery, and the Union in Antebellum Georgia*, 242. For a breakdown by county of the popular vote, see Johnson, "A New Look at the Popular Vote for Delegates to the Georgia Secession Convention."

In their statistical study of the secession vote in the Deep South, McCrary, Miller, and Baum confirm both Lipset's and Wooster's earlier findings of a considerable degree of regionwide polarization between those who owned slaves and those who did not. See Lipset, "The Emergence of the One-Party South: The Election of 1860," in *Political Man: The Social Bases of Politics*, 344–54; Wooster, *Secession Conventions of the South*, 256–66; McCrary, Miller, and Baum, "Class and Party in the Secession Crisis: Voting Behavior in the Deep South, 1856–1861," 430, 455.

18. *Athens Southern Watchman*, January 16, 1861; Hodler and Schretter, *Atlas of Georgia*, 80; James Eason file, Campbell County, Ga., Archives 044 42, Southern Claims Commission.

19. *Thomaston Upson Pilot*, December 22, 1860.

20. *Journal of the Public and Secret Proceedings of the Convention of the People of Georgia, 1861*, 15–23, 31–40; Grant, *The Way It Was in the South*, 81; *Augusta Chronicle and Sentinel*, February 1, 1861.

21. *Rome Tri-Weekly Courier*, January 1, 1861; Toombs, *Speech on the Crisis Delivered before the Georgia Legislature*; *Thomaston Upson Pilot*, December 8, 1860.

22. Candler, *Confederate Records of Georgia*, 1: 349–61; *Augusta Chronicle and Sentinel*, January 3, 1861; *Columbus Sun*, January 23, 1861; *Milledgeville Southern Recorder* in *Thomasville Southern Enterprise*, January 30, 1861.

23. Bryan, *Confederate Georgia*, 11.

24. *Augusta Chronicle and Sentinel*, October 2, 1860; *Albany Patriot*, November 15, 1860; *Thomaston Upson Pilot*, February 2, 1861.

25. See Potter, *Lincoln and His Party in the Secession Crisis*.

26. *Boston Herald* in Stampp, *Causes of the Civil War*, 68.

27. *Rochester Union* in *Augusta Chronicle and Sentinel*, January 24, 1861.

28. *Blakely (Ga.) Reporter*, March 22, 1900, in Whitehead, *Collections of Early County Historical Society*, 1: 134.

29. Chapman, *A Georgia Soldier in the Civil War*, 6.

30. Some of these are suggested in Wynne and Harrison, "'Plain Folk' Coping in the Confederacy: The Garrett-Asbell Letters," 102.

31. *Milledgeville Southern Recorder*, May 7, 1861. McCurry, in *Masters of Small Worlds*, suggests a further explanation for yeoman volunteerism. She argues that with emphasis placed on the status of mastery rather than on the ownership of slaves (thus strengthening ties between nonslaveholders and slaveholders), an attack on the status of any master was perceived as an attack on the status of all. The nature and valuation of social status based on a broad concept of mastery drew together a herrenvolk society. All that was needed for mastery was land and a family, not slaves. If yeomen perceived northern aggression as aiming to destroy slavery, that change might redefine property and mastery at all levels. This redefinition might destroy yeoman mastery of the household. Thus, argues McCurry, nonslaveholding yeomen fought primarily to protect their concept of household mastery, not necessarily for slavery itself. If McCurry is correct, then the concept

proved to be a double-edged sword that also cut against the Confederacy. As conditions worsened on the homefront, obligations of yeoman mastery drew soldiers back to their families at the call of what historian Mark Weitz called "a higher duty." See Weitz, *A Higher Duty: Desertion among Georgia Troops during the Civil War*.

32. *Augusta Chronicle and Sentinel*, January 24, 1861; Mamie L. Folsom to the *Dahlonega (Ga.) Nugget*, January 29, 1897, in Cain, *History of Lumpkin County*, 87; Avery, *History of the State of Georgia*, 186–88; *Augusta Chronicle and Sentinel*, January 24, 1861; R. Davis, "Memoirs of a Partisan War," 104–5; Swift, *Last Battle of the Civil War*, 27.

33. Aiken to Brown, February 15, 1861, Cuyler Collection; Constantine Wood to Brown, April 11, 1861, Governor's Incoming Correspondence.

34. George M. Franklin to Lincoln, January 24, 1861, in E. W. Solomons to Brown, February 12, 1861, Governor's Incoming Correspondence; Francis B. Drake to Brown, May 28, 1861, ibid.; W. A. Campbell to Brown, February 23, 1861, ibid. Sion A. Darnell of Pickens County expressed a similar opinion about unionist motives among mountain folk. See R. Davis, "Memoirs of a Partisan War," 103.

35. Alfred Prescott to P. Looney, February 27, 1865, Confederate Bible Records; Channing, *Confederate Ordeal*, 75.

36. Brown to A. I. Whitten, T. H. Callaway, and others, April 24, 1861, Governor's Letter Book; *Macon Telegraph*, May 1, 1861; Johnson, *Toward a Patriarchal Republic*, 63–64.

37. McGee, *Claybank Memories*, 42.

38. Crawford to Brown, July 31, 1861, Governor's Incoming Correspondence.

39. J. A. Maxwell to H. C. Wayne, August 10, 1861, Cuyler Collection; Wood to his wife, Ella, October 20, 1861, Civil War Miscellany.

40. Phillips, *Correspondence of Toombs, Stephens, and Cobb*, 580; Atkins Diary, December 15 and 16, 1861; Atkins file, Compiled Service Records.

41. *Augusta Chronicle and Sentinel*, March 10, 1861; *Rome Tri-Weekly Courier*, May 25, 1861; *Macon Telegraph*, June 25, 1861.

42. *Augusta Chronicle and Sentinel*, December 31, 1861.

43. Green Moore to Joseph E. Brown, October 4, 1861, Cuyler Collection; Crist and Dix, *Papers of Jefferson Davis*, 7: 361; Byrd to Brown, February 20, 1862, Cuyler Collection; *Augusta Chronicle and Sentinel*, February 12, 1862.

44. Gaulden to Brown, February 19, 1862, Governor's Incoming Correspondence; Johnson to Brown, February 17, 1862, ibid.

45. *Rome Tri-Weekly Courier*, April 23 and December 21, 1861.

46. *Turnwold Countryman*, April 15, 1862.

47. Escott, *After Secession*, 115; Candler, *Confederate Records of Georgia*, 2: 44.

48. *Rome Tri-Weekly Courier*, September 26, 1861; *Rome Weekly Courier*, October 4, 1861.

49. *Macon Telegraph*, January 24, 1861; *Columbus Times* in *Columbus Sun*, April 12, 1861.

50. Sarah S. Wright to Brown, May 27, 1861, Governor's Incoming Correspondence; *Milledgeville Federal Union*, December 11, 1860.

Chapter 2. "Far Greater Enemies to the South": Cotton Planters and Speculators

1. *Early County News*, September 28, 1864.
2. Gates, *Agriculture and the Civil War*, 6–7.
3. Range, *A Century of Georgia Agriculture*, 28; Barney, *Secessionist Impulse*, 159; *Eufaula Express*, September 1, 1860; *Report of the Chief Engineers*, 399–505. For an overview of problems with food production in Georgia during the 1850s, see Crawford, "Cotton, Land, and Sustenance."
4. *Macon Telegraph*, January 25, 1861; *Atlanta Southern Confederacy*, May 28, 1861; *Macon Telegraph*, May 3 and 4, 1861, March 21, 1863.
5. *Macon Telegraph*, March 11 and February 25, 1862; *Savannah Morning News*, April 12, 1862.
6. *Atlanta Southern Confederacy*, March 20, 1862; *Americus Sumter Republican*, May 9, 1862.
7. *Macon Telegraph*, April 5, 1862; *Turnwold Countryman*, May 10, 1864.
8. Wallenstein, *From Slave South to New South*, 100.
9. *Early County News*, March 8, 1865; Fields to Brown, November 8, 1864, Cuyler Collection.
10. *Columbus Times* in *Milledgeville Southern Recorder*, April 30, 1861. On July 25, 1862, the *Atlanta Southern Confederacy* reported that cotton was selling for fifty cents a pound in New York markets. Less than two years later, on February 18, 1864, the *Augusta Chronicle and Sentinel* listed it at nearly a dollar.
11. *Macon Telegraph*, June 16, 17, and July 10, 1862; *Athens Southern Watchman*, July 16, 1862.
12. Phillips, *Correspondence of Toombs, Stephens, and Cobb*, 595.
13. *Atlanta Southern Confederacy* in *Rome Tri-Weekly Courier*, June 4, 1861.
14. *War of the Rebellion: A Compilation of the Official Records of the Union and Confederate Armies* (hereafter cited as O.R.), ser. 1, vol. 35, pt. 2, pp. 93–96; O.R., ser. 1, vol. 53, pp. 274–75; *Columbus Enquirer*, May 13, 1862.
15. Frederick Burtz to Brown, March 29, 1862, Governor's Incoming Correspondence. For commentary on the Burtz letter, see Formwalt, "Planters and Cotton Production as a Cause of Confederate Defeat."
16. Wm. L. Gordon to Brown, March 29, 1862, Governor's Incoming Correspondence.
17. *Milledgeville Confederate Union*, January 20, 1863; *Athens Southern Watchman*, March 25, 1863; *Augusta Chronicle and Sentinel*, January 29, 1864; Anonymous to Brown, August 7, 1863, Cuyler Collection.

18. Brown to Stephens, February 25, 1862, Governor's Letter Book.
19. Bryan, *Confederate Georgia*, 118; Candler, *Confederate Records of Georgia*, 2: 370.
20. *Columbus Enquirer*, September 16, 1862.
21. Candler, *Confederate Records of Georgia*, 2: 268–69; *Acts of the General Assembly of the State of Georgia, 1862*, 20–22.
22. Barnsley to Alfred A. Marsh, January 3, 1863, Barnsley Papers; Tatum, *Disloyalty in the Confederacy*, 19; Candler, *Confederate Records of Georgia*, 2: 367–68, 504–7, 591; Brown to T. D. Key, March 11, 1863, Governor's Letter Book.
23. *Savannah Republican*, August 13, 1862; *Savannah Morning News*, June 1, 1863; *Macon Confederate [Union]* in *Augusta Chronicle and Sentinel*, June 6, 1863; *Columbus Sun*, June 24, 1863; *Savannah Republican*, July 4, 1863; Lebergott, "Why the South Lost," 69; Lebergott, "Through the Blockade," 882–83. Figures rounded to the nearest 100,000 in table 10 of Lebergott's "Through the Blockade" show that of the 6.8 million bales produced in the South during the war, 0.4 was used in the South, 0.5 went to the United Kingdom and Europe, 0.9 went to the North, and 3.8 was destroyed by neglect, the Union army, or southerners themselves. The remaining 1.8 million bales were sold after the war.
24. John Smith to Brown, March 12, 1862, Governor's Incoming Correspondence; *Atlanta Southern Confederacy*, March 27 and April 9, 1862.
25. *Augusta Chronicle and Sentinel*, December 12, 1861; *Columbus Sun*, January 4, 1862; J. H. Jones and D. Dudley to Brown, March 5, 1862, Governor's Incoming Correspondence; R. K Hines to Brown, March 6, 1862, ibid.; *Savannah Republican*, July 4, 1863; N. McDuffie to Cobb, March 25, 1865, Cobb Papers.
26. *Albany Patriot* in *Macon Telegraph*, March 17, 1863; Howell Cobb to Brown, November 17, 1864, Governor's Incoming Correspondence.
27. Godfrey Barnsley to Alfred A. Marsh, January 3, 1863, Barnsley Papers; J. H. Jones and D. Dudley to Brown, March 5, 1862, Governor's Incoming Correspondence.
28. Lebergott, "Through the Blockade," 868; M. Sheftall to Brown, May 28, 1864, Governor's Incoming Correspondence.
29. *Edgefield (S.C.) Advertiser* in *Augusta Southern Cultivator*, January 1862.
30. Lamar to Cobb, November 3, 1861, in R. Brooks, "Howell Cobb Papers," 360; Mrs. A. E. Moore to Joseph E. Brown, October 7, 1862, Cuyler Collection.
31. Hague, *Blockaded Family*, 101; Bryan, *Confederate Georgia*, 61; Standard, *Columbus in the Confederacy*, 47; Reiger, "Deprivation, Disaffection, and Desertion in Confederate Florida," 280.
32. Standard, *Columbus in the Confederacy*, 46; *Albany Patriot*, November 28, 1861; Godfrey Barnsley to Thomas C. Gilmour, April 8, 1862, Barnsley Papers. For an in-depth treatment of entrepreneurial activity in Georgia during the war, particularly in the larger urban centers, see DeCredico, *Patriotism for Profit*.
33. William C. Butler to Stephens, November 11, 1861, Stephens Papers; *Early County News*, December 2, 1863, and January 13, 1864.

34. *Athens Southern Watchman*, February 19, 1861.

35. *Thomaston Upson Pilot*, October 19, 1861.

36. *Augusta Chronicle and Sentinel*, March 23, 1862.

37. R. S. Taylor to Joseph E. Brown, June 26, 1862, Cuyler Collection; Mrs. Dr. Wellborn to Brown, November 16, 1862, Governor's Incoming Correspondence; A. E. Moore to Joseph E. Brown, October 7, 1862, Cuyler Collection; *Early County News*, November 18, 1863.

38. *Macon Telegraph*, November 13, 1861; *O.R.*, ser. 1, vol. 14, pp. 682–83.

39. Chapman, *Georgia Soldier*, 5.

40. Davidson, *Brooks of Honey and Butter*, 1: 203; *Early County News*, January 6, 1864; *Rome Tri-Weekly Courier*, October 14, 1862.

41. *Early County News*, April 6, 1864; *Thomaston Upson Pilot*, December 14, 1861.

42. *Acts of the General Assembly of the State of Georgia, 1861*.

43. *Early County News*, January 20, 1864.

44. Brown to Zebulon B. Vance, September 26, 1862, Brown Papers, Library of Congress; Cumming, *Journal of Kate Cumming*, 67.

45. *Macon Telegraph*, October 24, 1863; Berrien County Superior Court, Minute Book 1858–1865, 169; Dooly County Superior Court, Minute Book 1857–1871, 348.

46. *Columbus Enquirer*, August 26, 1862; Citizens of Pierce County to Brown, December 15, 1862, Governor's Petitions; *Albany Patriot*, April 13, 1865. McGregor's claim of exemption flew in the face of a recent Bibb County Superior Court ruling. Judge Osborn A. Lochrane, himself an Irish immigrant, ruled that all foreigners residing within the Confederate States at the time of the signing of the Ordinance of Secession were automatically made citizens of the Confederacy, unless proper notification was filed with a local clerk of the court of their intention not to become citizens. McGregor's particular circumstance is not known, but the timing of the Blackshear petition was probably not a coincidence. The citizens were angered not only by McGregor's speculating but also by his flagrant violation of the law in proclaiming himself a resident alien.

47. *Rome Tri-Weekly Courier*, November 12 and December 19, 1863.

48. *O.R.*, ser. 1, vol. 14, pp. 682–83.

49. *Atlanta Southern Confederacy*, November 9, 1861; *Athens Southern Watchman*, April 15, 1863.

50. Hunt to Brown, February 19, 1862, Adjutant and Inspector General's Incoming Correspondence; *Acts of the General Assembly of the State of Georgia, 1862*; Paine to Brown, March 28, 1864, Cuyler Collection.

51. Hunt to Brown, February 19, 1862, Adjutant and Inspector General's Incoming Correspondence; Greenwood to Brown, February 23, 1862, Governor's Incoming Correspondence.

52. *Macon Telegraph*, November 20, 1861, July 30, 1862.

53. Smith to Brown, October 17, 1864, Governor's Incoming Correspondence; *Macon Telegraph,* November 20, 1861, July 30 and October 17, 1862.

54. *Albany Patriot,* January 28, 1864.

55. *Historical Background of Dougherty County,* 9–17.

56. Ibid.

57. *History and Reminiscences of Dougherty County,* 54; Dougherty County Superior Court, Deed Book 3, 587; *Albany Patriot,* June 3, 1864.

58. Dougherty County Superior Court, Minute Book L, 139–41; *Albany Patriot,* April 14, 1864.

59. Dougherty County Superior Court, Minute Book L, 139–42; *Albany Patriot,* April 13, 1865; *History and Reminiscences of Dougherty County,* 54.

60. Edwards, *Scarlett Doesn't Live Here Anymore,* 95; *Athens Southern Watchman,* June 25, 1862.

Chapter 3. "God Help the Poor": Impressment, Hunger, and the Failure of Relief

1. *O.R.,* ser. 1, vol. 35, pt. 2, pp. 394–95; *Macon Telegraph,* November 10, 1863; *Athens Southern Watchman,* May 18, 1864.

2. *O.R.,* ser. 4, vol. 3, p. 944.

3. Candler, *Confederate Records of Georgia,* 3: 132, 134; Riley, "Desertion and Disloyalty," 27.

4. *Milledgeville Southern Recorder,* March 17, 1863; *Columbus Sun,* November 28, 1862; Phillips, *Correspondence of Toombs, Stephens, and Cobb,* 660.

5. Christian, "Georgia and the Confederate Policy of Impressing Supplies," 13, 16; *O.R.,* ser. 4, vol. 3, p. 968; Fleming, *Civil War and Reconstruction in Alabama,* 176.

6. *Savannah Morning News,* June 14, 1862; Cain to Brown, September 28, 1863, Governor's Incoming Correspondence; Shackelford to Brown, September 27, 1863, ibid.; Humphreys to Brown, November 27, 1863, ibid.

7. Jordan to Brown, November 18, 1861, Governor's Incoming Correspondence.

8. E. J. Hikes to Brown, March 31, 1862, Governor's Incoming Correspondence; G. W. Lamar to Brown, December 16, 1862, ibid.; *Columbus Sun,* September 10, 1863, and January 20, 1864.

9. *Athens Southern Watchman,* October 23, 1861; Anonymous to Brown, n.d., Governor's Incoming Correspondence.

10. *Early County News,* April 19, 1865.

11. Christian, "Georgia and the Confederate Policy of Impressing Supplies," 14–15.

12. Ibid., 20.

13. *Macon Telegraph,* October 31, 1863; *Milledgeville Confederate Union,* January 3, 1865; *Americus Sumter Republican* in *Columbus Sun,* November 14, 1863; *Augusta Chronicle and Sentinel,* October 12, 1864; Bryan to Brown, October 10, 1864,

Governor's Incoming Correspondence; Candler, *Confederate Records of Georgia*, 2: 802–3.

14. William K. Oxford to Howell Cobb, November 27, 1864, Cobb Papers; *Augusta Chronicle and Sentinel*, May 31, 1864; *Atlanta Southern Confederacy*, February 27, 1863; *Early County News*, April 6, 1864.

15. *Early County News*, April 20, 1864; Nancy Mann to Thomas Mann, January 2, 1864, Mann Civil War Papers.

16. *Milledgeville Confederate Union*, June 30, 1863.

17. Knight to Brown, February 22, 1864, Governor's Incoming Correspondence.

18. Lane to Brown, November 12, 1864, Cuyler Collection.

19. William A. Clarke to E. Cody, September 7, 1861, in Burnett, "Letters of Barnett Hardeman Cody and Others," 290; *Early County News*, August 10, 1864.

20. *Augusta Chronicle and Sentinel*, August 7, 1862; *Americus Sumter Republican*, August 8, 1862; Castleberry to Brown, August 1, 1862, Governor's Incoming Correspondence; *Augusta Chronicle and Sentinel*, November 4, 1862.

21. *Early County News*, June 15, 1864.

22. Edwards, *Scarlett Doesn't Live Here Anymore*, 89; *Early County News*, March 16, 1864.

23. Flynt, *Poor but Proud*, 41.

24. *Columbus Sun*, October 13, 1863; *Savannah Republican*, June 13, 1863.

25. *Macon Telegraph*, January 3, 1863.

26. *Columbus Sun*, October 29, 1861.

27. *Athens Southern Watchman*, May 1, 1861.

28. *Macon Telegraph*, May 23, 1861.

29. *Milledgeville Confederate Union* in *Savannah Morning News*, February 19, 1862; *Milledgeville Confederate Union*, May 12, 1863; *LaGrange Reporter*, March 4, 1865.

30. *Athens Southern Watchman*, January 21, 1863.

31. *Augusta Chronicle and Sentinel*, March 10, 1865.

32. *Atlanta Southern Confederacy*, March 31, 1864.

33. Cale to Brown, September 9, 1862, Governor's Incoming Correspondence.

34. *Atlanta Southern Confederacy*, March 23, 1862; *Augusta Chronicle and Sentinel*, November 1, 1862; *Milledgeville Confederate Union*, October 27, 1863; *Atlanta Southern Confederacy*, September 1, 1861.

35. *Atlanta Southern Confederacy*, November 3, 1861.

36. *Milledgeville Confederate Union*, January 13, 1863.

37. Furlow to Brown, February 15, 1862, Governor's Incoming Correspondence.

38. Cotton cards were small hand-held paddles with approximately ⅛-inch wire bristles embedded in one side. A pair was used to line up cotton fibers in preparation for spinning.

39. Fisher to Brown, October 6, 1862, Governor's Incoming Correspondence; Petition from Bartow County to Brown, October 10, 1862, Cuyler Collection.
40. Anonymous to Brown, August 7, 1863, Cuyler Collection.
41. *Savannah Republican*, May 26, 1863.
42. Russell to Brown, March 13, 1863, Governor's Incoming Correspondence.
43. *Columbus Sun* in *Milledgeville Confederate Union*, April 14, 1863.
44. *Athens Southern Watchman*, October 30, 1861.
45. *Augusta Chronicle and Sentinel*, August 28, 1864.
46. *Savannah Republican*, August 18, 1862; *Augusta Chronicle and Sentinel*, March 24, 1863; *Columbus Times* in *Macon Telegraph*, February 24, 1865; *LaGrange Reporter*, March 3, 1865.
47. *Augusta Chronicle and Sentinel*, October 27, 1864.
48. Mohr, "Slavery and Class Tensions in Confederate Georgia," 65.
49. John Henderson to Brown, July 8, 1863, Governor's Incoming Correspondence; Dorris to Brown, April 19, 1864, Cuyler Collection.
50. M. H. Gofer to Brown, January 5, 1864, Cuyler Collection.
51. Hammack to Brown, April 23, 1864, Cuyler Collection.
52. *Savannah Morning News*, August 2, 1861.
53. *Savannah Republican*, December 13, 1862; *Savannah Morning News*, March 4, 1862.
54. *Macon Telegraph*, April 2, 1863; *Savannah Republican*, April 14, 1862.
55. *Athens Southern Watchman*, June 12, 1861.
56. Sumter County Superior Court Records, Presentments of the Grand Jury, October 15, 1863; Lonn, *Desertion during the Civil War*, 115.
57. Mary Malory to Brown, February 23, 1862, Cuyler Collection.
58. Wallenstein, "Rich Man's War, Rich Man's Fight," 25.
59. J. Heard and J. Leadbetter to Brown, July 8, 1863, Governor's Incoming Correspondence; Knight to Brown, July 16, 1864, ibid.
60. J. B. Guest to Brown, May 20, 1862, Governor's Incoming Correspondence.
61. Brown to May and others, November 27, 1861, Governor's Letter Book; Escott, "Joseph E. Brown, Jefferson Davis, and the Problem of Poverty in the Confederacy," 61; Sandwich to Brown, December 16, 1861, Governor's Incoming Correspondence; W. R. Singleton to Brown, December 16, 1861, ibid.
62. Brown to J. L. Whitaker, December 16, 1862, Governor's Letter Book; Guest to Brown, May 20, 1862, Governor's Incoming Correspondence; James C. Cothern to Brown, January 15, 1862, ibid.
63. Cleveland to Brown, November 3, 1865, Governor's Incoming Correspondence; Cain to Brown, May 5, 1863, ibid.
64. Paine to Brown, March 28, 1864, Cuyler Collection.
65. Blake to Brown, May 6, 1863, Governor's Incoming Correspondence; Harris to Brown, April 3, 1864, Cuyler Collection.
66. Hudlow to Brown, May 22, 1864, Cuyler Collection; J. W. Henson, Max-

well Chastain, Jasper Ashworth, L. B. Crawford, and S. W. Bates to Brown, July 1, 1864, ibid.

67. Brown to Brown, November 2, 1863, Governor's Incoming Correspondence; Bachlott to Brown, February 12, 1864, ibid.

68. Booth to Brown, September 14, 1863, Governor's Incoming Correspondence; Sumner to Brown, March 22, 1865, Cuyler Collection.

69. Paxton to Brown, April 11, 1864, Governor's Incoming Correspondence.

70. Lane to Brown, February 27, 1865, Cuyler Collection.

71. J. Clements and Isabella [illegible] to Brown, October 8, 1863, Cuyler Collection; Pollie Heptinstall to Brown, May 22, 1864, ibid.

72. Pollie Heptinstall to Brown, May 22, 1864, Cuyler Collection; Clemmons to Brown, April 17, 1864, ibid.; Tyler to Brown, October 11, 1864, Governor's Incoming Correspondence.

73. Captain Elkanah Johnson to Brown, February 18, 1865, Governor's Incoming Correspondence.

74. *Augusta Chronicle and Sentinel*, October 21, 1862; Lyon to Brown, November 29, 1862, Cuyler Collection. Lyon may have had other than altruistic motives. The position of judge for the Georgia southwestern judicial circuit was open at the time. Lyon, a Whig, may have seen the donation as a way to curry favor with Brown to influence the General Assembly, which controlled judicial appointments at the circuit level. If so, the effort failed. A month after Lyon announced his donation, the assembly named Richard H. Clark, a long-time Democratic rival, to the seat.

75. Brown to Justices of the Inferior Court of Bartow (Cass) County (and other selected counties), January 5, 1863, Governor's Letter Book.

76. Brown to A. E. Cochran, January 1, 1863, Governor's Letter Book; *Macon Telegraph*, March 18, 1863.

77. *Americus Sumter Republican*, July 17, 1863.

78. *Early County News*, March 30 and August 24, 1864.

79. Adair to Brown, November 25, 1862, Cuyler Collection; *Early County News*, May 4, 1864.

80. *Early County News*, March 8, 1865.

81. *Athens Southern Watchman*, January 13, 1864; *Turnwold Countryman*, November 13, 1863.

82. Sarah S. Wright to Brown, May 27, 1861, Governor's Incoming Correspondence.

83. *Macon Telegraph* in *Savannah Republican*, January 19, 1864.

Chapter 4. "The Women Rising": Letters of Despair and Acts of Desperation

1. Eubanks to Brown, July 18, 1864, Governor's Incoming Correspondence.

2. Green to Brown, December 11, 1863, Governor's Incoming Correspondence.

3. Petition from Ladies of the County of Schley to Brown, August [illegible], 1864, Governor's Incoming Correspondence; Brooks to Brown, June 22, 1864, ibid.; Mansfield to Brown, September 1, 1862, Cuyler Collection.

4. Nichols to Brown, April 17, 1862, Governor's Incoming Correspondence.

5. Hill to Brown, July 28, 1863, Cuyler Collection.

6. Tillery to Brown, July 26, 1864, Governor's Incoming Correspondence.

7. Jones to Brown, August 22, 1864, Governor's Incoming Correspondence. For more on the incident, see chapter 7 of this volume and Meyers, "'The Wretch Vickery' and the Brooks County Civil War Slave Conspiracy."

8. Owen to Brown, February 28, 1862, Governor's Incoming Correspondence. Owen used the term "myrmadons" (correctly spelled "myrmidons"), or unquestioning followers, in reference to Yankee soldiers. The Confederate Congress finally authorized the use of black troops in March 1865.

9. Wheeler to Brown, October 31, 1864, Governor's Incoming Correspondence; Ladies of Baker County to Brown, October 26, 1864, Cuyler Collection.

10. Mary Frances Brooks to Rhodam Maxie Brooks, September 3, 1862, Confederate Letters; J. Boyd to his brother, February 16, 1862, Boyd Letters.

11. William Asbell to his wife, Sarah Asbell, October 19 and November 19, 1863, in Wynne and Harrison, "'Plain Folk' Coping in the Confederacy," 114, 116–17; Huguley to commander of the Third Brigade, April 9, 1862, Cuyler Collection.

12. S. A. Foster to G. Foster, March 6, 1862, Cuyler Collection; G. Foster to O. C. Myers, March 10, 1862, ibid.; W. W[illegible] to Charlton H. Way, July 21, 1862, ibid.

13. G. Ward, *Civil War*, 201; Andrews, *Footprints of a Regiment*, 20.

14. Watkins, *Co. Aytch*, 194.

15. Lonn, *Desertion during the Civil War*, 57–59; Owens, "Penalties for Desertion," 235.

16. E. J. Fritz to Brown, April 16, 1861, Governor's Incoming Correspondence.

17. Thurman to Brown, October 11, 1864, Governor's Incoming Correspondence; Williams to Brown, June 20, 1864, ibid.

18. Mrs. S. E. Cook to Brown, August 16, 1864, Governor's Incoming Correspondence.

19. *Clarke County (Ga.) Banner*, May 10, 1895, Civil War Miscellany.

20. McDonald to Brown, October 12, 1864, Governor's Incoming Correspondence.

21. William Asbell to Sarah Asbell, November 1 and 19, 1863, in Wynne and Harrison, "'Plain Folk' Coping in the Confederacy," 115, 117.

22. Petition from Women of Miller County, Georgia, to Secretary of War James Seddon and President Jefferson Davis, September 8, 1863, Letters Received, Confederate Secretary of War, RG 109, Microcopy M 437, Roll 80, 776–80.

23. *O.R.*, ser. 1, vol. 30, pt. 2, pp. 629–31, 635–36; Henderson, *Roster of the Confederate Soldiers of Georgia*, 5: 775–86.

24. *Augusta Chronicle and Sentinel*, August 8, 1861.

25. Hurst to C. H. May, April 1, 1862, Cuyler Collection.

26. *Atlanta Southern Confederacy*, February 11, 1863.

27. Dupree to Brown, March 5, 1862, Governor's Incoming Correspondence.

28. George Fowler to Tabetha C. Fowler, October 7, 1863, Civil War Miscellany.

29. *Americus Sumter Republican* in *Athens Southern Watchman*, April 3, 1863.

30. *Atlanta Southern Confederacy*, June 17 and November 7, 1862. For a concise overview of women's riots in Georgia and the factors contributing to them, see Williams and Williams, "'The Women Rising': Cotton, Class, and Confederate Georgia's Rioting Women." See also T. Williams, "'The Women Rising': Class and Gender in Civil War Georgia."

31. Amos, "'All Absorbing Topics': Food and Clothing in Confederate Mobile"; Chesson, "Harlots or Heroines? A New Look at the Richmond Bread Riot"; Tice, "'Bread or Blood!': The Richmond Bread Riot"; Escott, *Many Excellent People*, 65; Graham, "Women's Revolt in Rowan County"; Coulter, *Confederate States of America*, 423; Young, "Some Florida Soldiers"; Chesson, "Bread Riots."

32. Similarly, in *The Flour War: Gender, Class, and Community in Late Ancien Régime French Society*, Cynthia A. Bouton identifies four common types of riots: (1) those in smaller towns focused on a local market, where rioters forced sales at a "just price"; (2) those in larger urban centers of distribution such as Paris, where rioters went after stores of "hoarded" goods; (3) seizing of goods in transit; and (4) attacks on large food producers in the countryside. Confederate Georgia saw all these types, though the state's rail system made some smaller towns into centers of distribution where goods were stockpiled.

33. George Rudé, in his works *The Crowd in the French Revolution* and *The Crowd in History: A Study of Popular Disturbances in France and England, 1730–1848*, concludes that rioters were often driven as much by political motives as by economic necessity. Though Georgia's Civil War riots were primarily need based, they were also largely class based, and the potential for political consequences was surely not lost on many of the participants.

34. *Americus Sumter Republican*, March 27, 1863; *Atlanta Southern Confederacy*, April 24, 1863.

35. *Augusta Chronicle and Sentinel*, April 4 and 11, 1863; *Augusta Constitutionalist*, April 11, 1863.

36. *Columbus Sun*, April 11, 1863; *Augusta Chronicle and Sentinel*, November 23, 1863.

37. *Columbus Sun*, April 14, 1863; *Savannah Morning News*, April 3, 1863; *Macon Telegraph*, April 2, 1863.

38. *Macon Telegraph*, April 22, 1863.

39. *Macon Telegraph*, July 2 and 23, 1862; *Milledgeville Confederate Union*, April 28, 1863.

40. *Troy Southern Advertiser*, April 22, 1863; *Columbus Sun*, April 8, 1863.

41. *Turnwold Countryman*, April 7, 1863.

42. *Atlanta Southern Confederacy*, April 24, 1863; *Athens Southern Watchman*, April 8, 1863; *Troy Southern Advertiser*, April 22, 1863.

43. *Athens Southern Watchman*, April 8, 1863.

44. *Augusta Constitutionalist*, April 11, 1863; *Athens Southern Watchman*, July 23, 1862.

45. *O.R.*, ser. 4, vol. 2, p. 468; *Early County News*, April 27, 1864. At war's end, Augusta alone still had some five hundred families on its indigent rolls. Whites, *The Civil War as a Crisis in Gender*, 81.

46. A. J. Glen to Joseph E. Brown, August 7, 1863, Cuyler Collection.

47. Thomas County Superior Court, December 1863, Minute Book 1858–1865; Wisenbaker Reminiscences, 19–20.

48. Thomas County Superior Court, December 1863, Minute Book 1858–1865; Coulter, *Confederate States of America*, 423. There was also a tradition in English common law dating back to the seventeenth century that women who engaged in rioting would not be prosecuted so long as their actions were spontaneous and driven by dire necessity. Though there is no evidence of a direct link, that may have helped local justices rationalize the lack of prosecutions. See Hufton, *The Prospect before Her: A History of Women in Western Europe*, 1: 468–69.

49. *Columbus Sun*, April 22, 1864; *Augusta Constitutionalist*, April 23 and 24, 1864; Savannah, Georgia, City Council Minutes, April 1864.

50. E. Yulee to Joseph E. Brown, April 19, 1864, Governor's Incoming Correspondence.

51. *Augusta Constitutionalist*, April 23, 1864.

52. Union Primitive Baptist Church Minutes, May 7 and June 11, 1864.

53. B. D. Smith to Brown, May 16, 1864, Governor's Incoming Correspondence. Campbell County, along with its seat of Campbellton, merged with Fulton County in 1932.

54. *O.R.*, ser. 1, vol. 35, pt. 2, p. 544.

55. *Early County News*, February 8, 1865.

56. Barnsley to Thomas C. Gilmour, January 26 and December 31, 1862, Barnsley Papers.

57. *Macon Telegraph*, February 24, 1865; *Augusta Chronicle and Sentinel*, March 8, 1865.

58. *Milledgeville Confederate Union*, March 7, 1865.

59. Barfield, *History of Harris County*, 758.

60. *Savannah Republican*, January 19, 1864.

61. *O.R.*, ser. 4, vol. 2, p. 721.

62. Andrews, *Footprints of a Regiment*, 39.

63. Ibid.

Chapter 5. "Worse Than Slaves": Military Conscription

1. Kirkland file, Compiled Service Records; Henderson, *Roster of the Confederate Soldiers of Georgia*, 5: 372; Union Missionary Baptist Church Cemetery Records. After the war, Kirkland moved to neighboring Miller County and served for some years as county treasurer and tax collector. He was also a trustee of Union Missionary Baptist Church. He died in 1904 at age seventy-five and was laid to rest in the church cemetery beside his wife, Amanda Bush Kirkland.

2. *Early County News*, May 4, 1864.

3. Barrow to Colonel W. M. Browne, May 3, 1863, Barrow Papers; *Savannah Republican*, June 15, 1863.

4. *O.R.*, ser. 4, vol. 2, pp. 160–68.

5. "'Miss Abby's' Diary," January 20, 1864; Mercer Diary, March 3, 1862; Edward Harden to his mother, April 17, 1862, Harden Papers; Andrews, *Footprints of a Regiment*, 121–23.

6. *Atlanta Southern Confederacy*, October 30, 1862.

7. *Milledgeville Confederate Union*, March 31, 1863.

8. *Macon Telegraph*, July 14, 1863.

9. Millican to Brown, June 20, 1862, Cuyler Collection; Lee Dupont to his wife, Dupont Letters.

10. Cobb, *Digest of the Statutes of the State of Georgia*, 2: 967.

11. *O.R.*, ser. 4, vol. 1, pp. 1085, 1156. Although the Confederate Constitution called for the creation of a Confederate supreme court, none was ever established; hence the reliance on state supreme courts. A system of Confederate state courts was created to replace the abolished United States state courts to hear cases of habeas corpus as well as confiscation. For further information on the Confederate court system, see Grice, "The Confederate States Court for Georgia," and Hamilton, "State Courts and the Confederate Constitution."

12. Lester, *Cases in Law*, 33: 347–71. In Georgia, state forces consisted at various times of the Georgia Militia, the Georgia State Line, the Georgia State Guard, the Georgia Reserve Force, and three "state armies" raised in 1861. For further details on these forces, see Bragg, *Joe Brown's Army*, vii–xi.

13. *Macon Telegraph*, November 13, 1862; A. Moore, *Conscription and Conflict*, 34, 69. Sums in excess of two thousand dollars for substitutes were not unusual. One man advertised for a substitute in the spring of 1863 offering $2,500. See *Augusta Chronicle and Sentinel*, April 7, 1863.

14. *Augusta Chronicle and Sentinel*, August 21 and September 30, 1862; *Savannah Morning News*, November 10, 1863; quote from *Augusta Chronicle and Sentinel*, August 20, 1862.

15. *Milledgeville Confederate Union*, May 5, 1863.

16. *Milledgeville Southern Recorder*, January 5, 1864.

17. *Augusta Chronicle and Sentinel*, December 31, 1864.

18. Brooks County Militia to Brown, July 24, 1864, Governor's Petitions;

Wiley W. Groover to Brown, August 10, 1864, ibid.; Citizens of Stockton to Brown, July 28, 1864, ibid.

19. Knight to Brown, September 14, 1861, Governor's Incoming Correspondence.

20. Candler, *Confederate Records of Georgia*, 2: 224–25; Anonymous to H. C. Wayne, September 1862, Adjutant and Inspector General's Incoming Correspondence; Edwards, *Scarlett Doesn't Live Here Anymore*, 89.

21. It is also a "perplexing thing" that Nisbet would write so nostalgically about the war years. While captain of Company H of the Twenty-first Georgia Infantry Regiment, Nisbet was court-martialed for (1) taking his company on a "drunken debauch for several days" near Madison Court House, Virginia, during which he took his men to a house of "lewd women"; (2) assisting a private to desert from a hospital by hiding him in an ambulance from pursuing guards; and (3) fleeing the battlefield at Sharpsburg, Maryland. Nisbet did not stop running until he was on the Virginia side of the Potomac River. Candler, *Confederate Records of Georgia*, 2: 433–34; Nisbet, *Four Years on the Firing Line*, 39; Nisbet file, Compiled Service Records.

22. *Atlanta Southern Confederacy*, April 10 and 16, 1862.

23. Riley, "Desertion and Disloyalty," 84; *Augusta Chronicle and Sentinel*, December 10, 1862; *Turnwold Countryman*, January 19, 1864; Prescott Reminiscences; Bryan, *Confederate Georgia*, 90.

24. Bush to Brown, October 16, 1863, Governor's Incoming Correspondence; Mrs. B. J. Smith to Brown, August 13, 1864, ibid.

25. *Milledgeville Southern Recorder*, November 15, 1864; Whitehead, *Collections of Early County Historical Society*, 1: 134; Riley, "Desertion and Disloyalty," 64.

26. *Americus Sumter Republican*, December 12, 1862; *Milledgeville Southern Recorder*, January 5, 1864; Cobb to Brown, April 21, 1864, Brown Papers, Hargrett Library; *O.R.*, ser. 4, vol. 3, pp. 868–70.

27. Head to Brown, September 21, 1861, Governor's Incoming Correspondence; Riley, "Desertion and Disloyalty," 75.

28. *Augusta Constitutionalist*, June 24 and July 24, 1862; *Milledgeville Southern Federal Union*, July 29, 1862.

29. *Augusta Constitutionalist*, July 26, 1862.

30. *American Annual Cyclopedia, 1862*, 16; "Muster Roll of Company D, Fifty-Second Regiment, Georgia Volunteer Infantry, Army of Tennessee" (Boyd Guards) and "Muster Roll of Company E, Phillips' Legion Ga. Infantry, Army of Northern Virginia" (Blue Ridge Rifles), in Cain, *History of Lumpkin County*, 158–64, 165–68; *O.R.*, ser. 4, vol. 2, p. 786.

31. Purcell, "Military Conscription in Alabama," 104; Andrews, *Footprints of a Regiment*, 110.

32. *Savannah Republican*, May 29, 1863.

33. *Early County News*, March 30, 1864.

34. Knight to Brown, February 22, 1864, Governor's Incoming Correspondence.

35. *Savannah Republican* in *Macon Telegraph*, January 7, 1864; *Rome Tri-Weekly Courier*, October 23, 1862; Wm. M. Grunz to Brown, January 18, 1864, Governor's Incoming Correspondence.

36. *Atlanta Southern Confederacy*, April 4, 1862; Wm. Hauser to Brown, March 7, 1862, Governor's Incoming Correspondence; Walls to Brown, October 15, 1864, ibid.

37. *Savannah Republican*, March 5, 1863; G. W. Lee to H. C. Wayne, September 18, 1864, Cuyler Collection; *Savannah Republican*, August 22, 1862.

38. Although modern dictionaries spell "aide-de-camp" with the intervening "*e*" (as in the original French), Georgia records of the nineteenth century do not. When used in this work, "aid-de-camp" is spelled without the first "*e*" in place.

39. *Macon Telegraph*, December 24, 1863; Bragg, *Joe Brown's Army*.

40. Styles to Wayne, January 5, April 11 and 13, 1864, Adjutant and Inspector General's Incoming Correspondence; Wayne to Styles, Adjutant General's Letter Books, no. 23: 446.

41. Chaires to C. Lumpkin, October 1, 1863, Chaires file, Compiled Service Records.

42. Wayne to Major Thomas Arrington, Adjutant General's Letter Books, no. 20: 142.

43. The Brooks County Inferior Court eventually ordered all the men released under writs of habeas corpus and indicted Chaires on two counts of false imprisonment. There is no record of Creech being brought to trial for his participation. Brooks County Inferior Court, Minute Book 1, 187–90; Thomas County Superior Court, Minute Book 1858–1865, 481–82; Thomas County Superior Court, Minute Book K, 224, 231; Brooks County Inferior Court, Minute Book 1, 187–90; Brooks County Superior Court, Minute Book A, 238.

44. Thomas County Superior Court, Minute Book 1858–1865, 550, 557.

45. Traveling salesmen of the time were called *drummers*. The term originated with men hired to stand outside general stores—sometimes with actual drums—to draw attention to the merchandise. Rogers, *Thomas County during the Civil War*, 66; MacIntyre to H. C. Wayne, November 17, 1864, Adjutant and Inspector General's Incoming Correspondence.

46. Thomas County Superior Court, Minute Book 1858–1865, 227; Thomas County Superior Court, Minute Book K, 482; Dougherty County Superior Court, Minute Book L, 105.

47. MacIntyre to Wayne, August 8 and September 6, 1864, Adjutant and Inspector General's Incoming Correspondence; MacIntyre to Joseph E. Brown, September 27, 1864, MacIntyre Papers.

48. MacIntyre to James T. Hall, n.d., MacIntyre Papers.

49. MacIntyre to Brown, September 27, 1864, MacIntyre Papers.

50. Styles to Henry Wayne, January 5, 1864, Adjutant and Inspector General's Incoming Correspondence.

51. Davidson to Ben L. Yancey, September 5, 1864, Adjutant General's Letter Books, no. 26: 188; Ben L. Yancey to Styles, September 5, 1864, ibid., 189–90; Ben L. Yancey to Overstreet, September 17, 1864, Adjutant and Inspector General's Incoming Correspondence, 275–76.

52. Ben L. Yancey to Hilliard, September 8, 1864, Adjutant and Inspector General's Incoming Correspondence, 209; L. Walker, *History of Ware County Georgia*, 98–99.

53. *Savannah Republican*, June 28, 1862.

54. Murray, *South Georgia Rebels*, 40–41.

55. Ben L. Yancey to Styles, September 20, 1864, Adjutant General's Letter Books, no. 26: 325; Styles to Henry Wayne, October 12 and 18, 1864, Adjutant and Inspector General's Incoming Correspondence; Henry Wayne to Styles, October 15, 1864, Adjutant General's Letter Books, no. 27: 42; Styles to Henry Wayne, November 5, 1864, Adjutant and Inspector General's Incoming Correspondence.

56. *Albany Patriot*, February 23, 1865.

Chapter 6. "Distemper of the Time": The Courts and Planter Privilege

1. Wooster, *People in Power*, 71–72; Hall, *Politics of Justice*, 160, 166, 169–70. For further reading on the relationship between planters and local courts, see Carlson, "'The Distemper of the Time': Conscription, the Courts, and Planter Privilege in Civil War South Georgia." See also Carlson, "Wiregrass Runners."

2. Bleckley, *Cases in Law*, 34: 142–43.

3. The Confederate Congress ended all hope of a dominant national judiciary when it delayed forming a Confederate supreme court and then declared that no power, not even the nonexistent Confederate supreme court, could review a state supreme court decision. For more information on the Civil War drafts, conscientious objectors, draft evasion, and draft riots, see O'Sullivan and Meckler, *The Draft and Its Enemies: A Documentary History*; Murdock, *Patriotism Limited*; Lonn, *Desertion during the Civil War*; A. Moore, *Conscription and Conflict in the Confederacy*.

4. The framers of the Confederate Constitution envisioned a system of national courts composed of several Confederate state courts operating in the same manner as the U.S. state courts they were to replace. The state court judges, when seated together, would form a Confederate supreme court vested with the power to review Confederate state court and state supreme court decisions. But, while Confederate state courts were established, a national supreme court was not, due in part to the impracticability of having Confederate state court judges act as Confederate supreme court judges. Also, while Confederate founding fathers saw such a court as a necessary nationalizing ingredient, traditional fear of a centralized national judiciary threatening state sovereignty was another factor that led Congress to delay its establishment. As one historian wrote, the battle over the Confederate

supreme court serves as one example of how Confederate nationalism gave way to Confederate antinationalism.

Without a unified legal voice, judicial interpretation of the Confederate Constitution varied throughout the upper and lower level state courts and Confederate district courts, resulting in disputes over not only interpretation but also jurisdiction. Did states hold primary jurisdiction over violations of Confederate law? Who held appellate powers or the right of view of congressional actions? The Confederate attorney general declared that "any matter over which the Confederate laws operate, the State Judge or State Court can proceed no further," undoubtedly drawing his interpretation from Justice James Kent's assertion that only those courts with complete jurisdiction had any jurisdiction. Kent wrote that because federal courts were established and fully competent to try cases involving federal law, there was no need for state court interference. The attorney general simply replaced the word *Federal* with *Confederate*. Fehrenbacher, *Constitutions and Constitutionalism in the Slaveholding South*, 68–73; Robbins, "The Confederacy and the Writ of Habeas Corpus," 86, 89.

5. Judge Fleming did remark that although plaintiffs had the right to petition any court of proper jurisdiction, it was his personal preference that conscripts refer all enrollment questions to the Confederate courts at Savannah. Superior court records show that Fleming did not hear another habeas corpus case until May 1864, a considerable length of time given the numbers of troops that moved through or were stationed in and around Savannah. The four writ cases presented to him all dealt with short-term problems of execution following both the First and Third Conscription Acts. Chatham County Superior Court, Minute Book 24, 491; Chatham County Superior Court, Minute Book 25, 196; Lester, *Cases in Law*, 33: 596.

6. Elbert County Superior Court, Minute Book 1862–1868, 64, 80; Bibb County Superior Court, Minute Book 10, 215.

7. For more information on the writ of habeas corpus, see Robbins, "The Confederacy and the Writ of Habeas Corpus"; Neely, *Southern Rights*; and Duker, *Constitutional History of Habeas Corpus*.

8. Brown to Wilbur, September 1, 1864, Governor's Letter Book.

9. *O.R.*, ser. 4, vol. 2, pp. 655–56.

10. Ibid.

11. Fehrenbacher, *Constitutions and Constitutionalism in the Slaveholding South*, 74–81; Robbins, "The Confederacy and the Writ of Habeas Corpus," 83–97.

12. *Early County News*, February 10 and 24, 1864.

13. *Augusta Chronicle and Sentinel*, September 12, 1862; *Americus Sumter Republican*, December 17, 1864.

14. Lester, *Cases in Law*, 33: 347–71.

15. Bibb County Superior Court, Minute Book 10, 639, 628; U.S. Bureau of the Census, *Population Schedule, 1860*.

16. Bibb County Superior Court, Minute Book 10, 236, 240, 246; Lester, *Cases in Law*, 33: 450.

17. Bibb County Superior Court, Minute Book 10, 558, 587; U.S. Bureau of the Census, *Population Schedule, 1860*.

18. *Macon Telegraph*, May 7, 1861.

19. Bibb County Superior Court, Minute Book 10, 213; Lonn, *Foreigners in the Confederacy*, 394. Lonn writes that all claims for exemption by foreigners were denied based on this law. Bibb County Superior Court records do not bear this out. In 1864, all foreigners in Bibb County who claimed exemption from service were granted their discharges.

20. *Atlanta Intelligencer* in *Columbus Enquirer*, August 26, 1862; Lonn, *Foreigners in the Confederacy*, 389. Judge Hull of the Georgia Supreme Court agreed. Hull held in 1862 that all foreign-born citizens who claimed exemption from military service should be prosecuted and sent to the state penitentiary.

21. *Atlanta Intelligencer* in *Columbus Enquirer*, August 26, 1862.

22. *Augusta Chronicle and Sentinel*, July 22, 1863.

23. Bibb County Superior Court, Minute Book 10, 729–42.

24. *Southern Recorder*, March 14, 1865; Sumter County Superior Court, Minute Book, 381; Dougherty County Superior Court, Minute Book L, 174; Bleckley, *Cases in Law*, 34: 181; U.S. Bureau of the Census, *Population Schedule, 1860*. Clark was known to be stubborn in his judicial and political views. Wrote a contemporary of him: "It is doubtful whether, in a single instance, he ever accepted a reversal of one of his judgements by the Supreme Court with anything approaching full mental acquiescence. When reversed he remained of the same opinion still—was not convinced against his will nor convinced at all. It sometimes required all his amiability and gentleness of disposition to keep him from breaking into open insubordination and treating the official court with official discourtesy. His political opinions were equally fixed, and immovable and his allegiance to his party [Democratic] was constant." Wylie, *Memoirs of Judge Richard H. Clark*, 1–2.

25. Elbert County Superior Court, Book 1862–1868, 156; *Augusta Chronicle and Sentinel*, August 19, 1863; Lester, *Cases in Law*, 33a: 136.

26. *Milledgeville Southern Recorder*, November 1, 1864.

27. Gilmore, *Ages of American Law*, 37–38.

28. *Augusta Chronicle and Sentinel*, December 30, 1862; Brown to Thomas, December 17, 1862, Governor's Letter Book.

29. Brown to Thomas, December 17, 1862, and January 1, 1863, Governor's Letter Book.

30. *Macon Telegraph*, August 23, 1862; Bibb County Superior Court, Minute Book 10, 598, 628, 666, 670; Lester, *Cases in Law*, 33a: 67.

31. *Augusta Chronicle and Sentinel*, December 21, 1862.

32. Moore, *Conscription and Conflict*, 53, 56–57; Lester, *Cases in Law*, 33: 365–67.

33. Elbert County Superior Court, Minute Book 1862–1868, 62–71, 73–76,

77–80, 81–86, 149–51; Holmes to Brown, October 27, 1862, Cuyler Collection; Brown to Howell Cobb, March 7, 1863, Governor's Letter Book.

34. It probably also did not help that the enrolling officer was a cousin of the judge's wife. Talbot County Superior Court, Minute Book, 155.

35. Enrollment officials had conscripted Humphries, who promptly made application for light duty. Denied that, Humphries accepted the position as constable, hoping to use this new position as an exemption. Humphries's election was something of a mystery to Colonel A. T. MacIntyre, gubernatorial aid-de-camp for Thomas County. Humphries and his suspected accomplice, J. S. Parramore, had been arrested in Thomasville in January 1863 for carrying two hundred thousand dollars in counterfeit bank notes. After several months in prison at Savannah, Humphries returned to Thomasville, where he successfully ran for office. *Savannah Morning News* in *Augusta Chronicle and Sentinel*, January 5, 1863; *Savannah Morning News* in *Macon Telegraph*, January 7, 1863; A. T. MacIntyre to Henry C. Wayne, April 4, 1864, Adjutant and Inspector General's Incoming Correspondence; Thomas County Superior Court, Minute Book 1858–1865, 522.

36. Brown to [illegible], May 21, 1864, Governor's Letter Book.

37. Officers usually did not have a problem being discharged after election to office; they simply resigned their commissions. First Lieutenant Reuben Mayo was elected sheriff of Washington County, Georgia, and resigned his commission in February 1864 with little or no difficulty. Enlisted men in similar circumstances, however, routinely encountered blocks to an early release following their election. Lester, *Cases in Law*, 33: 166; Mayo file, Compiled Service Records.

38. Dougherty County Superior Court, Minute Book L, 172–74, 176–77; Bleckley, *Cases in Law*, 34: 200–202; Sumter County Superior Court, Minute Book, 321, 378–79; Adams to Brown, February 13 and 20, 1865, Governor's Incoming Correspondence; Clark to Adams, February 11, 1865, Governor's Incoming Correspondence.

39. Bleckley, *Cases in Law*, 34: 72–77; *Augusta Chronicle and Sentinel*, October 1, 1864.

40. *Columbus Sun*, January 27, 1864.

41. William Keen to Brown, July 21, 1864, Governor's Petitions; *Albany Patriot*, September 29, 1864; *Milledgeville Southern Recorder*, September 13, 1864.

42. *Albany Patriot*, September 29, 1864; *Milledgeville Confederate Union* in *Albany Patriot*, September 29, 1864.

43. Fieri facias, or fi fas, are court-ordered seizures of money or property to repay a debt in default.

44. *Columbus Enquirer*, September 29, 1863.

45. *Columbus Enquirer*, October 20, 1863.

46. Ibid.

47. *Macon Telegraph*, January 2, 1864.

48. *Albany Patriot*, May 29, 1863; *Milledgeville Southern Recorder*, June 2, 1863; Lester, *Cases in Law*, 33: 563.

49. Lester, *Cases in Law*, 33: 561–64.

50. Clark to Brown, July 16, 1862, Governor's Incoming Correspondence.

51. Under the exemption laws, any planter or overseer enrolled in the Confederate army who had under his control a certain number of slaves could be exempted with the payment of a surety bond and proof that he was in continuous practice of his profession. Governor Brown's act reorganizing the militia, on the other hand, required that all white males not in military service in the Confederate army be enrolled for mandatory militia duty. Under this law, Colonel Edwin T. Jones, aid-de-camp for the Tenth Militia District, arrested the three men and ordered them to make arrangements to be forwarded to Macon for enlistment. Bleckley, *Cases in Law*, 34: 28–42; Dougherty County Superior Court, Minute Book L, 153–56, 158–61.

52. *Albany Patriot*, November 10, 1864; Dougherty County Superior Court, Minute Book L, 160–61; Bleckley, *Cases in Law*, 34: 28–42.

53. Bleckley, *Cases in Law*, 34: 28–42.

54. Dougherty County Superior Court, Minute Book L, 149, 152; Brooks County Inferior Court, Minute Book 1, 246.

55. *Augusta Chronicle and Sentinel*, August 27, 1862, February 12, 1863.

56. Under the First Conscription Act, all white males over age thirty-five were eligible substitutes. With the Second Conscription Act in September 1862, men between thirty-five and forty-five were eligible for conscription in their own right and thus were not legal substitutes. Principals who had put in substitutes within this age range now either had to report for duty or supply a new substitute. In December 1863, the practice of substitution was eliminated completely. On January 9, 1864, all principals were required to report for duty as volunteers by February 1 or be conscripted. For a synopsis of substitution, see A. Moore, *Conscription and Conflict*, 27–51.

57. Elbert County Superior Court, Minute Book 1862–1868, 89, 92, 141.

Chapter 7. "Very Improper Conduct": Slaves and Plain Folk

1. Such worries had been common in the slaveholding South for some time. See Bolton, *Poor Whites of the Antebellum South*, 107–10. The most thorough study of the relationship between nonslaveholding whites and African Americans in the Old South is Lockley, *Lines in the Sand: Race and Class in Lowcountry Georgia, 1750–1860*.

2. *Augusta Constitutionalist*, May 5, 1864; Clements, *History of Irwin County*, 134–35.

3. *Rome Courier* in *Cassville Standard*, August 15, 1860; *Thomaston Upson Pilot*, September 15, 1860; *Columbus Sun*, February 6, 1861.

4. *Rome Tri-Weekly Courier*, October 16, 1860.

5. *Albany Patriot*, November 22, 1860.

6. *Macon Telegraph*, November 9, 1860; *Milledgeville Southern Recorder* in *Augusta Chronicle and Sentinel*, November 10, 1860.

7. *Albany Patriot*, November 22, 1860; *Columbus Enquirer*, October 9, 1860; *Cuthbert Reporter* in *Macon Telegraph*, October 5, 1860.

8. Campbell to Brown, February 23, 1861, Governor's Incoming Correspondence.

9. Wm. P. Harrison to Brown, April 29, 1861, Cuyler Collection; *Augusta Chronicle and Sentinel*, May 30, 1861; James Hicks to Brown, June 19, 1861, Governor's Incoming Correspondence; William Gleeman to Brown, June 20, 1861, ibid.

10. *Columbus Sun*, July 15, 1861.

11. L. R. Ramsaur to Brown, December 14, 1861, Governor's Incoming Correspondence.

12. *Early County News* in *Augusta Constitutionalist*, June 24, 1862.

13. Harrison to Joseph E. Brown, April 29, 1861, Cuyler Collection. For a discussion of wartime slave resistance in the Deep South and associated literature, see D. Williams, ""'The 'Faithful Slave'" Is About Played Out': Civil War Slave Resistance in the Lower Chattahoochee Valley."

14. *O.R.*, ser. 1, vol. 47, pt. 2, p. 40; Rawick, *American Slave*, ser. 2, vol. 12, pt. 1, p. 258.

15. Rawick, *American Slave*, ser. 1, vol. 6, p. 297; ibid., ser. 2, vol. 12, pt. 2, p. 17; ibid., supplement, ser. 1, vol. 1, p. 257.

16. Rawick, *American Slave*, ser. 2, vol. 12, pt. 2, pp. 26–27; ibid., supplement, ser. 1, vol. 3, pt. 1, p. 315.

17. *Albany Patriot*, May 23, 1861.

18. *Albany Patriot*, November 7, 1861.

19. *Macon Telegraph*, January 25, March 26, 1861; *New York Times*, January 25 and February 8, 1863; *Columbus Enquirer*, March 31, 1863.

20. Beals, *War within a War*, 142–43; *Albany Patriot*, May 30, 1861.

21. Sumter County Superior Court, Minute Book, 47; Lowndes County Superior Court, Minute Book A, 234, 277, 291; Thomas County Superior Court, Minute Book 1858–1865, 494.

22. Sumter County Superior Court, Minute Book, 231; Clay County Superior Court, Minute Book, 455; Thomas County Superior Court, Minute Book 1858–1865, 401–2; *Albany Patriot*, June 13, 1861.

23. Lowndes County Superior Court, Minute Book A, 288; Citizens of Sumter, Webster, and Marion counties to H. C. Wayne, July 31, 1863, Governor's Petitions; Citizens of Stewart County to Brown, July 21, 1864, ibid.; *Columbus Enquirer*, June 23, 1863.

24. MacIntyre to H. C. Wayne, August 8, 1864, Adjutant and Inspector General's Incoming Correspondence; Lowndes County Superior Court, Minute Book A, 317.

25. Bryan, *Confederate Georgia*, 125; Grant, *The Way It Was in the South*, 83.

26. Bryan, *Confederate Georgia*, 124–25.

27. Rawick, *American Slave*, ser. 2, vol. 12, pt. 1, p. 24; ibid., ser. 2, vol. 12, pt. 2, p. 17.

28. Rawick, *American Slave*, ser. 2, vol. 12, pt. 1, p. 25.

29. Rawick, *American Slave*, ser. 2, vol. 13, pt. 3, p. 187.

30. Rawick, *American Slave*, ser. 2, vol. 12, pt. 1, pp. 24–25.

31. Rawick, *American Slave*, ser. 2, vol. 12, pt. 1, p. 24.

32. Grant, *The Way It Was in the South*, 83, 87; *Columbus Enquirer*, September 18, 1862; Bryan, *Confederate Georgia*, 127; *LaGrange Reporter*, March 3, 1865.

33. *Atlanta Southern Confederacy*, December 19, 1862; Clements, *History of Irwin County*, 134–35; Clay County Superior Court, Minute Book, December Term, 1863; Lee County Superior Court, Minute Book C, September Term, 1863; Kinsland, "The Civil War Comes to Lumpkin County," 24.

34. *O.R.*, ser. 1, vol. 15, p. 947; *Atlanta Southern Confederacy*, October 4, 1862; Massey to Brown, March 9, 1865, Governor's Incoming Correspondence; *Early County News*, April 6, 1864.

35. *Albany Patriot*, April 25, 1861; *Savannah Republican* in *Augusta Chronicle and Sentinel*, July 14, 1861; *Columbus Sun*, March 29, 1862.

36. Bryan, *Confederate Georgia*, 126.

37. L. H. Briscoe to Justices of the Inferior Court of Brooks County, August 4, 1864, Adjutant General's Letter Books, no. 25: 217; *Augusta Chronicle and Sentinel*, August 24 and 31, 1864.

38. *Early County News*, March 16, 1864; Suarez, *Source Book on the Early History of Cuthbert and Randolph County*, 130–31.

39. Mohr, *On the Threshold of Freedom*, 164; Bryan, *Confederate Georgia*, 131.

40. Bryan, *Confederate Georgia*, 131; Suarez, *Source Book on the Early History of Cuthbert and Randolph County*, 125.

41. Rawick, *American Slave*, ser. 2, vol. 13, pt. 3, p. 5; ibid., supplement, ser. 1, vol. 3, pt. 1, pp. 4–5.

42. L. H. Briscoe to Justices of the Inferior Court of Brooks County, August 4, 1864, Adjutant General's Letter Books, no. 25: 217; L. H. Briscoe to Justices of the Inferior Court of Early County, August 4, 1864, ibid., no. 25: 282; L. H. Briscoe to Justices of the Inferior Court of Lowndes County, August 11, 1864, ibid., no. 25: 285; L. H. Briscoe to Justices of the Inferior Court of Dooly County, August 12, 1864, ibid., no. 25: 311; L. H. Briscoe to Justices of the Inferior Court of Decatur County, August 14, 1864, ibid., no. 25: 345.

43. Brooks County Militia to Brown, July 24, 1864, Governor's Petitions; D. P. Holloway to Brown, n.d., Governor's Incoming Correspondence; A. T. MacIntyre to H. C. Wayne, August 8, 1864, Adjutant and Inspector General's Incoming Correspondence; L. H. Briscoe to Justices of Inferior Court of Brooks County, August 4, 1864, Adjutant General's Letter Books, no. 25: 217.

44. The 1830 census shows both men with sons in the "under five" category. Based on the proximity of Vickery homes to that of Henry Holliday, Elias is the probable father. U.S. Bureau of the Census, *Population Schedule, 1830*; U.S. Bureau

of the Census, *Population Schedule, 1840*; U.S. Bureau of the Census, *Population Schedule, 1850*; U.S. Bureau of the Census, *Population Schedule, 1860*.

45. Meyers, "'The Wretch Vickery,'" 32; Georgia Department of Defense, Lists of Men Enrolled in the Georgia Militia.

46. *Columbus Sun*, August 27, 1864; *Augusta Chronicle and Sentinel*, August 26, 1864; *Augusta Constitutionalist*, August 26, 1864; *Macon Telegraph*, August 26, 1864; Sarah Jones to Brown, August 22, 1864, Governor's Incoming Correspondence.

47. *Columbus Sun*, August 27, 1864; *Augusta Chronicle and Sentinel*, August 26, 1864; *Augusta Constitutionalist*, August 26, 1864; *Macon Telegraph*, August 26, 1864; Meyers, "'The Wretch Vickery,'" 27–38.

48. Unfortunately, the one piece of definitive evidence, the list of police appointments, has not survived or was never recorded. Searches of both the Inferior and Superior Court records show no mention of any appointment being made.

49. Durham probably had a closer relationship with Vickery than the other planned victims. Sam, one of Durham's slaves, was convicted not only of insurrection but inducement to insurrection, suggesting that Sam was a close assistant to Vickery in the planning and organization. For Vickery to have had such access to Sam could mean that he was Durham's overseer or a sharecropper farmer on Durham's. Huxford, *History of Brooks County*, 123–27; Georgia Department of Defense, Lists of Men Enrolled in the Georgia Militia; *Augusta Constitutionalist*, August 31, 1864.

50. Brooks County Militia to Brown, Governor's Petitions; U.S. Bureau of the Census, *Population Schedule, 1860*.

51. Georgia Department of Defense, Lists of Men Enrolled in the Georgia Militia; A. T. MacIntyre to H. C. Wayne, August 8, 1864, Adjutant and Inspector General's Incoming Correspondence.

52. *O.R.*, ser. 1, vol. 35, pt. 2, pp. 359–60.

53. *O.R.*, ser. 1, vol. 35, pt. 2, p. 607.

54. *O.R.*, ser. 1, vol. 14, p. 752; *Augusta Chronicle and Sentinel*, August 26, 1864.

55. *Augusta Constitutionalist*, August 24 and 31, 1864; Huxford, *History of Brooks County*, 127.

56. *Augusta Constitutionalist*, August 31, 1864; Georgia Department of Defense, Lists of Men Enrolled in the Georgia Militia.

57. *Augusta Constitutionalist*, August 31, 1864.

58. Ibid.; Georgia Department of Defense, Lists of Men Enrolled in the Georgia Militia.

59. *Augusta Constitutionalist*, August 31, 1864; Georgia Department of Defense, Lists of Men Enrolled in the Georgia Militia.

60. *Augusta Constitutionalist*, August 31, 1864; Georgia Department of Defense, Lists of Men Enrolled in the Georgia Militia.

61. Folsom to his wife, September 10, 1864, McLeod and McLeod, *Civil War Letters of Bryant Folsom*, 67.

Chapter 8. "We Are Fighting Each Other Harder Than We Ever Fought the Enemy": Georgia's Inner Civil War

1. *Savannah Morning News,* September 10, 1863.

2. Anonymous to Brown, n.d., Governor's Incoming Correspondence; *Early County News,* December 14, 1864.

3. *Americus Sumter Republican,* August 21, 1863; *Milledgeville Confederate Union,* August 25, September 8 and 22, 1863; *Augusta Chronicle and Sentinel,* June 6, 1863; Martis, *Atlas of the Congresses of the Confederate States,* 87.

4. *Savannah Morning News,* October 1, 1863.

5. *Turnwold Countryman,* May 26, 1863; *Athens Southern Watchman,* April 29, May 27, June 3, 1863.

6. Barnsley to Thomas C. Gilmour, December 31, 1862, Barnsley Papers.

7. *Milledgeville Confederate Union,* November 3, 1863; Martis, *Atlas of the Congresses of the Confederate States,* 87, 110–13. See also Percy, "Localizing the Context of Confederate Politics: The Congressional Election of 1863 in Georgia's First District."

8. *Columbus Enquirer,* October 9, 1863; *Columbus Sun,* October 13, 1863.

9. *Columbus Enquirer,* October 9, 1863.

10. *O.R.,* ser. 4, vol. 3, pp. 393–95.

11. *O.R.,* ser. 4, vol. 3, p. 397.

12. *O.R.,* ser. 1, vol. 32, pt. 3, pp. 682–83; *O.R.,* ser. 4, vol. 3, p. 397.

13. Longstreet, *From Manassas to Appomattox,* 651; *O.R.,* ser. 1, vol. 28, pt. 2, p. 411; *O.R.,* ser. 1, vol. 35, pt. 1, pp. 529–32; Tatum, *Disloyalty in the Confederacy,* 68–69.

14. One hundred thousand white southerners who served in the Union military were from Confederate states. Two hundred thousand were from the Border South states. See Freehling, *The South vs. the South,* xiii; Current, *Lincoln's Loyalists,* 218.

15. Watson, Small Print Collection; Fife file, Compiled Service Records; *Pioneers of Wiregrass Georgia,* 8: 82; Harris file, Murray County, Ga., Archives 004 143B, Southern Claims Commission; R. Davis, "Forgotten Union Guerrilla Fighters from the North Georgia Mountains," 32; R. Davis, "Memoirs of a Partisan War," 113; Current, *Lincoln's Loyalists,* 217; R. Davis, "White and Black in Blue," 348.

16. Bonner, "David R. Snelling," 275–82.

17. O'Connor to Brown, March 10, 1862, Governor's Incoming Correspondence; Mueller, *Perilous Journeys,* 109.

18. *O.R.,* ser. 4, vol. 3, pp. 1119–20; *Milledgeville Southern Recorder,* November 17, 1863; Houghton and Houghton, *Two Boys in the Civil War and After,* 237–41; John W. Riley to Brown, July 22 (no year), Governor's Incoming Correspondence.

19. Riley, "Desertion and Disloyalty," 69; Bohannon, "They Had Determined to Root Us Out," 105; *Athens Southern Watchman,* November 12, 1862; *O.R.,* ser. 1, vol. 28, pt. 2, p. 273; Sarris, "An Execution in Lumpkin County," 141–42; Kins-

land, "The Civil War Comes to Lumpkin County," 23–24. The *Watchman* gives forty as the number of men involved in the White County jailbreak.

20. M. E. Mills to Brown, January 29, 1864, Governor's Incoming Correspondence.

21. Walker to Brown, January 18, 1864, Governor's Incoming Correspondence; Knight to Brown, February 22, 1864, ibid.

22. Morton to Brown, December 24, 1863, Governor's Incoming Correspondence; Evers to Margaret Evers, January 11, 1863, *Confederate Reminiscences and Letters*, 6: 210.

23. M. N. Cody to Charlton A. May, February 13, 1862, Cuyler Collection; Atkins Diary, January 22, 1862; Milo W. Grow to his wife, Kate Baughn Grow, June 26, 1862, *Confederate Reminiscences and Letters*, 5: 156.

24. *Columbus Sun*, November 18, 1863; Brooks to his wife, July 25, 1863, Brooks Letters; Dupont to his wife, Dupont Letters.

25. *Atlanta Southern Confederacy*, February 4, 1863; Andrews, *Footprints of a Regiment*, 39; "Samuel Henderson Frier, 1833–1863: AWOL from the Confederate Army," 81; *O.R.*, ser. 4, vol. 2, p. 721.

26. Escott, *After Secession*, 127; *Columbus Enquirer*, August 11, 1863; *Savannah Republican*, September 15, 1863.

27. Cobb to his wife, February 4, 1864, Cobb Papers; *Athens Southern Watchman*, September 28, 1864.

28. Mason file, Union County, Ga., Archives 0044 24C, Southern Claims Commission.

29. R. Davis, "White and Black in Blue," 357; Inscoe, "Moving through Deserter Country," 162.

30. D. J. Burt to Brown, February 26, 1864, Governor's Incoming Correspondence; *O.R.*, ser. 1, vol. 44, p. 977; *O.R.*, ser. 1, vol. 44, pp. 827–28; Riley, "Desertion and Disloyalty," 59; R. Davis, "White and Black in Blue," 357.

31. Turner, *Navy Gray*, 130–31, 325 n. 6.

32. Turner, *Navy Gray*, 130; [name illegible] to Brown, October 5, 1864, Governor's Incoming Correspondence; *O.R.*, ser. 1, vol. 23, pt. 2, p. 738; *Milledgeville Confederate Union*, November 24, 1863.

33. *Macon Telegraph*, September 15, 1862.

34. W. W. Findley to Brown, July 26, 1862, Governor's Incoming Correspondence; W. A. Campbell to Brown, July 12, 1862, and February 28, 1863, ibid.; Josiah A. Woody to Brown, September 6, 1862, ibid.; *Dahlonega Signal* in *Augusta Chronicle and Sentinel*, January 30, 1863.

35. Bohannon, "They Had Determined to Root Us Out," 98–106.

36. *O.R.*, ser. 4, vol. 2, pp. 360–61.

37. Henry C. Wayne to E. M. Galt, January 17, 1863, Adjutant General's Letter Books; *Atlanta Southern Confederacy*, February 4, 1863; G. W. Lee to Brown, February 5, 1863, Governor's Incoming Correspondence; Citizens of Dahlonega, Ga.,

to Joseph E. Brown, March 4, 1863, Cuyler Collection; *Athens Southern Watchman*, June 17, 1863.

38. W. A. Campbell to Brown, August 4, 1863, Governor's Incoming Correspondence; T. J. Haralson and others to Brown, August 7, 1863, Governor's Petitions; Brown to Davis, August 25, 1863, Governor's Letter Book; G. W. Lee to Joseph E. Brown, October 6, 1863, Cuyler Collection.

39. *Savannah Morning News*, November 16, 1863; *Athens Southern Watchman*, November 25, 1863.

40. Henry C. Wayne to G. W. Lee, January 23, 1864, Adjutant General's Letter Books.

41. *Atlanta [Southern] Confederacy* in *Augusta Chronicle and Sentinel*, October 28, 1862; *O.R.*, ser. 1, vol. 23, pt. 2, p. 738.

42. *O.R.*, ser. 1, vol. 23, pt. 2, pp. 737–38; *Augusta Constitutionalist*, May 7, 1864.

43. Mary Noble to Lelia Montan, November 20, 1864, Noble-Attaway Papers; Battey, *History of Rome and Floyd County*, 1: 206–7.

44. *Albany Patriot*, May 23, 30, and September 5, 1861.

45. For an ethnography of southerners of Scots, Irish, and Welsh descent, see McWhiney, *Cracker Culture: Celtic Ways in the Old South*. For a physical, social, and economic description of the antebellum Wiregrass region, see chapter 1 of Wetherington, *The New South Comes to Wiregrass Georgia, 1860–1910*. For a concise treatment of draft evasion in south Georgia, see Carlson, "The 'Loanly Runagee.'" See also Carlson, "Wiregrass Runners."

46. Sumter County Superior Court, Minute Book, April 1861; Harwell and Racine, *Fiery Trail*, 61; A. T. MacIntyre to H. C. Wayne, April 21, 1865, Adjutant and Inspector General's Incoming Correspondence.

47. *Milledgeville Confederate Union*, January 3, 1865; Rawick, *American Slave*, supplement, ser. 1, vol. 4, pt. 2, p. 392; *Albany Patriot*, September 9, 1864.

48. *Milledgeville Confederate Union*, January 3, 1865.

49. *Atlanta Southern Confederacy*, June 21, 1864.

50. *Southern Recorder*, June 30, 1863; *Augusta Chronicle and Sentinel*, May 31, 1863; Dougherty County Superior Court, Minute Book L, 77, 78.

51. Clements, *History of Irwin County*, 134–35.

52. Hewett, *Supplement to the Official Records*, pt. 2, vol. 5, p. 479; G. Davis et al., *Official Military Atlas of the Civil War*, plate 145; Brown file, Compiled Service Records; Fourth Georgia Cavalry, Compiled Service Records.

53. *Valdosta Times*, December 20, 1884; Trowell, *Exploring the Okefenokee*, 62.

54. *O.R.*, ser. 1, vol. 28, pt. 2, p. 411.

55. Hewett, *Supplement to the Official Records*, pt. 2, vol. 5, p. 488; *Macon Telegraph*, December 10, 1863.

56. *O.R.*, ser. 1, vol. 28, pt. 2, p. 411; *Macon Telegraph*, December 10, 1863; U.S. Bureau of the Census, *Population Schedule, 1860*. Three Union soldiers, members of the Forty-seventh New York Infantry Regiment, were arrested at Homerville.

They claimed they had been cut off from their units at Olustee. All were remanded to the custody of Allen Smith, the local enrolling officer. *Macon Telegraph*, March 5, 1864.

57. *Macon Telegraph*, December 10, 1863, March 10, 1864; Rogers, *Thomas County during the Civil War*, 66.

58. Henry Wayne to A. T. MacIntyre, August 10, 1864, MacIntyre Papers.

59. Edwin T. Jones to Henry Wayne, August 18, 1864, Adjutant and Inspector General's Incoming Correspondence.

60. *O.R.*, ser. 4, vol. 2, pp. 655–56; Smith to General Henry Wayne, August 20, 1864; Adjutant and Inspector General's Incoming Correspondence; Smith to Henry Wayne, August 25, 1864, ibid.; Smith to Henry Wayne, August 26, 1864, ibid.; McKinnon to Henry Wayne, September 20, 1864, ibid.; Styles to Henry Wayne, October 18, 1864, ibid.

61. L. H. Briscoe to Justices of the Inferior Court of Brooks County, August 4, 1864, Adjutant General's Letter Books, no. 25: 217; L. H. Briscoe to Justices of the Inferior Court of Early County, August 4, 1864, ibid., 282; L. H. Briscoe to Justices of the Inferior Court of Lowndes County, August 11, 1864, ibid., 285; L. H. Briscoe to Justices of the Inferior Court of Dooly County, August 12, 1864, ibid., 311; L. H. Briscoe to Justices of the Inferior Court of Decatur County, August 14, 1864, ibid., 345.

62. Camfield file, Compiled Service Records; *Albany Patriot*, April 27, 1865.

63. *Albany Patriot*, November 3, 1864; Lawton to G. W. Randolph, October 4, 1862, Lawton file, Compiled Service Records; Brimberry to Joseph Davis, February 3, 1893, ibid.; Lawton to Jefferson Davis, August 24, 1863, ibid.

64. *Albany Patriot*, November 3, 1864, February 23, 1865; Dunlap to Billie Dunlap, August 11, 1864, *Confederate Reminiscences and Letters*, 6: 179; Citizens of Worth County to Brown, October 4, 1864, Governor's Petitions; Fields to Brown, November 8, 1864, Cuyler Collection.

65. W. Ward, *Ward's History of Coffee County*, 141–42.

66. Carey W. Styles to H. C. Wayne, November 5, 1864, Adjutant and Inspector General's Incoming Correspondence.

67. Bryan, *Confederate Georgia*, 153–54; *O.R.*, ser. 1, vol. 47, pt. 2, p. 1391; Clinch file, Compiled Service Records.

68. *O.R.*, ser. 1, vol. 46, pt. 3, pp. 1353–56; Hardee file, Compiled Service Records; Hardee to Colonel A. T. MacIntyre, January 30, 1865, MacIntyre Papers.

Chapter 9. "Don't Think There Is Much Regret for the Loss"

1. *Early County News*, March 30 and October 5, 1864.

2. Bryan, *Confederate Georgia*, 148.

3. Celathiel Helms to his wife, Mary Helms, July 6, 1864, Confederate Letters.

4. Brown to Jefferson Davis, July 19, 1864, Governor's Letter Book; J. A. Seddon to Brown, July 21, 1864, ibid.; Brown to J. A. Seddon, July 22, 1864, ibid.

5. Anonymous to Brown, June 6, 1864, Governor's Incoming Correspondence; Moses W. Finger to Brown, May 14, 1864, Governor's Incoming Correspondence; Henry Collom to Brown, May 27, 1864, ibid.

6. *Milledgeville Confederate Union*, June 28, 1864.

7. "Dobbin" is a colloquialism referring to a farm horse or a plodding workhorse.

8. John D. Palmour and others to Brown, March 20, 1865, Governor's Incoming Correspondence; J. Moore, "Sherman's 'Fifth Column,'" 386; Dyer, *Secret Yankees*, 149, 151; R. Davis, "White and Black in Blue," 357; Bryan, *Confederate Georgia*, 150; *O.R.*, ser. 1, vol. 38, pt. 2, p. 866; *O.R.*, ser. 1, vol. 52, pt. 1, p. 107; *O.R.*, ser. 1, vol. 38, pt. 5, p. 299.

9. R. Davis, "Forgotten Union Guerrilla Fighters from the North Georgia Mountains," 30–33; Sarris, "Anatomy of an Atrocity," 704–5. For more on the First Georgia State Troops Volunteer Battalion, see R. Davis, "White and Black in Blue," 360–66.

10. Dickey to his wife, Anna, October 26, 1864, Civil War Miscellany; *Albany Patriot*, November 10, 1864; Dougherty County Superior Court, Minute Book L, 160–61; Bleckley, *Cases in Law*, 34: 28–42. Named for Alexander H. Stephens, Camp Stephens was located in Spalding County north of Griffin on McIntosh Road. See Krakow, *Georgia Place-Names*, 34.

11. Dickey to his wife, Anna, October 26, 1864, Civil War Miscellany.

12. The militia's only major stand came at Griswoldville on November 22, 1864, where it was defeated with heavy losses.

13. Smith to Brown, February 25, 1865, Governor's Incoming Correspondence.

14. Kinsland, "The Civil War Comes to Lumpkin County," 23–24; Covington, *History of Colquitt County*, 37.

15. Clements, *History of Irwin County*, 134–35; U.S. Bureau of the Census, *Population Schedule, 1860*; Irwin County Court of the Ordinary, Inventories, Appraisements, Returns, Sales, and Miscellaneous Estate Records, Book No. 12, 1864–1871, 32; Irwin County Inferior Court, Minute Book, 1852–1878, January 1862, March 1864, and September 1864.

16. *Albany Patriot*, February 23, 1865.

17. Prescott to P. Looney, February 27, 1865, Confederate Bible Records; *Albany Patriot*, March 23, 1865; B. F. White to Lamar Cobb, January 6, 1865, Cobb Papers; J. Williams to J. A. Davis, February 26, 1865, ibid.; Clinch to Howell Cobb, April 4, 1865, ibid.

18. Andrew J. Hansell to Howell Cobb, January 10, 1865, Cobb Papers; Joseph Henry Lumpkin to J. A. Campbell, December 31, 1864, ibid.; *O.R.*, ser. 1, vol. 49, pt. 1, p. 963; *O.R.*, ser. 1, vol. 45, pt. 2, p. 805; Findley to Brown, January 26, 1865, Governor's Incoming Correspondence; A. W. Reynolds to Howell Cobb, January 22, 1865, Cobb Papers.

19. B. J. Fry to Howell Cobb, December 16, 1864, Cobb Papers; T. T. Eason to

Howell Cobb, March 28 1865, ibid.; Bryan, *Confederate Georgia*, 264 n. 84; *Milledgeville Confederate Union*, December 20, 1864; James J. Findley to Brown, January 26, 1865, Governor's Incoming Correspondence; *Augusta Constitutionalist*, March 10, 1865.

20. *Athens Southern Watchman*, January 25, 1865; Findley to Brown, January 26, 1865, Governor's Incoming Correspondence; *Augusta Chronicle and Sentinel*, January 29, 1865; *Athens Southern Watchman*, January 18, 1865.

21. *Augusta Chronicle and Sentinel*, February 26, 1865; W. A. Thomas to Howell Cobb, January 18, 1865, Cobb Papers; J. T. Smith to Brown, February 25, 1865, Governor's Incoming Correspondence.

22. *Milledgeville Confederate Union*, February 28, 1865; Citizens of Wilcox County to Brown, January 14, 1865, Brown Papers, Hargrett Library; *Augusta Chronicle and Sentinel*, February 2, 1865; Berrien County Inferior Court, Minutes, January 18[?], 1865; *O.R.*, ser. 1, vol. 47, pt. 3, p. 262; *O.R.*, ser. 1, vol. 44, pp. 827–28; *Augusta Register* in *Sumter Republican*, January 21, 1865; *O.R.*, ser. 1, vol. 47, pt. 2, p. 31.

23. *Augusta Chronicle and Sentinel*, February 11, 1865; *Columbus Sun*, February 5, 1865.

24. Rogers, *Antebellum Thomas County*, 112, 115–17; *Turnwold Countryman*, February 14, 1865.

25. Griffin, Ga., Cotton Receipts, Box 20, Folder 23, Cuyler Collection; Columbus, Ga., Cotton Receipts, Box 20, Folder 23, ibid.; Cotton Receipts, Box 20, Folder 25, and Box 21, Folder 2, ibid.; Sherman, *Memoirs*, 2: 231; D. Williams, *Rich Man's War*, 181.

26. *Augusta Constitutionalist*, March 10, 1865.

27. *Augusta Chronicle and Sentinel*, December 3, 1864; Cumming, *Journal of Kate Cumming*, 244. Coffee was one of the rarest commodities in the Confederacy and so expensive that poorer folk used everything from peanuts to pecan shells as substitutes. Though most plain folk had run out of coffee by the summer of 1861, it was the next year before one plantation mistress noticed with astonishment that some people were drinking a brew of parched rye instead. See Chesnut, *Mary Chesnut's Civil War*, 285.

28. *Augusta Chronicle and Sentinel*, December 21, 1864; *Columbus Sun*, February 24, 1865; *Early County News*, April 5, 1865.

29. Julia A. Brooks and others to Brown, June 22, 1864, Governor's Petitions; Daniel Chessy to Brown, October 7, 1864, Governor's Incoming Correspondence; West Sheffield to Brown, September 30, 1864, ibid.

30. Cleveland, *Alexander H. Stephens*, 721; *Columbus Sun*, January 5 and March 22, 1865.

31. Nolan, *Lee Considered*, 175–77.

32. Sherman, *Memoirs*, 2: 250–52; Foner, *Reconstruction*, 70–71; *Albany Patriot*, February 23, 1865.

33. *O.R.*, ser. 4, vol. 3, pp. 1009–10.

34. Candler, *Confederate Records of Georgia*, 2: 832–35; Bryan, *Confederate Georgia*, 134; *Athens Southern Watchman*, March 15, 1865; *Early County News*, January 18, 1865.

35. *Columbus Times*, February 15, 1865. At least a few blacks seem to have served unofficially and sporadically in the role of Confederate soldiers. See Jordan, *Black Confederates and Afro-Yankees in Civil War Virginia*.

36. Mohr, *On the Threshold of Freedom*, 283–84. For the most complete treatment of emancipation as an issue in the Civil War South, including the question of arming the slaves, see Durden, *Gray and the Black*. An excellent study of how the issue of arming slaves developed at the local level in Georgia is Dillard, "Arming the Slaves."

37. Mohr, *On the Threshold of Freedom*, 283–84; *Early County News*, April 5, 1865.

38. Coulter, *Confederate States of America*, 105.

39. Cleveland, *Alexander H. Stephens*, 721.

40. *O.R.*, ser. 1, vol. 19, pt. 2, p. 622.

41. Beringer et al., *Why the South Lost the Civil War*, 13; *Athens Southern Watchman*, September 28, 1864; Freehling, *The South vs. the South*, xiii.

42. Escott, *After Secession*, 63; Owsley, "Defeatism in the Confederacy," 456. Owsley was the first prominent historian to argue that the causes of Confederate defeat were primarily internal. In his seminal work *State Rights in the Confederacy*, Owsley identified the concept of state sovereignty written into the Confederate constitution—and the weakness it imposed on the central government—as the leading factor in the Confederacy's collapse.

43. *Columbus Sun* in *Augusta Chronicle and Sentinel*, February 17, 1865.

44. Andrews, *Footprints of a Regiment*, 184.

Bibliography

Newspapers

Albany (Ga.) Patriot, 1860–61, 1863–65.
Americus (Ga.) Sumter Republican, 1862–64.
Athens (Ga.) Southern Watchman, 1861–65.
Atlanta (Ga.) Gate City Guardian, 1861.
Atlanta (Ga.) Southern Confederacy, 1861–64.
Augusta (Ga.) Chronicle and Sentinel, 1860–65.
Augusta (Ga.) Constitutionalist, 1862–65.
Augusta (Ga.) Southern Cultivator, 1862.
Cassville (Ga.) Standard, 1860.
Charleston (S.C.) Mercury, 1860.
Clarke County (Ga.) Banner, 1895.
Columbus (Ga.) Enquirer, 1860, 1862–63.
Columbus (Ga.) Sun, 1861–65.
Columbus (Ga.) Times, 1865.
Early County (Ga.) News, 1863–65.
Eufaula (Ala.) Express, 1860.
Frank Leslie's Illustrated Newspaper (N.Y.), 1861–65.
Griffin (Ga.) American Union, 1860.
Harper's Weekly (N.Y.), 1861–65.
Harris County (Ga.) Enterprise, 1860.
LaGrange (Ga.) Reporter, 1865.
Macon (Ga.) Journal and Messenger, 1864.
Macon (Ga.) Telegraph, 1860–65.

Milledgeville (Ga.) *Confederate Union*, 1863–65.
Milledgeville (Ga.) *Federal Union*, 1860.
Milledgeville (Ga.) *Southern Federal Union*, 1862.
Milledgeville (Ga.) *Southern Recorder*, 1861, 1863–65.
New York Times, 1863.
Richmond (Va.) *Examiner*, 1862.
Rome (Ga.) *Tri-Weekly Courier*, 1860–63.
Rome (Ga.) *Weekly Courier*, 1861.
Savannah (Ga.) *Morning News*, 1861–63.
Savannah (Ga.) *Republican*, 1862–64.
Thomaston (Ga.) *Upson Pilot*, 1860–61.
Thomasville (Ga.) *Southern Enterprise*, 1861.
Troy (Ala.) *Southern Advertiser*, 1863.
Turnwold (Ga.) *Countryman*, 1862–65.
Valdosta (Ga.) *Times*, 1884.

Books, Articles, and Other Materials

Acts of the General Assembly of the State of Georgia, 1861. Milledgeville, Ga.: Boughton, Nisbet, and Barnes, 1862.

Acts of the General Assembly of the State of Georgia, 1862. Milledgeville, Ga.: Boughton, Nisbet, and Barnes, 1863.

Adjutant and Inspector General's Incoming Correspondence. Georgia Department of Archives and History, Atlanta.

Adjutant General's Letter Books. Georgia Department of Archives and History, Atlanta.

Ambrose, Stephen E. "Yeoman Discontent in the Confederacy." *Civil War History* 8 (1962): 259–68.

American Annual Cyclopedia, 1862. New York: D. Appleton, 1862.

Amos, Harriet E. "'All Absorbing Topics': Food and Clothing in Confederate Mobile." *Atlanta Historical Journal* 22 (1978): 17–28.

Andrews, William H. *Footprints of a Regiment: A Recollection of the First Georgia Regulars, 1861–1865*. Introduction by Richard M. McMurry. Atlanta: Longstreet Press, 1992.

Atkins, James. Diary. Civil War Miscellany, Personal Papers. Georgia Department of Archives and History, Atlanta.

Avery, I. W. *History of the State of Georgia*. New York: Brown and Derby, 1881.

Bailey, Fred A. *Class and Tennessee's Confederate Generation*. Chapel Hill: University of North Carolina Press, 1987.

Baker, Robin E. "Class Conflict and Political Upheaval: The Transformation of North Carolina Politics during the Civil War." *North Carolina Historical Review* 69 (1992): 148–78.

Barfield, Louise Calhoun. *History of Harris County, Georgia, 1827–1961*. Columbus, Ga.: Columbus Office Supply, 1961.

Barnesly, Godfrey. Papers. Felix Hargrett Rare Book and Manuscript Library, University of Georgia, Athens.
Barney, William L. *The Road to Secession: A New Perspective on the Old South.* New York: Praeger, 1972.
———. *The Secessionist Impulse: Alabama and Mississippi in 1860.* Princeton: Princeton University Press, 1974.
Barrow, David C. Papers. Felix Hargrett Rare Book and Manuscript Library, University of Georgia, Athens.
Bartley, Numan V. *The Creation of Modern Georgia.* 2d ed. Athens: University of Georgia Press, 1990.
Battey, George Magruder, Jr. *A History of Rome and Floyd County.* Vol. 1. Atlanta: Webb and Vary, 1922.
Beals, Carleton. *War within a War: The Confederacy against Itself.* Philadelphia and New York: Chilton, 1965.
Beringer, Richard E., Herman Hattaway, Archer Jones, and William N. Still. *Why the South Lost the Civil War.* Athens: University of Georgia Press, 1986.
Berrien County, Ga., Inferior Court. Minutes. Georgia Department of Archives and History, Atlanta.
Berrien County, Ga., Superior Court. Minute Book, 1858–1865. Berrien County Courthouse, Nashville.
Bibb County, Ga., Superior Court. Minute Book 10. Bibb County Courthouse, Macon.
Blair, William. *Virginia's Private War: Feeding Body and Soul in the Confederacy, 1861–1865.* New York: Oxford University Press, 1998.
Blakey, Arch Fredric, Ann Smith Lainhart, and Winston Bryant Stephens, Jr., eds. *Rose Cottage Chronicles: Civil War Letters of the Bryant-Stephens Families of North Florida.* Gainesville: University Press of Florida, 1998.
Bleckley, Logan E., comp. *Cases in Law and Equity Argued and Determined in the Supreme Court of the State of Georgia.* Vol. 34. Charlottesville, Va.: Michie, 1904.
Bohannon, Keith S. "They Had Determined to Root Us Out: Dual Memoirs by a Unionist Couple in Blue Ridge Georgia." In *Enemies of the Country: New Perspectives on Unionists in the Civil War South,* edited by John C. Inscoe and Robert C. Kenzer. Athens: University of Georgia Press, 2001.
Bolton, Charles C. *Poor Whites of the Antebellum South: Tenants and Laborers in Central North Carolina and Northeast Mississippi.* Durham, N.C.: Duke University Press, 1994.
Boney, F. N. *Southerners All.* Macon, Ga.: Mercer University Press, 1984.
Bonner, James C. "David R. Snelling: A Story of Desertion and Defection in the Civil War." *Georgia Review* 10 (1955): 275–82.
Bouton, Cynthia A. *The Flour War: Gender, Class, and Community in Late Ancien Régime French Society.* University Park: Pennsylvania State University Press, 1993.
Boyd Letters. Columbus State University Archives, Columbus, Ga.

Bragg, William Harris. *Joe Brown's Army: The Georgia State Line, 1862–1865*. Macon, Ga.: Mercer University Press, 1987.
Briant, Huldah Annie Fain. Papers. Duke University, Durham, N.C.
Brooks County, Ga., Inferior Court. Minute Book 1. Brooks County Courthouse, Quitman.
Brooks County, Ga., Superior Court. Minute Book A. Microfilm, Ellen Odom Genealogical Library, Moultrie.
Brooks, R. P., ed. "Howell Cobb Papers." *Georgia Historical Quarterly* 6 (1922): 355–94.
Brooks, William. Civil War Letter. AC 00-268. Georgia Department of Archives and History, Atlanta.
Brown, Joseph E. Papers. Felix Hargrett Rare Book and Manuscript Library, University of Georgia, Athens.
Brown, Joseph E. Papers. Library of Congress, Washington, D.C.
Bryan, T. Conn. *Confederate Georgia*. Athens: University of Georgia Press, 1953.
Burnett, Edmund Cody, ed. "Letters of Barnett Hardeman Cody and Others, 1861–1864." *Georgia Historical Quarterly* 23 (1939): 265–99, 362–80.
Bynum, Victoria E. *Mississippi's Longest Civil War: Memory, Community, and the Free State of Jones*. Chapel Hill: University of North Carolina Press, 2001.
———. Review of *Poor Whites of the Antebellum South*, by Charles C. Bolton. *Journal of Southern History* 61 (1995): 601–2.
———. "Telling and Retelling the Legend of the 'Free State of Jones.'" In *Guerrillas, Unionists, and Violence on the Confederate Home Front*, edited by Daniel E. Sutherland. Fayetteville: University of Arkansas Press, 1999.
———. *Unruly Women: The Politics of Social and Sexual Control in the Old South*. Chapel Hill: University of North Carolina Press, 1992.
Cain, Andrew W. *History of Lumpkin County*. Atlanta: Stein, 1932.
Candler, Allen D., comp. *The Confederate Records of Georgia*. 6 vols. (vol. 5 never published). Atlanta: State Printing Office, 1909–11.
Carey, Anthony Gene. *Parties, Slavery, and the Union in Antebellum Georgia*. Athens: University of Georgia Press, 1997.
Carlson, David. "'The Distemper of the Time': Conscription, the Courts, and Planter Privilege in Civil War South Georgia." *Journal of Southwest Georgia History* 14 (1999): 1–24.
———. "The 'Loanly Runagee': Draft Evaders in Confederate South Georgia." *Georgia Historical Quarterly* 84 (2000): 589–615.
———. "Wiregrass Runners: Conscription, Desertion, and the Origins of Discontent in Civil War South Georgia." Master's thesis, Valdosta State University, 1999.
Cecil-Fronsman, Bill. *Common Whites: Class and Culture in Antebellum North Carolina*. Lexington: University of Kentucky Press, 1992.
Channing, Steven A. *Confederate Ordeal: The Southern Home Front*. Alexandria, Va.: Time-Life Books, 1984.

Chapman, R. D. *A Georgia Soldier in the Civil War, 1861–1865.* Houston: n.p., 1923.
Chatham County, Ga., Superior Court. Minute Book 24. Microfilm 0183766. Church of Jesus Christ of Latter-day Saints, Salt Lake City, Utah.
Chatham County, Ga., Superior Court. Minute Book 25. Microfilm 0183766. Church of Jesus Christ of Latter-day Saints, Salt Lake City, Utah.
Chesnut, Mary Boykin Miller. *Mary Chesnut's Civil War.* Edited by C. Vann Woodward. New Haven: Yale University Press, 1981.
Chesson, Michael B. "Bread Riots." In *The Encyclopedia of the Confederacy,* edited by Richard N. Current. New York: Simon and Schuster, 1993.
———. "Harlots or Heroines? A New Look at the Richmond Bread Riot." *Virginia Magazine of History and Biography* 92 (1984): 131–75.
Christian, Rebecca. "Georgia and the Confederate Policy of Impressing Supplies." *Georgia Historical Quarterly* 28 (1944): 1–33.
Civil War Miscellany. Georgia Department of Archives and History, Atlanta.
Clay County, Ga., Superior Court. Minute Book. Clay County Courthouse, Fort Gaines.
Clements, J. B. *History of Irwin County.* 1932. Reprint, Spartanburg, S.C.: Reprint Company, 1997.
Cleveland, Henry. *Alexander H. Stephens in Public and Private with Letters and Speeches, Before, During, and Since the War.* Philadelphia: National Publishing, 1866.
Clinton, Catherine. *The Plantation Mistress: Woman's World in the Old South.* New York: Pantheon, 1982.
———. *Tara Revisited: Women, War, and the Plantation Legend.* New York: Abbeville Press, 1995.
Cobb, Howell. Papers. Felix Hargrett Rare Book and Manuscript Library, University of Georgia, Athens.
Cobb, Thomas R. R. *A Digest of the Statutes of the State of Georgia in Force Prior to the Session of the General Assembly of 1851.* Vol. 2. Athens: Georgia General Assembly, 1851.
Compiled Service Records of the Confederate Soldiers Who Served in Organizations from the State of Georgia. Microcopy 266. National Archives, Washington, D.C.
Confederate Bible Records. United Daughters of the Confederacy. Georgia Department of Archives and History, Atlanta.
Confederate Letters. United Daughters of the Confederacy. Georgia Department of Archives and History, Atlanta.
Confederate Reminiscences and Letters. 7 vols. Atlanta: United Daughters of the Confederacy, Georgia Division, 1997.
Co-Operation Meeting of the Citizens of Stewart County, December 18, 1860. Broadside in Stewart, Archives Folder, File 2, Counties. Georgia Department of Archives and History, Atlanta.

Coulter, E. Merton. *The Confederate States of America, 1861–1865.* Baton Rouge: Louisiana State University Press, 1950.
Covington, W. A. *History of Colquitt County.* Atlanta: Foote and Davies, 1937.
Crawford, George B. "Cotton, Land, and Sustenance: Toward the Limits of Abundance in Late Antebellum Georgia." *Georgia Historical Quarterly* 72 (1988): 215–47.
Crist, Lynda Lasswell, and Mary Seaton Dix, eds. *The Papers of Jefferson Davis.* Vol. 7. Baton Rouge: Louisiana State University Press, 1992.
Cumming, Kate. *Gleanings from Southland: Sketches of Life and Manners of the People of the South Before, During, and After the War of Secession.* Birmingham, Ala.: Roberts and Sons, 1895.
———. *The Journal of Kate Cumming—A Confederate Nurse, 1862–1865.* Edited by Richard Harwell. Savannah, Ga.: Beehive Press, 1975.
Current, Richard Nelson. *Lincoln's Loyalists: Union Soldiers from the Confederacy.* 1992. Reprint, New York: Oxford University Press, 1994.
Cuyler, Talemon. Collection. Felix Hargrett Rare Book and Manuscript Library, University of Georgia, Athens.
Davidson, William H. *Brooks of Honey and Butter: Plantations and People of Meriwether County, Georgia.* 2 vols. Alexander City, Ala.: Outlook, 1971.
Davis, George B., et. al. *Official Military Atlas of the Civil War.* 1894–95. Reprint, New York: Fairfax Press, 1983.
Davis, Robert S. "White and Black in Blue: The Recruitment of Federal Units in Civil War North Georgia." *Georgia Historical Quarterly* 85 (2001): 347–74.
———. "Forgotten Union Guerrilla Fighters from the North Georgia Mountains." *North Georgia Journal* 5 (Summer 1988): 30–40.
———, ed. "Memoirs of a Partisan War: Sion Darnell Remembers North Georgia." *Georgia Historical Quarterly* 80 (1996): 93–116.
Davis, William C. *The Cause Lost: Myths and Realities of the Confederacy.* Lawrence: University Press of Kansas, 1996.
DeBats, Donald A. *Elites and Masses: Political Structure, Communication, and Behavior in Ante-Bellum Georgia.* New York: Garland, 1990.
DeCredico, Mary A. *Patriotism for Profit: Georgia's Urban Entrepreneurs and the Confederate War Effort.* Chapel Hill: University of North Carolina Press, 1990.
Degler, Carl. *The Other South: Southern Dissenters in the Nineteenth Century.* 1974. Reprint, Boston: Northeastern University Press, 1982.
Devens, Richard M. *The Pictorial Book of Anecdotes and Incidents of the War of the Rebellion.* Hartford, Conn.: Hartford Publishing, 1866.
Dillard, Philip David. "Arming the Slaves: Transformation of the Public Mind." Master's thesis, University of Georgia, 1994.
Dooly County, Ga., Superior Court. Minute Book, 1857–1871. Dooly County Courthouse, Vienna.
Dougherty County, Ga., Superior Court. Deed Book 3. Dougherty County Courthouse, Albany.

Dougherty County, Ga., Superior Court. Minute Book L. Dougherty County Courthouse, Albany.

Duker, William F. *A Constitutional History of Habeas Corpus.* Contributions in Legal Studies, no. 13. Westport, Conn.: Greenwood Press, 1980.

Dupont Letters. Valdosta–Lowndes County Historical Society, Valdosta, Ga.

Durden, Robert F. *The Gray and the Black: The Confederate Debate on Emancipation.* Baton Rouge: Louisiana State University Press, 1972.

Durrill, Wayne K. *War of Another Kind: A Southern Community in the Great Rebellion.* New York: Oxford University Press, 1990.

Dyer, Thomas G. *Secret Yankees: The Union Circle in Confederate Atlanta.* Baltimore: Johns Hopkins University Press, 1999.

Edwards, Laura F. *Scarlett Doesn't Live Here Anymore: Southern Women in the Civil War Era.* Urbana: University of Illinois Press, 2000.

Elbert County, Ga., Superior Court. Minute Book, 1862–1868. Microfilm no. 0209478. Church of Jesus Christ of Latter-day Saints, Salt Lake City, Utah.

Ellis, Daniel. *The Thrilling Adventures of Daniel Ellis.* New York: Harper and Brothers, 1867.

Escott, Paul D. *After Secession: Jefferson Davis and the Failure of Confederate Nationalism.* Baton Rouge: Louisiana State University Press, 1978.

———. "Joseph E. Brown, Jefferson Davis, and the Problem of Poverty in the Confederacy." *Georgia Historical Quarterly* 61 (1977): 59–71.

———. *Many Excellent People: Power and Privilege in North Carolina, 1850–1900.* Chapel Hill: University of North Carolina Press, 1985.

———. "Southern Yeomen and the Confederacy." *South Atlantic Quarterly* 77 (1978): 146–58.

Faust, Drew Gilpin. *Mothers of Invention: Women of the Slaveholding South in the American Civil War.* Chapel Hill: University of North Carolina Press, 1996.

Fehrenbacher, Don. E. *Constitutions and Constitutionalism in the Slaveholding South.* Mercer University Lamar Memorial Lectures, no. 31. Athens, Ga., 1989.

Fitzhugh, George. *Sociology for the South, or the Failure of Free Society.* New York: Burt Franklin, 1854.

Fleming, Walter L. *Civil War and Reconstruction in Alabama.* New York: Columbia University Press, 1905.

Flynt, Wayne. *Poor but Proud: Alabama's Poor Whites.* Tuscaloosa: University of Alabama Press, 1989.

Foner, Eric. *Reconstruction: America's Unfinished Revolution, 1863–1877.* New York: Harper and Row, 1988.

Formwalt, Lee W. "Planters and Cotton Production as a Cause of Confederate Defeat: Evidence from Southwest Georgia." *Georgia Historical Quarterly* 74 (1990): 269–76.

Fox-Genovese, Elizabeth. *Within the Plantation Household: Black and White Women of the Old South.* Chapel Hill: University of North Carolina Press, 1988.

Freehling, William W. *The Road to Disunion: Secessionists at Bay, 1776–1854*. New York: Oxford University Press, 1990.
———. *The South vs. the South: How Anti-Confederate Southerners Shaped the Course of the Civil War*. New York: Oxford University Press, 2001.
Freehling, William W., and Craig M. Simpson, eds. *Secession Debated: Georgia's Showdown in 1860*. New York: Oxford University Press, 1992.
Gallagher, Gary W. *The Confederate War*. Cambridge: Harvard University Press, 1997.
Gates, Paul W. *Agriculture and the Civil War*. New York: Knopf, 1965.
Genovese, Eugene. *The World the Slaveholders Made*. New York: Pantheon, 1969.
Georgia Department of Defense. Lists of Men Enrolled in the Georgia Militia by Militia Districts as required by the Act of 14 December 1863, for Re-organizing the Militia of the State. Georgia Department of Archives and History, Atlanta.
Gienapp, William E., ed. *The Civil War and Reconstruction: A Documentary Collection*. New York: Norton, 2001.
Gillespie, Michelle. *Free Labor in an Unfree World: White Artisans in Slaveholding Georgia, 1789–1860*. Athens: University of Georgia Press, 2000.
Gilmore, Grant. *The Ages of American Law*. New Haven: Yale University Press, 1977.
Goodman, Paul. "White Over White: Planters, Yeomen, and the Coming of the Civil War: A Review Essay." *Agricultural History* 54 (1980): 446–52.
Governor's Incoming Correspondence, 1861–65. Georgia Department of Archives and History, Atlanta.
Governor's Letter Book, 1861–65. Georgia Department of Archives and History, Atlanta.
Governor's Petitions, 1861–65. Georgia Department of Archives and History, Atlanta.
Graham, Christopher A. "Women's Revolt in Rowan County." *Columbiad: A Quarterly Review of the War between the States* 3 (1999): 131–47.
Grant, Donald L. *The Way It Was in the South: The Black Experience in Georgia*. Edited with introduction by Jonathan Grant. New York: Birch Lane Press, 1993.
Grice, Warren. "The Confederate States Court for Georgia." *Georgia Historical Quarterly* 9 (1925): 131–58.
Hague, Parthenia A. *A Blockaded Family: Life in Southern Alabama during the Civil War*. 1888. Reprint, Freeport, N.Y.: Books for Libraries Press, 1971.
Hahn, Steven. *The Roots of Southern Populism: Yeoman Farmers and the Transformation of the Georgia Upcountry, 1850–1890*. New York: Oxford University Press, 1983.
Hall, Kermit. *The Politics of Justice: Lower Federal Judicial Selection and the Second Party System, 1829–1861*. Lincoln: University of Nebraska Press, 1979.
Hamilton, J. G. De Roulhac. "The State Courts and the Confederate Constitution." *Journal of Southern History* 4 (1938): 425–48.
Harden, Edward. Papers. Duke University, Durham, N.C.

Harris, J. William. *Plain Folk and Gentry in a Slave Society: White Liberty and Black Slavery in Augusta's Hinterlands*. Middletown, Conn.: Wesleyan University Press, 1985.
Harwell, Richard, and Philip N. Racine, eds. *The Fiery Trail: A Union Officer's Account of Sherman's Last Campaign*. Knoxville: University of Tennessee Press, 1986.
Helper, Hinton Rowan. *The Impending Crisis of the South*. New York: Burdick Brothers, 1857.
Henderson, Lillian, comp. *Roster of the Confederate Soldiers of Georgia, 1861–1865*. 6 vols. Hapeville, Ga.: Longina and Porter, 1959–64.
Hewett, Janet B., ed. *Supplement to the Official Records of the Union and Confederate Armies*. 85 vols. Wilmington, N.C.: Broadfoot Publishing, 1995.
Hill, Benjamin H., Jr. *Senator Benjamin H. Hill of Georgia: His Life, Speeches, and Writings*. Atlanta: H. C. Hudgins, 1891.
Historical Background of Dougherty County, 1836–1940. Atlanta: Cherokee Publishing, 1981.
History and Reminiscences of Dougherty County, Georgia. Albany, Ga.: Daughters of the American Revolution, Thronateeska Chapter, 1924.
Hodler, Thomas W., and Howard A. Schretter. *The Atlas of Georgia*. Athens, Ga.: Institute of Community and Area Development, 1986.
Houghton, W. R., and M. B. Houghton. *Two Boys in the Civil War and After*. Montgomery, Ala.: Paragon Press, 1912.
Hufton, Olwen. *The Prospect before Her: A History of Women in Western Europe*. Vol. 1, *1500–1800*. New York: Knopf, 1996.
Huxford, Folks. *The History of Brooks County, Georgia*. 1948. Reprint, Spartanburg, S.C.: Reprint Company, 1978.
Inscoe, John C. "'Moving Through Deserter Country': Fugitive Accounts of the Inner Civil War in Southern Appalachia." In *The Civil War in Appalachia: Collected Essays*, edited by Kenneth W. Noe and Shannon H. Wilson. Knoxville: University of Tennessee Press, 1997.
Inscoe, John C., and Robert C. Kenzer, eds. *Enemies of the Country: New Perspectives on Unionists in the Civil War South*. Athens: University of Georgia Press, 2001.
Irwin County, Ga., Court of the Ordinary. Inventories, Appraisement, Returns, Sales, and Miscellaneous Estate Records, Book No. 12, 1864–71. Irwin County Courthouse, Ocilla.
Irwin County, Ga., Inferior Court. Minute Book, 1852–1878. Irwin County Courthouse, Ocilla.
Johnson, Michael P. "A New Look at the Popular Vote for Delegates to the Georgia Secession Convention." *Georgia Historical Quarterly* 56 (1972): 259–75.
———. *Toward a Patriarchal Republic: The Secession of Georgia*. Baton Rouge: Louisiana State University Press, 1977.
Jordan, Ervin L. *Black Confederates and Afro-Yankees in Civil War Virginia*. Charlottesville: University Press of Virginia, 1995.

Journal of the Public and Secret Proceedings of the Convention of the People of Georgia, 1861. Milledgeville, Ga.: Boughton, Nisbet, and Barnes, 1861.

Kibler, Lillian A. "Unionist Sentiment in South Carolina in 1860." *Journal of Southern History* 4 (1938): 346–66.

Kinsland, William S. "The Civil War Comes to Lumpkin County." *North Georgia Journal* 1 (Summer 1984): 21–26.

Krakow, Kenneth K. *Georgia Place-Names*. Macon, Ga.: Winship Press, 1975.

Lebergott, Stanley. "Through the Blockade: The Profitability and Extent of Cotton Smuggling, 1861–1865." *Journal of Economic History* 41 (1981): 867–88.

———. "Why the South Lost: Commercial Purpose in the Confederacy." *Journal of American History* 70 (1983): 58–74.

Lee County, Ga., Superior Court. Minute Book C. Lee County Courthouse, Leesburg.

Lester, George N., comp. *Cases in Law and Equity Argued and Determined in the Supreme Court of the State of Georgia*. Vols. 33 and 33a. 1870. Reprint, Atlanta: Franklin-Turner, 1907.

Letters Received, Confederate Secretary of War. National Archives, Washington, D.C.

Lipset, Seymour Martin. *Political Man: The Social Bases of Politics*. Expanded ed. Baltimore: Johns Hopkins University Press, 1981.

Lockley, Timothy James. *Lines in the Sand: Race and Class in Lowcountry Georgia, 1750–1860*. Athens: University of Georgia Press, 2001.

Longstreet, James. *From Manassas to Appomattox: Memoirs of the Civil War in America*. Philadelphia: Lippincott, 1896.

Lonn, Ella. *Desertion during the Civil War*. 1928. Reprint, with a new introduction by William Blair. Lincoln: University of Nebraska Press, 1998.

———. *Foreigners in the Confederacy*. 1940. Reprint, Gloucester, Mass.: Peter Smith, 1965.

Lowndes County, Ga., Superior Court. Minute Book A. Valdosta–Lowndes County Historical Society, Valdosta.

MacIntyre, Archibald T. Papers. Record Group 1097-1. Georgia Department of Archives and History, Atlanta.

Mann Civil War Papers. Georgia Department of Archives and History, Atlanta.

Martis, Kenneth C. *The Historical Atlas of the Congresses of the Confederate States of America, 1861–1865*. Gyula Pauer, cartographer. New York: Simon and Schuster, 1994.

McCrary, Peyton, Clark Miller, and Dale Baum. "Class and Party in the Secession Crisis: Voting Behavior in the Deep South, 1856–1861." *Journal of Interdisciplinary History* 8 (1978): 429–57.

McCurry, Stephanie. *Masters of Small Worlds: Yeoman Households, Gender Relations, and the Political Culture of the Antebellum South Carolina Low Country*. New York: Oxford University Press, 1995.

McGee, Val L. *Claybank Memories: A History of Dale County, Alabama*. Ozark, Ala.: Dale County Historical Society, 1989.
McLeod, Roscoe H., and Maryann McLeod, eds. *The Civil War Letters of Bryant Folsom*. Quitman, Ga.: Brooks County Genealogical Society, 1990.
McPherson, James M. "American Victory, American Defeat." In *Why the Confederacy Lost*, edited by Gabor S. Boritt. New York: Oxford University Press, 1992.
———. *Drawn with the Sword*. New York: Oxford University Press, 1996.
McWhiney, Grady. *Cracker Culture: Celtic Ways in the Old South*. Tuscaloosa: University of Alabama Press, 1988.
Mercer, George A. Diary. Southern Historical Collection, University of North Carolina, Chapel Hill.
Meyers, Christopher C. "'The Wretch Vickery' and the Brooks County Civil War Slave Conspiracy." *Journal of Southwest Georgia History* 12 (1997): 27–38.
Miller, Caroline. *Lamb in His Bosom*. New York: Harper and Brothers, 1933.
"Miss Abby's" Diary. Felix Hargrett Rare Book and Manuscript Library, University of Georgia, Athens.
Mitchell, Margaret. *Gone with the Wind*. New York: Macmillan, 1936.
Mohr, Clarence L. *On the Threshold of Freedom: Masters and Slaves in Civil War Georgia*. Athens: University of Georgia Press, 1986.
———. "Slavery and Class Tensions in Confederate Georgia." *Gulf Coast Historical Review* 4 (1989): 58–72.
Moneyhon, Carl H. "Disloyalty and Class Consciousness in Southwestern Arkansas, 1852–1865." *Arkansas Historical Quarterly* 52 (1993): 223–43.
Moore, Albert Burton. *Conscription and Conflict in the Confederacy*. 1924. Reprint, Columbia: University of South Carolina Press, 1996.
Moore, John Hammond. "Sherman's 'Fifth Column': A Guide to Unionist Activity in Georgia." *Georgia Historical Quarterly* 68 (1984): 382–409.
Mueller, Edward A. *Perilous Journeys: A History of Steamboating on the Chattahoochee, Apalachicola, and Flint Rivers, 1828–1928*. Eufaula, Ala.: Historic Chattahoochee Commission, 1990.
Murdock, Eugene Converse. *Patriotism Limited, 1862–1865: The Civil War Draft and the Bounty System*. Kent, Ohio: Kent State University Press, 1967.
Murray, Alton J. *South Georgia Rebels: The True Wartime Experiences of the 26th Regiment Georgia Volunteer Infantry, Lawton-Gordon-Evans Brigade, Confederate States Army, 1861–1865*. St. Marys, Ga.: Alton J. Murray, 1976.
Neely, Mark E. *Southern Rights: Political Prisoners and the Myth of Confederate Constitutionalism*. Charlottesville: University Press of Virginia, 1999.
Nisbet, James Cooper. *Four Years on the Firing Line*. Edited by Bell Irvin Wiley. Jackson, Tenn.: McCowat-Mercer Press, 1963.
Noble-Attaway Papers. Southern Historical Collection, University of North Carolina, Chapel Hill.
Nolan, Alan T. *Lee Considered: General Robert E. Lee and Civil War History*. Chapel Hill: University of North Carolina Press, 1991.

Oakes, James. *Slavery and Freedom: An Interpretation of the Old South*. New York: Vintage, 1990.
O'Donovan, Susan E., ed. "The Journal of Nelson Tift." *Journal of Southwest Georgia History* 3 (1985): 64–100.
O'Sullivan, John, and Alan M. Meckler, eds. *The Draft and Its Enemies: A Documentary History*. Urbana: University of Illinois Press, 1974.
Owens, Thomas. "Penalties for Desertion." *Confederate Veteran* 2 (1894): 235.
Owsley, Frank L. "Defeatism in the Confederacy." *North Carolina Historical Review* 3 (1926): 446–56.
———. *Plain Folk of the Old South*. Baton Rouge: Louisiana State University Press, 1949.
———. *State Rights in the Confederacy*. 1925. Reprint, Gloucester, Mass.: Peter Smith, 1961.
Pendleton, Louis B. *In the Okefenokee: A Story of War Time and the Great Georgia Swamp*. Boston: Roberts Brothers, 1895.
Percy, William Alexander. "Localizing the Context of Confederate Politics: The Congressional Election of 1863 in Georgia's First District." *Georgia Historical Quarterly* 79 (1995): 192–209.
Phillips, Ulrich B., ed. *The Correspondence of Robert Toombs, Alexander H. Stephens, and Howell Cobb*. Washington, D.C.: Government Printing Office, 1913.
Pioneers of Wiregrass Georgia. Vol. 8. Homerville, Ga.: Huxford Genealogical Society, 1988.
Potter, David M. *Lincoln and His Party in the Secession Crisis*. 1942. Reprint, with a new introduction by Daniel W. Crofts, Baton Rouge: Louisiana State University Press, 1995.
Prescott, Emma J. Slade. Reminiscences. Atlanta Historical Society Archives, Atlanta.
Purcell, Douglas Clare. "Military Conscription in Alabama during the Civil War." *Alabama Review* 34 (1981): 94–106.
Rable, George C. *Civil Wars: Women and the Crisis of Southern Nationalism*. Urbana: University of Illinois Press, 1989.
Range, Willard. *A Century of Georgia Agriculture, 1850–1950*. Athens: University of Georgia Press, 1954.
Rawick, George P., ed. *The American Slave: A Composite Autobiography*. Series 1 and 2. 19 vols. Supplement, Series 1. 12 vols. Westport, Conn.: Greenwood Press, 1972 and 1977.
Reiger, John F. "Deprivation, Disaffection, and Desertion in Confederate Florida." *Florida Historical Quarterly* 48 (1969–70): 279–98.
Report of the Chief Engineers, Presidents, and Superintendents of the Southwestern Railroad Company of Georgia from No. 1 to 22 Inclusive with the Charter and Amendments Thereto. Macon, Ga.: J. W. Burke, 1869.
Riley, James A. "Desertion and Disloyalty in Georgia during the Civil War." Master's thesis, University of Georgia, 1951.

Robbins, John B. "The Confederacy and the Writ of Habeas Corpus." *Georgia Historical Quarterly* 55 (1971): 83–101.
Rogers, William Warren. *Antebellum Thomas County, 1825–1861.* Tallahassee: Florida State University, 1963.
———. *Thomas County during the Civil War.* Tallahassee: Florida State University, 1964.
Rudé, George. *The Crowd in the French Revolution.* New York: Oxford University Press, 1959.
———. *The Crowd in History: A Study of Popular Disturbances in France and England, 1730–1848.* New York: Wiley, 1964.
Rutledge, Stephen W. "Stephen W. Rutledge: His Autobiography and Civil War Journal." *East Tennessee Roots* 6 (Fall 1989): 101–12.
"Samuel Henderson Frier, 1833–1863: AWOL from the Confederate Army." *Huxford Genealogical Society Magazine* 26 (1999): 81–83.
Sarris, Jonathan D. "Anatomy of an Atrocity: The Madden Branch Massacre and Guerrilla Warfare in North Georgia, 1861–1865." *Georgia Historical Quarterly* 77 (1993): 679–710.
———. "An Execution in Lumpkin County: Local Loyalties in North Georgia's Civil War." In *The Civil War in Appalachia: Collected Essays*, edited by Kenneth W. Noe and Shannon H. Wilson. Knoxville: University of Tennessee Press, 1997.
Savannah, Ga., City Council. Minutes. Georgia Department of Archives and History, Atlanta.
Sherman, William T. *Memoirs of General William T. Sherman.* 2 vols. New York: D. Appleton, 1875.
Shugg, Roger W. *Origins of Class Struggle in Louisiana.* Baton Rouge: Louisiana State University Press, 1939.
Southern Claims Commission Approved Claims, 1871–80. National Archives, microfiche, Washington, D.C.
Stampp, Kenneth M., ed. *The Causes of the Civil War.* Englewood Cliffs, N.J.: Prentice Hall, 1974.
Standard, Diffee William. *Columbus, Georgia, in the Confederacy: The Social and Industrial Life of the Chattahoochee River Port.* New York: William-Frederick Press, 1954.
Stephens, Alexander H. Papers. Library of Congress, Washington, D.C.
Suarez, Annette McDonald. *A Source Book on the Early History of Cuthbert and Randolph County, Georgia.* Atlanta: Cherokee Publishing, 1982.
Sumter County, Ga., Superior Court. Minute Book. Sumter County Courthouse, Americus.
Sumter County, Ga., Superior Court Records. Georgia Department of Archives and History, Atlanta.
Sutherland, Daniel E. "The Absence of Violence: Confederates and Unionists in Culpeper County, Virginia." In *Guerrillas, Unionists, and Violence on the Confed-*

erate Home Front, edited by Daniel E. Sutherland. Fayetteville: University of Arkansas Press, 1999.

———, ed. *Guerrillas, Unionists, and Violence on the Confederate Home Front*. Fayetteville: University of Arkansas Press, 1999.

Swift, Charles Jewett. *The Last Battle of the Civil War*. Columbus, Ga.: Gilbert Printing, 1915.

Talbot County, Ga., Superior Court. Minute Book. Talbot County Courthouse, Talbotton.

Tatum, Georgia Lee. *Disloyalty in the Confederacy*. 1934. Reprint, with a new introduction by David Williams, Lincoln: University of Nebraska Press, 2000.

Thomas County, Ga., Superior Court. Minute Book, 1858–1865. Thomas County Courthouse, Thomasville.

Thomas County, Ga., Superior Court. Minute Book K. Thomas County Courthouse, Thomasville.

Tice, Douglas O. "'Bread or Blood!': The Richmond Bread Riot." *Civil War Times Illustrated* 12 (1974): 12–19.

Toombs, Robert. *Speech on the Crisis Delivered before the Georgia Legislature*. Washington, D.C.: Lemuel Towers, 1860.

Trowell, C. T. *Exploring the Okefenokee: The Richard L. Hunter Survey of the Okefenokee Swamp, 1856–57*. Research Paper No. 1. Douglas, Ga.: n.p., 1988.

Turner, Maxine. *Navy Gray: A Story of the Confederate Navy on the Chattahoochee and Apalachicola Rivers*. Tuscaloosa: University of Alabama Press, 1988.

Union Missionary Baptist Church Cemetery Records. Miller County, Ga.

Union Primitive Baptist Church, Lanier County, Ga. Minutes. Huxford Genealogical Society Library, Homerville, Ga.

U.S. Bureau of the Census. *Population Schedules of the Fifth Census of the United States: Population Schedule, 1830*. National Archives Microfilm Publications, Washington, D.C.

———. *Population Schedules of the Sixth Census of the United States: Population Schedule, 1840*. National Archives, Washington, D.C.

———. *Population Schedules of the Seventh Census of the United States: Population Schedule, 1850*. National Archives, Washington, D.C.

———. *Population Schedules of the Eighth Census of the United States: Population Schedule, 1860*. National Archives, Washington, D.C.

Walker, Laura Singleton. *The History of Ware County, Georgia*. Macon, Ga.: J. W. Burke, 1934.

Walker, Sandra D. "Living on the Southern Frontier: Georgia Novelist Caroline Miller's View of One Woman's Life in the Other Old South." *Journal of Southwest Georgia History* 13 (1998): 50–61.

Wallenstein, Peter. *From Slave South to New South: Public Policy in Nineteenth-Century Georgia*. Chapel Hill: University of North Carolina Press, 1987.

———. "Rich Man's War, Rich Man's Fight: Civil War and the Transformation of Public Finance in Georgia." *Journal of Southern History* 50 (1984): 15–42.

War of the Rebellion: A Compilation of the Official Records of the Union and Confederate Armies. 128 parts in 70 vols. and atlas. Washington, D.C.: Government Printing Office, 1880–1901. This work is cited in the endnotes as *O.R.*

Ward, Geoffrey C. *The Civil War.* New York: Knopf, 1992.

Ward, Warren P. *Ward's History of Coffee County.* 1930. Reprint, Spartanburg, S.C.: Reprint Company, 1985.

Watkins, Sam R. *"Co. Aytch": A Side Show of the Big Show.* 1882. Reprint, Wilmington, N.C.: Broadfoot Publishing, 1987.

Watson, Thomas A. Small Print Collection, Box 18, No. 79. Georgia Department of Archives and History, Atlanta.

Weitz, Mark A. *A Higher Duty: Desertion among Georgia Troops during the Civil War.* Lincoln: University of Nebraska Press, 2000.

Wetherington, Mark V. *The New South Comes to Wiregrass Georgia, 1860–1910.* Knoxville: University of Tennessee Press, 1994.

Whitehead, Mary Grist, ed. *Collections of Early County Historical Society.* Vol. 1. Colquitt, Ga.: Automat Printers, 1971.

———. *Collections of Early County Historical Society.* Vol. 2. Tallahassee, Fla.: Rose Printing, 1979.

Whites, LeeAnn. *The Civil War as a Crisis in Gender: Augusta, Georgia, 1860–1890.* Athens: University of Georgia Press, 1995.

Wiley, Bell I. *The Plain People of the Confederacy.* 1943. Reprint, with a new introduction by Paul D. Escott, Columbia: University of South Carolina Press, 2000.

———, ed. "The Confederate Letters of John W. Hagan." *Georgia Historical Quarterly* 38 (1954): 170–200, 268–89.

Williams, David. "'The "Faithful Slave" is About Played Out': Civil War Slave Resistance in the Lower Chattahoochee Valley." *Alabama Review* 52 (1999): 83–104.

———. *Johnny Reb's War: Battlefield and Homefront.* Abilene, Tex.: McWhiney Foundation Press, 2000.

———. *Rich Man's War: Class, Caste, and Confederate Defeat in the Lower Chattahoochee Valley.* Athens: University of Georgia Press, 1998.

Williams, Teresa Crisp. "'The Women Rising': Class and Gender in Civil War Georgia." Master's thesis, Valdosta State University, 1999.

Williams, Teresa Crisp, and David Williams. "'The Women Rising': Cotton, Class, and Confederate Georgia's Rioting Women." *Georgia Historical Quarterly* 86 (2002): 49–83.

Wisenbaker, Thannie. Reminiscences. South Georgia Regional Library, Valdosta.

Woodward, C. Vann, ed. *Mary Chesnut's Civil War.* New Haven: Yale University Press, 1981.

Wooster, Ralph. *The People in Power: Courthouse and Statehouse in the Lower South, 1850–1860.* Knoxville: University of Tennessee Press, 1969.

———. *The Secession Conventions of the South.* Princeton: Princeton University Press, 1962.

Wright, Gavin. *The Political Economy of the Cotton South: Households, Markets, and Wealth in the Nineteenth Century.* New York: Norton, 1978.

Wylie, Lollie Belle, ed. *The Memoirs of Judge Richard H. Clark.* Atlanta: Franklin Printing and Publishing, 1898.

Wynne, Lewis N., and Guy Porcher Harrison. "'Plain Folk' Coping in the Confederacy: The Garrett-Asbell Letters." *Georgia Historical Quarterly* 72 (1988): 102–18.

Young, Mary J. "Some Florida Soldiers." United Daughters of the Confederacy Scrapbooks. Vol. 1. Florida State Archives, Tallahassee.

Index

Abingdon, Va., 80
Abolitionism, 11, 133, 136, 190
Abram's Creek, 171
"Absence of Violence: Confederates and Unionists in Culpepper County, Virginia, The," 196n.1
Adair, J. B., 69
Adams, Capt. Asbury A., 122
After Secession: Jefferson Davis and the Failure of Confederate Nationalism, 195n.1, 197n.4
Agriculture and the Civil War, 26
Aids-de-camp, 105, 106, 108, 109–11, 116, 123, 127, 144, 147, 173; spelling of, 215n.38
Aiken, James, 18
Albany, Ga., 32, 33, 39, 40, 49, 69, 103, 122, 136, 171, 174, 188
Albany Bridge Company, 42, 43
Aldrich, A. P., 2
Alexander, M. T., 38
Altamaha River, 32, 169, 171, 172, 177
Amanda, USS, 163
Ambrose, Stephen, 195n.1
Americus, Ga., 57, 69
Amnesty, 162
Anderson, Jeff, 141, 165, 166
Anderson, John, 140

Andersonville prison, 183
Andrews, Sgt. William, 75, 89, 90, 94, 103, 194
Antiwar meetings, 185–87
Apalachicola, Fla., 32, 163–64
"Appeal to the People of Georgia," 30
Appling County, Ga., 50, 65, 184
Appomattox, Va., 194
Archer, Fla., 80
Army of Northern Virginia, 89, 162
Army of Tennessee, 70, 89
Arrington, Maj. Thomas W., 106
Artisans, 196n.2
Asbell, Sarah, 77
Asbell, William, 74, 77
Athens, Ga., 37, 152
Atkins, James, 21, 161
Atlanta, Ga., 4, 37, 39, 62, 76, 80, 82, 115, 124, 130, 140, 163, 166, 179, 181, 187
Aucilla River, 147
Augusta, Ga., 4, 48, 58, 59, 60, 64, 82, 84, 89, 100, 102, 116, 185, 188
Avery, Celestia, 139

Bachlott, John, 66
Bailey, Fred A., 196n.1
Bainbridge, Ga., 32, 126, 174
Baker, Robin E., 195n.1

Baker County, Ga., 29, 41, 73, 137, 144
Baldwin County, Ga., 54, 55, 56, 157
Banks County Guards, 103
Barber v. Irwin, 128
Barnsley, Godfrey, 31, 33, 88, 153
Barrow, David, 92
Barter system, 38, 39, 87. *See also* Currency; Promissory notes
Bartow, Francis, 15
Bartow County, Ga., 18, 31, 38, 58, 80, 88
Bartow Light Infantry, 110
Baum, Jacob, 106
Bear Wallow, La., 6
Benning, Henry L., 13
Beringer, Richard, 199n.20
Berrian County, Ga., 39, 65, 174, 179, 184, 186
Bezley, Robert, 140
Bibb County, Ga., 50, 54, 117, 120, 128, 182, 185, 218n.19
Bigham, Judge Benjamin H., 122, 123
Billingslea, Francis, 128
Bill (slave), 140
Blackjack Island, 172
Black market, 3, 47
Blackshear, Ga., 39, 64, 88, 177, 184, 205n.46
Black soldiers, 136
Blair, B., 54
Blair, William, 196n.1
Blake, H. W., 66
Blakely, Ga., 17, 21, 25, 141, 143
Blasdell, Dr. A., 169
Blockade: Union, 32, 34, 35, 58, 64, 135, 140, 163, 188
Blue and the Gray, The, 6
Blue Ridge Rifles, 103
Bogg's Chapel, Ga., 76
Bolton, Charles C., 196n.1
Bonds, 62
Bone, Mildred, 76–77
Bone, Willis J., 131, 140, 183
Bone Pond, 183
Boney, F. N., 197n.2
Booth, John, 66
Bouton, Cynthia A., 211n.32
Boyd Guards, 103

Brinson, Isaac, 127–28
Britain, 118, 192
Brooks, Pvt. B. F., 72, 189
Brooks, Julia A., 72, 189
Brooks, Mary, 74
Brooks, R. H., 161
Brooks, Rhodam, 74
Brooks County, Ga., 22, 47, 73, 98, 99, 106, 110, 128, 138, 144–50, 174, 177, 215n.43, 223n.48
Brookville, Ga., 72
Brown, Cpl. George, 171
Brown, G. R., 66
Brown, James George, 180
Brown, John, 136
Brown, Gov. Joseph E., 10, 11, 27, 180, 209n.74; and arming of slaves, 190; and class-based politics, 153; and conscription, 96, 99, 105; and corn supplies, 68; and cotton production limitations, 29, 30, 31; and cotton smuggling, 32; and cotton trade, 34; and defense of Atlanta, 179, 181; and deserter roundups, 166; and exemptions, 122; and impressment, 46, 47, 50; letters to, 2, 4, 5, 18, 22, 24, 28, 33, 38, 44, 48, 49, 52, 56, 58, 61, 63, 64, 65, 67, 68, 69, 70, 71–2, 73, 76, 78, 85, 86, 87, 95, 99, 102 ,104, 109, 115, 120, 121, 123, 133, 134, 142, 151, 159, 160, 164, 168, 176, 179, 182, 185, 186; and police patrols, 147; and poor relief, 89; and proclamation on treason, 166; and reorganization of state militia, 160, 220n.51; and salt, 64–65; and secession convention, 13, 20; and slave impressment, 53; and speculation, 39; and state rights, 127
Brucetown, Va., 150
Brunswick, Ga., 136
Brushy Creek Primitive Baptist Church, 162
Bryan, John, 50
Bryan, Soloman, 167
Buchanan, Col. James, 17
Bull Run, Battle of. *See* Manassas (First Battle of, Second Battle of)
Burke County, Ga., 66, 71–72, 121, 132
Burns, John, 102

Burns, Ken, 6
Bush, Isaac, 100
Bush, Judge James, 17, 50, 70
Butts County, Ga., 83
Bynum, Victoria, 195n.1
Byrd, W. H., 22

Cain, John W., 47, 65
Cale, W. C., 56
Calhoun County, Ga., 41, 47, 133, 134–35, 161
Calloway, Mirrel, 122
Camden County, Ga., 171
Camfield, Capt. Caleb H., 126, 174
Campbell, J. A., Assistant Secretary of War, 115
Campbell, W. A., 133
Campbell County, Ga., 14, 87
Camp Jackson, 78
Camp Lamar Cobb, 76, 106
Camp Lee, 171
Camp Oglethorpe, 130
Camp Stephens, 182
Carey, Anthony, 200n.12
Carroll County, Ga., 102
Carrollton, Ga., 102
Cartersville, Ga., 80
Cass County, Ga., 18
Cass Depot, Ga., 80
Castleberry, William, 53
Catoosa County, Ga., 151
Cecil-Fronsman, Bill, 195n.1, 196n.2
Cedar Grove, Ga., 102
Chaires, Capt. Joseph J., 106, 215n.43
Chancellorsville, Battle of, 92
Charlton County, Ga., 171
Chatham County, Ga., 86, 113, 114, 115, 217n.5
Chattahoochee County, Ga., 141, 185
Chattahoochee River, 32, 64, 140, 159–60
Chattanooga, Tenn., 32, 163, 178
Chattooga County, Ga., 13, 95, 160
Cherokee County, Ga., 68
Chessy, Daniel, 189
Chitty, Rachel, 87
Citizenship, Confederate, 117, 205n.46
Civil War: and antiwar sentiments, 160, 191; calls for end to, 152; lower-class perceptions of, 16; northern support for, 17; popular perceptions of, 6–7; southern support for, 36
Civil War, The, 6
Civil War as a Crisis in Gender: Augusta, Georgia, 1860–1890, The, 198n.13
Civil War Journal, 6
Civil Wars: Women and the Crisis of Southern Nationalism, 198n.13
Clark, Judge Richard Henry, 118, 122, 126–28, 130, 209n.74, 218n.24
Clarke, Judge James T., 124–25
Clarke County, Ga., 27, 40, 62, 140
Class: and clothing, 57; distinctions within military, 21, 70; and honor, 79; and impressment, 49; and nationalism, 187; and political consciousness, 152–53; and rioting, 80, 83, 84, 88, 211n.33; and slave impressment, 53; and taxation, 50; tensions, 1, 2, 7, 9–10, 23–24, 70, 188, 193–94, 195n.1, 196n.1; and trade unions, 60; and women's concerns, 71, 72
Class and Tennessee's Confederate Generation, 196n.1
"Class Conflict and Political Upheaval: The Transformation of North Carolina Politics during the Civil War," 195n.1
Clay County, Ga., 53, 137, 140
Clemmons, Mary A., 67
Cleveland, George W., 65
Clinch, Col. Duncan L., 171, 177, 184
Clinch County, Ga., 47, 65, 98, 105, 121, 157, 172, 184
Clinton, Catherine, 198n.13
Cloth, 58, 82. *See also* Thread; Wool; Yarn
Clothing, 48, 93; homespun, 56–57; shoes, 56, 82
Clyattville, Ga., 105
Cobb, Gen. Howell, 14, 32, 100, 102, 126, 146, 159, 160, 162, 184, 185
Cobb County, Ga., 68, 82, 168
Cobb's Legion, 174
Cochran, Peterson B., 132
Cody, Pvt. M. N., 161
Coffee County, Ga., 103, 105, 109, 170, 171, 172, 174, 176, 184

Cole, Sheriff, 86
Collins, Jasper, 3
Colonization, 136
Colquitt, Ga., 4, 80, 88–89, 100
Colquitt, Capt. Jack, 168
Colquitt County, Ga., 28, 65, 68, 106, 176, 183
Columbia County, Ga., 71, 73, 99
Columbus, Ga., 4, 18, 24, 30, 32, 35, 54, 62, 64, 80, 82, 89, 123, 130, 135, 139, 141, 142, 143, 153, 154, 161, 180, 186, 187, 188
Columbus Artillery, 22
Columbus Naval Iron Works, 60
Comer, Laura, 138
Comet, 32
Committees of Public Safety, 28. *See also* Police patrols; Slave patrols; Vigilance committees
Common Whites: Class and Culture in Antebellum North Carolina, 195n.1, 196n.2
Compromise of 1850, 186
Concurrent jurisdiction, 113
Conecuh County, Ala., 140
Confederacy: attorney general of, 113, 217n.4; constitution of, 96, 213n.11, 216n.4, 217n.4; contemporary predictions of defeat of the, 7, 13; lack of support for the, 1, 2, 17, 30, 39, 50, 197n.3; secretary of war of, 128, 179; state courts of, 213n.11, 216n.4, 217n.5
Confederate Bureau of Conscription, 159. *See also* Conscription
Confederate Commissary Bureau, 128; commissary agents, 40, 187
Confederate Congress, 30, 91, 96, 112, 115, 128, 185, 190, 216n.3; First, 153; Second, 5, 153
Confederate Conscription Act, 103, 112–13, 160, 185; of April 1862, 1, 72, 91, 92, 96–97, 105, 112, 137, 193, 217n.5, 220n.56; constitutionality of, 96–97; exemptions from, 92, 220n.51; of February 1864, 97, 217n.5; of September 1862, 97, 127, 220n.56. *See also* Conscription; Exemptions

Confederate States Laboratory, 59
Confederate Supreme Court, 213n.11, 216n.3, 216n.4
Confederate War, The, 199n.20
Confederate War Department, 48, 172
Confiscation, 213n.11
Conscript companies, 166
Conscription, 71, 87, 92–102, 108, 126–27, 128, 138, 142, 153, 162, 174, 185, 191, 217n.5; evasion of, 159; favoritism in, 107–9; officers, 94, 95, 103–4, 105, 127, 164, 184, 196n.1; terms of, 91; Union, 17. *See also* Confederate Conscription Act; Enrollment; Exemptions
Contract theory, 129–30
Cook House, 188
Cooper, Bennett, 69
Cooperationists, 13, 200n.14
Cooper Union, 136
Corn combinations, 41–42
Cotton, 45, 68, 80, 188; "bugs," 29; cards, 58, 207n.38; export bans on, 25, 30; factories, 38; material, 57; and northern industry, 16; overproduction of, 28–32, 124, 191, 193, 196n.1; smuggling of, 25, 32, 33, 100; state limitations on production of, 30–31; tax on seed, 30–31; and voluntary production limits, 27–28, 30, 94; wartime production of, 3, 35, 128, 204n.23; wartime profits from, 33–34
Coulter, Merton E., 191
Coweta County, Ga., 186
Cracker Culture: Celtic Ways in the Old South, 196n.2
Crawford, J. T., 148
Crawford, Joel, 20
Crawford County, Ga., 132
Crawford (deserter), 168
Crawfordville, Ga., 13
Creech, David, 147, 148
Creech, James B., 106, 215n.43
Crime: arson, 87–88, 100, 132, 133, 141, 145, 148, 188; bribery, 32–33, 111; burglary, 75; counterfeiting, 219n.34; disorderly conduct, 86; embezzlement, 48; false imprisonment, 215n.43; inciting slaves, 148; murder, 123, 132; theft, 80,

82, 138, 141, 145, 165, 198n.13; treason, 166. *See also* Deserter gangs; Desertion; Layout gangs; Riots
Croft, Capt. Edward, 22
Cromarty (bounty hunter), 107
Crops: corn, 26, 34, 38, 40, 49, 52, 63, 66, 68, 69, 88, 89, 128; grain, 28, 37; oats, 26; planting of, 68, 76, 128, 161; rice, 86; rye, 40; wheat, 40, 68. *See also* Cotton
Crowd in History: A Study of Popular Disturbances in France and England, 1730–1848, The, 211n.33
Crowd in the French Revolution, The, 211n.33
Crystal Lake, Ga., 183
Cuba, 116, 136
Culpepper, Capt. Marion J., 148
Cumberland Gap, Tenn., 78
Cumberland Island, Ga., 136
Cumming, Kate, 39
Currency: Confederate, 37, 38, 45, 69, 70, 74, 87, 123–25, 130; U. S., 124. *See also* Barter system; Promissory notes
Cuthbert, Ga., 28, 100, 143
Cutliff, John, 128

Dade County, Ga., 18, 65, 168
Dahlonega, Ga., 18, 66, 141, 166, 167, 172, 184
Dalton, Ga., 61, 75
Daniel, William A., 103
Darien, Ga., 20, 171
Darnel, Elias, 180
Davidson, Cullen, 133
Davidson, Capt. David, 109
Davis, President Jefferson, 5, 46, 47, 57, 92, 96, 115, 136, 138, 162, 167, 189, 190, 191, 193
Davis, John, 88
Dawson, Cornelius, 157
Dawson County, Ga., 63, 66
Dawsonville, Ga., 163, 180
Deadman's Bay, Fla., 146, 147
Decatur County, Ga., 16, 74, 77, 106, 126, 144, 174, 189
deGraffenreid, William K., 119

Democratic Party, 186
Deserter gangs, 50, 131–32, 141, 147, 164, 176, 179, 185. *See also* Layout gangs
Deserters, 5, 67, 88, 107, 111, 121, 128, 141, 144, 159, 160, 165, 168, 169, 184, 188; execution of, 75, 78, 90, 162; harboring of, 182–83; and slaves, 131, 174
Desertion, 1, 2, 21, 51, 66, 78, 79, 89, 90, 102, 157, 161, 162, 178, 188, 191, 193, 214n.21
Dickey, William, 182
Dillard, Powell, and Company, 30
Dirt Town, Ga., 95
Discharges, 109, 188, 219n.34; class preference in, 75; forged, 105, 106; medical, 119, 130; as overage, 118; and resignation, 20–21, 219n.34; as underage, 117, 130
Disease, 119; asthma, 76; bronchitis, 76; consumption, 104; epilepsy, 103; pneumonia, 75; tuberculosis, 104; typhoid fever, 76
"Disloyalty and Class Consciousness in Southwestern Arkansas, 1852–1865," 195n.1
Disloyalty in the Confederacy, 195n.1, 197n.3
Dooly County, Ga., 39, 144, 174
Dorris, Francis A., 61
Dougherty, John, 121
Dougherty County, Ga., 40, 41–44, 92, 118, 127, 137, 173, 174
Draft. *See* Confederate Conscription Act; Conscription
"Drummers," 106; definition of, 215n.45
Du Bois, W.E.B., 140
Dunlap, Mollie, 174
Dupont, Lee, 161
Dupree, Jason L., 78
Durham, Lindsey H., 140
Durham, Robert A., 145, 223n.49
Durrill, Wayne K., 196n.1
Dyer, Thomas, 197n.3

Early County, Ga., 17, 38, 50, 69, 70, 72, 80, 88, 91, 100, 141, 143, 144, 174, 188
Early Volunteers, 91, 92

Echols County, Ga., 65, 172, 184, 186
Edgerly, A. S., 97
Edwards, Laura F., 198n.13
Edwards, Samuel, 134
Effingham County, Ga., 134, 141, 160
Elbert County, Ga., 113, 120, 121, 130
Elections: candidate fraud in, 14; class tensions and, 153; of 1861, 23; of 1863, 152, 193; to gain exemptions, 100–102; to Georgia secession convention, 13, 14. *See also* Georgia secession convention
Eleventh Florida Infantry Regiment, 106
Ellijay, Ga., 40
Elliott, Capt. Bufort, 145–46, 148
Emancipation, 135–36, 189–91
Emancipation Proclamation, 135, 192
Emmanuel County, Ga., 18, 66
Enemies of the Country, 197n.3
England, 26, 117, 118, 153, 192
Enrollment, 76; bonuses for, 91, 129; class disparity in, 23, 70, 94; decline in, 2, 21–22; reasons for, 17, 200n.14; and reenlistments, 22. *See also* Conscription; Enrollment officers
Enrollment officers, 72, 99, 100, 106, 109, 116, 120, 121, 122, 169, 172, 177, 219n.33, 219n.34, 227n.56; and corruption, 172–74. *See also* Conscription (officers)
Ersatz, 55–56
Escaped prisoners, 183
Escott, Paul, 23, 193, 195n.1, 197n.4
Espionage, 180
Eubanks, Jane, 71
Eufaula, Ala., 28
Evers, William J., 161
Exemption, 39, 72, 78, 92–94, 97, 100, 106, 109, 128, 173, 182, 191, 219n.34; black market in, 109–10; class disparity in, 104, 111; eligibility for, 92; fees for, 2, 92, 126; medical, 104, 106, 110, 119; repeal of, 92. *See also* Confederate Conscription Act; Conscription; Substitution
Extortionists. *See* Speculation

Fannin County, Ga., 18, 66, 133, 157, 164–65, 167, 181

Farrell, Joseph, 118
Farrell, William, 118
Farrensides, Dr. H. M., 148
Faust, Drew Gilpin, 198n.13
Fayette County, Ga., 13
Fernandina, Fla., 136
Fields, Elizabeth A., 28, 176
Fife, William, 157
Fifteenth Alabama Infantry Regiment, 20
Fifth Tennessee Mounted Infantry, 181
Fifty-first Georgia Infantry Regiment, 122, 161
Findley, James J., 167, 184, 185
Finger, Maj., 167
First Georgia Infantry Regiment, 75, 94, 105, 194
First Georgia State Troops Volunteer Battalion, 181
First Regiment Georgia Reserves, 122
Fisher, Julia, 57
Fitzhugh, George, 11
Fleeman, Richard S., 120
Fleming, Walter, 5
Fleming, Judge William B., 113, 217n.5
Fleming, W. W., 38
Flint River, 32, 41, 42
Florida, 136. *See also under various towns and counties*
Flour War: Gender, Class, and Community in Late and Ancien Régime French Society, The, 211n.32
Floyd County, Ga., 23, 75, 131, 168
Folsom, Bryant, 150
Folsom, Thomas, 148
Food: bacon, 35, 37, 38, 39, 47, 61, 74, 77, 82, 86, 87, 88; butter, 34; coffee, 35, 229n.27; flour, 35, 37; importation of, 26; lard, 38; rum, 35; salt, 34, 37, 64–65, 68, 74, 135, 140; sugar, 37, 38, 39, 86; suggestions to increase Georgia's supply of, 26; supply of, 4, 28–29, 34, 35, 37, 45, 61, 77, 84, 89, 138, 146, 193; syrup, 37; whiskey, 40–41, 76
Foreigners, 39, 218n.19; Irish, 117, 130, 205n.46
Forsyth, Ga., 80, 83
Fort Gaines, Ga., 32, 100, 159, 164

Fort Pulaski, 52
Fort Sumter, 2, 17, 22, 76
Fort Valley, Ga., 24, 37, 132
Forty-seventh New York Infantry Regiment, 226n.56
Foster, Second Lt. G., 75
Fourth Georgia Cavalry, 106, 171, 172, 177
Fox-Genovese, Elizabeth, 198n.13
France, 26, 192
Franklin County, Ga., 100, 160
Frazier, Rev. Garrison, 135
Fredericksburg, Battle of, 92
Free blacks, 132, 135, 136, 137, 143
Freehling, William, 9, 199n.20
Free Labor in an Unfree World: White Artisans in Slaveholding Georgia, 199n.9
French Revolution, 84
Friends of the Union, 186
Frier, Samuel Henderson, 162
Fry, B. J., 185
Fulton County, Ga., 102
Furloughs, 21, 67, 71, 74–75, 76, 78, 89, 100, 106, 110, 128, 161, 176, 188, 189; class preference in, 75
Furlow, T. M., 57

Gainesville, Ga., 166
Gallagher, Gary W., 199n.20
Gallaway (conscription officer), 100
Galt, Capt. E. M., 166
Gates, Paul W., 26
Gaulden, C. S., 22, 147
General Order No. 14, 190
George (slave), 148
Georgia: secession convention in, 13–16, 20; socioeconomic structure of, 8, 9; state arsenal in, 58; state constitution of, 200n.12; state penal code of, 141. *See also under various towns and counties*
—state military districts in: Fifth District (Clinch, Coffee, Ware Counties), 105, 109–11; Seventh District (Brooks, Colquitt, Thomas Counties), 106, 173; Tenth District (Dougherty, Lee, Worth Counties), 127, 173, 220n.51; Twelfth District (Quitman, Stewart, Webster Counties), 173
Georgia Adjutant General's Office, 111, 173. *See also* Wayne, Adjutant General Henry C.
Georgia General Assembly, 40, 141, 143, 152, 190, 209n.74; attempts to limit inflation and speculation, 38; and cotton production limitations, 30, 31; and impressment, 46, 50; and poor relief, 63, 68; and trade unions, 60; and wartime cotton profits, 34
Georgia legislature. *See* Georgia General Assembly
Georgia Reserves Forces, 99, 102, 109, 172, 213n.12
Georgia State Guard, 213n.12
Georgia State Line, 213n.12
Georgia State Supreme Court, 96, 112, 113, 116, 117, 119, 121, 127–28, 218n.24
Georgia v. Philpot, 120
Germany, 118
Gettysburg, 6
Gillespie, Michelle, 199n.9
Gilliland, John, 86
Gilmer County, Ga., 152, 164, 167
Gladdy, Mary, 135–36
Glenn, Joseph M. W., 120
Gone with the Wind, 6, 8, 198n.13
Gordon, Mary, 180
Gordon County, Ga., 13, 134, 180
Gordy, James T., 138
Goss, Horatio, 121
Gould, Judge, 116
Grand juries, 39, 45–46, 52; Baker County, 137; Lowndes County, 138; Muscogee County, 63; Sumter County, 137; Terrell County, 124; Webster County, 124–5; Worth County, 136
Green, George, 170–71
Green, John, 72
Green, Mrs. John, 71–72
Greene County, Ga., 11, 22, 40
Greenville, Ga., 67, 74
Greenwood, M., 41
Greer, Walter P., 116

Grier (merchant), 133
Griffin, Ga., 29, 37, 187
Griffin, Joshua, 65
Griffin, Thomas, 65
Griswoldville, Battle of, 228n.12
Grooverville, Ga., 98
Grouby, E. H., 25, 28, 35, 53, 69, 116, 178, 190
Grow, Milo, 161
Guerrilla bands. *See* Layout gangs
Guerrillas, Unionists, and Violence on the Confederate Homefront, 197n.3
Guerrilla war, 181
Gunpowder, 59

Habeas corpus, writ of, 108, 113–16, 120, 126, 130, 213n.11, 215n.43, 217n.5
Habersham County, Ga., 14, 132
Hahn, Stephen, 195n.1, 196n.2
Hall, James T., 108–9
Hall County, Ga., 66, 166, 179
Hamilton, Col. B. B., 116
Hamlin, Hannibal, 13
Hammack, J. D., 61
Hancock County, Ga., 11, 102
Hansell, Judge Augustin H., 106, 108, 122
Hardee, Capt. Robert A., 147, 148, 177
Hardee's Corps, 75
Harden, Edward, 94
Harris, Alfred, 66
Harris, Andrew T., 157
Harris, Judge L., 82
Harris, William J., 195n.1
Harris County, Ga., 13, 51, 89, 157
Harrison, William, 135
Harris (white man), 134
Hart, John, Jr., 132
Hart, John, Sr., 132
Hart County, Ga., 89, 185
Hartridge, Julian, 153
Harvey, John, 163
Hattaway, Herman, 199n.20
Hawkins, Ella, 136
Head, Capt. James, 102
Heard, Peter, 138
Heard County, Ga., 67
Helper, Hinton Rowan, 11, 132

Hennion, Horatio, 165–66
Henry, John, 60
Hickory Grove, Ga., 132–33
Hill, Sen. Benjamin H., 7, 13, 119
Hill, David P., 43
Hill, H. B., 98–99
Hill, Mrs. Richard B., 72
Hilliard, Rev. H. W., 152–53
Hilliard, Thomas, 109–10
Hoarding, 37, 40, 69. *See also* Speculation
Hog Mountain, Ga., 66
Holaman, J.M.C., 123
Holland, M. B., 20
Holliday, Henry J., 145, 222n.44
Holmes, Jenkins, 121
Holt, Hines, 139
Holt, Samuel, 3
Home guard, 85, 101, 179; Brooks County, 106; federal, 180–81
Homerville, Ga., 184, 226n.56
Homespun. *See* Clothing
Hood, Gen. John B., 106
Houston County, Ga., 172
Huchins, John, 103
Hudlow, Sarah, 66
Huguley, G. W., 75
Humphreys, William C., 47
Humphries, Hillary B., 122, 219n.34
Hunger, 27, 30, 53, 70, 80, 187, 191; as motivation to riot, 83, 84, 85. *See also* Food; Malnutrition; Starvation
Hunt, R. R., 40
Hunter, Lt. George R., 119, 120
Hunter, Richard, 172
Hurst, Eli, 78
Huskey, William F., 140

Immigrants. *See* Foreigners
Impending Crisis of the South, 11, 132
Impressment, 3–4, 45, 46, 50, 58, 77, 83, 153; agents, 49, 52, 164, 196n.1; committees, 47; of free blacks, 143; and impersonation of officers, 169; of livestock, 55; of slaves, 52, 53; by women, 87
Industry: and impressment, 47, 58; and northern pressure for war, 16; southern development of, 11; and trade unions,

60; and Union blockade, 58; and wages, 58–59; working conditions in, 59–60
Inferior courts, 56, 99, 141, 147; Brooks County, 98, 128, 144–50, 215n.43, 223n.48; Chatham County, 115; Cherokee County, 68; Clarke County, 62; Dougherty County, 42; Early County, 100; Fannin County, 66; Hall County, 66; Hart County, 89; Lowndes County, 61; Lumpkin County, 66; Miller County, 88; Muscogee County, 82; Pierce County, 64; Ware County, 66; Washington County, 100; Worth County, 123, 173
Inflation, 34–36, 38, 45, 47, 60, 63, 70, 77, 193. *See also* Barter system; Currency
Inscoe, John C., 197n.3
Irvin, C. M., 52
Irwin County, Ga., 61, 131, 140, 144, 162, 171, 174, 183, 184
Irwinville, Ga., 183, 191

Jackson, Miss., 57
Jackson Artillery, 24
Jackson County, Ala., 6
Jackson County, Ga., 185
Jacksonville, Fla., 136
Jasper County, Ga., 185
Jay, Simon, 117
Jefferson County, Ga., 104
Jeffers v. Fair, 96, 112, 116, 121
Jelks, Dr. E. A., 110–11
Jenkins, Justice Charles, 113, 128
"Jennie Freedom," 57
Jennings, Ira, 117
Johnny Reb's War: Battlefield and Homefront, 196n.1
Johnson, D. A., 179
Johnson, D. H., 152
Johnson, F. S., 22
Johnson, Michael, 200n.12
Johnson, M. W., 100
Johnson County, Ga., 134
Johnston, Gen. Joseph E., 61, 168, 178
Jones, Archer, 199n.20
Jones, Brad, 141

Jones, Col. Edwin T., 123, 127–28, 173, 220n.51
Jones, John, 40
Jones, Col. John J., 108
Jones, John R., 107
Jones, Mitchell, 145–46, 150
Jones, Mrs. Mitchell, 73, 145
Jones County, Ga., 22
Jones County, Miss., 6
Jordan, Duncan, 47, 48
Joyner, W. R., 98
Judiciary, members of: attorneys, 119; bailiffs, 87; judges, 112, 119; justices of the peace, 65, 87, 100, 121, 122, 179. *See also* Georgia Supreme Court; Inferior courts; Superior courts

Kent, Justice James, 217n.4
Kenzer, Robert C., 197n.3
Kierce, George M., 170–71, 183
Kierce, John, 170–71
Kinchafoonee Creek, 169
King, A. S., 103
King, Carrie, 180
King, James, 128
Kingdom of Jones, 6
Kirkland, Amanda Bush, 213n.1
Kirkland, Jacob, 92
Kirkland, Cpl. John Joseph, 91–92, 213n.1
Knight, Newton, 6
Knight, Samuel D., 104, 160
Knight, Thomas S. T., 99
Knight, Wiley, 64
Knowles, Daniel E., 109–10

Labor: and children, 59, 60; and northern whites, 16; and slaves, 11, 52, 60, 142, 199n.9; and women, 57–59. *See also* Industry; Trade unions
LaFayette, Ga., 168
Lafayette, La., 80
Lafayette County, Fla., 146
LaGrange Female College, 38
Lamar, John B., 34
Lamb in His Bosom, 198n.13
Lane, Capt., 148
Lane, Mary, 52, 67

Law: common, 113, 212n.48; martial, 96, 116
Lawton, Capt. Winburn J., 174
Layout gangs, 5, 6, 50, 71, 165, 176, 178. *See also* Deserter gangs
Leather, 56, 68, 85
Lee, Col. George Washington, 166, 172
Lee, Gen. Robert E., 76, 162, 189, 190, 191, 194
Lee County, Ga., 41, 52, 140, 169
Legal fees, 117
Lennard and Jordan, 47
Lester, David, 157–58
Letters: to Georgia government, 71, 100, 182, 198n.13; from soldiers, 79; to soldiers, 74, 76–79, 161. *See also* Brown (letters to); Petitions
Levy County, Fla., 146
Lewis, E. J., 102
Liberty County, Ga., 163, 186
Lincoln, President Abraham, 2, 10, 13, 18, 115, 136, 184, 185, 192, 200n.14
Linton, James A., 109
Liverpool, England, 32
Livestock, 26, 28, 38, 88
Lochrane, Judge Osborn A., 117–18, 120, 130, 205n.46
Longstreet, Gen. James, 157
Lost Cause, 8, 191, 194
Lott, Dr. Daniel, 109–10
Love, Judge Peter E., 186
Lovengard, Elias, 117–18
Lowndes County, Ga., 41, 61, 67, 85, 86, 105, 110, 137, 138, 144, 174
Lumpkin, Ga., 76, 124
Lumpkin County, Ga., 56, 66, 103, 140, 160, 165, 166, 182, 185
Lynching, 52, 133, 190
Lyon, Judge Richard, 68, 209n.74

MacGare, T. J., 188
MacIntyre, Col. Archibald Thomson, 106, 108–9, 138, 147, 173, 219n.34
Macon, Ga., 4, 32, 33, 62, 65, 70, 82–83, 123, 130, 173, 180, 186, 220n.51
Macon Arsenal, 177
Macon County, Ga., 133
Macon Volunteers, 21
Madden, John, 60
Madison, Fla., 145, 146, 147
Madison Court House, Va., 214n.21
Malnutrition, 34. *See also* Food; Hunger; Starvation
Manassas: First Battle of, 2, 20, 21, 34, 35; Second Battle of, 92
Mann, Nancy, 51
Mansfield, Lucius, 124
Mansfield, William, 72
Manufacturing. *See* Industry
Many Excellent People: Power and Privilege in North Carolina, 1850–1900, 195n.1
March to the Sea, 157, 163, 182, 184
Marietta, Ga., 21, 80, 82, 168
Marion County, Ga., 164, 170, 185
Martin, George, 168
Martin, Jere, 103
Martin, Mrs. Philip, 132
Mary Chesnut's Civil War, 198n.13
Mason, Austin, 163
Masonic Lodge No. 217, 110
Massey, S. S., 141
Masters of Small Worlds: Yeoman Households, Gender Relations, and the Political Culture of the Antebellum South Carolina Low Country, 196n.2, 200n.14
Maxwell, J. A., 21
May, Col. Robert, 64
Mayo, First Lt. Reuben, 219n.37
McBurney, James C., 180
McCurry, Stephanie, 196n.2, 200n.14
McDonald, Catherine, 77
McDonald, William, 131
McElrath, Jack, 60
McGlin, Anne, 86
McGregor, John L., 39, 205n.46
McIntosh County, Ga., 131
McIntyre, R., 86
McIntyre, W., 86
McKinney, Jeremiah, 120
McKinnon, Sheriff Duncan, 173
McKinnon, William G., 106

McLane, Julia, 86
McLendon, William, 134
McLeod, Ephraim, 134
McRae, Gustavus, 117
McRae, Hilliard, 117
McWhiney, Grady, 196n.2
Meadows, Louis, 135
Meads, David, 122
Mechanics' and Working Men's Ticket, 153
Medical examining boards, 119
Medicine, 40
Mercer, George A., 94
Mercer, Nathaniel, 127–28
Merchants, 33, 35, 39, 40, 45, 82, 85, 104, 106, 126, 146, 196n.2. See also Speculation
Meriwether County, Ga., 13, 23
Militia, 96, 99, 105, 126, 127, 128, 160, 177, 179, 180, 183, 184, 185, 213n.12; of Brooks County, 106, 147; reorganization of Georgia's, 144, 220n.51
Milledgeville, Ga., 13, 51, 62, 82, 157
Millen, Maj. M. B., 45
Miller, Caroline, 198n.13
Miller, Thomas, 102
Miller County, Ga., 64, 65, 77, 78, 80, 88, 161, 189, 213n.1
Miller County Wildcats, 17, 78
Millican, A. W., 94
Milton County, Ga., 61
Mira, A. F., 86
Miscegenation, 132
Missionary Ridge, Battle of, 157
Mitchell, Margaret, 198n.13. See also Gone with the Wind
Mitchell County, Ga., 45, 134
Mobile, Ala., 4, 80
Mobocracy, 84
Moncrief, Wiley, 117
Money. See Currency
Moneyhon, Carl H., 195n.1
Monroe County, Ga., 83, 134
Monticello, Fla., 146
Morale, 21, 36, 44, 46, 70, 179
Morgan, John C., 134

Morgan County, Ga., 40, 185
Morgan Restaurant, 188
Morgantown, Ga., 41
Morris, J. L., 102
Morton, Judge James O., 145
Morton, J. F., 160
Moseley, Capt. James L., 147
Mosely, Capt. B. F., 62
Mossy Creek, Ga., 165–66
Mothers of Invention: Women of the Slaveholding South in the American Civil War, 198n.13
Mott, Randolph L., 18
Mountain Rangers, 23
Murray County, Ga., 157, 180
Muscogee County, Ga., 63, 82, 123, 136

Nassau, Bahamas, 32, 34
Nationalism, 187, 216n.4, 217n.4
Naylor, Ga., 87
"Needle women," 58
Nelson (slave), 148
Nettles, Hattie, 135
Newton, Ga., 68
New York, N.Y., 32
Nichols, W. M., 72
Nisbet, Eugenius A., 15, 119
Nisbet, Col. James C., 100, 214n.21
Norman, J. B., Sr., 183
Norris, George A., 82
North and South, Book 2, 6

Oakes, James, 197n.2
Ocmulgee River, 32, 169, 171, 185
Oconee River, 32
O'Connor, John, 159
Oglesby's Mill, Ga., 60
Oglethorpe County, Ga., 40, 100, 120, 122
Ogletree (soldier), 24
Okefenokee Swamp, 88, 164, 172
O'Kelley, William, 179
Oliver, John, 160
Olustee, Battle of, 227n.56
O'Neal, J. W., 62
Order of the Heroes of America, 5
Ordinance of Secession, 205n.46

Origins of Class Struggle in Louisiana, 195n.1
O'Skellie, Thomas, 117
Overseers, 72, 92, 126, 127, 128, 130, 133, 138–39, 141, 174, 220n.51, 223n.49
Overstreet, W. B., 109
Owens, Mrs. C. J., 73
Owsley, Frank Lawrence, Sr., 193, 197n.2, 230n.41

Paine, J., 65
Panic of 1837, 9
Parker, William, 137
Parker (well digger), 133
Parramore, J. S., 219n.34
Parties, Slavery, and the Union in Antebellum Georgia, 200n.12
Partisan Rangers, 110
Patillo, James, 134
Patriotism, 182, 193
Patrol laws, 136–37
Patterson, William, 126
Patterson v. Camfield, 126
Paulding County, Ga., 69, 184
Paxton, Capt., 105
Paxton, Rebecca, 67
Peace and Constitutional Society, 5
Peace Society, 5, 155–57
Pearce, Gadwell Jefferson, 38
Pearson, Ben, 176
Peeples, R. A., 61
Peninsula campaign, 92
Perry, Joel, 38
Peters, Hetta, 87
Peters, W. S., 87
Petitions, 67, 72, 77, 92, 138, 145, 176, 188. *See also* Letters
Pickens County, Ga., 18, 67, 85, 180
Pierce County, Ga., 39, 64, 65, 80, 87, 184, 186
Pine Mount, Ga., 104
Pitchford, Lewis, 167
Plain folk, 34, 35, 40, 45, 46, 51, 83, 92, 99, 128, 130; definition of, 196n.2; and exemption requests, 71, 73; and slaves, 131, 135; and Unionism, 52. *See also* Poor whites

Plain Folk and Gentry in a Slave Society: White Liberty and Black Slavery in Augusta's Hinterlands, 195n.1
Plain Folk of the Old South, 197n.2
Plain People of the Confederacy, The, 195n.1
Plantation Mistress: Woman's World in the Old South, The, 198n.13
Planters, 30, 33, 34, 35, 40, 41, 45, 61, 70, 92, 127, 130, 144, 151, 188, 220n.51; attitudes of, toward plain folk, 9–10, 88; bonded, 27, 179; conscription exemptions for, 2–3, 71–73, 126, 128, 129; and debt repayment, 124; definition of, 196n.2; and impressment, 52; military enlistments of, 22; "new money," 13; "old money," 12; and poor relief, 54–55; poor white attitudes toward, 1, 3, 4; and wartime cotton production, 28–32, 196n.1
Poe, Washington, 117, 119
Police patrols, 141, 177; in Brooks County, 145, 147, 150. *See also* Slave patrols
Poor relief, 24, 54, 55, 61–69, 88
Poor whites, 3, 41; attitudes of, toward elites, 4, 30; attitudes of, toward military service, 5; attitudes of, toward slavery, 11, 133; competition of, with slave labor, 11, 199n.9; and debt repayment, 124; definition of, 196n.2; and support for the Confederacy, 30, 178, 193
Poor Whites of the Antebellum South: Tenants and Laborers in Central North Carolina and Northeast Mississippi, 196n.1
Potter, David M., 197n.4
Poverty gap, 9, 25
Pratt, Sergeant, 50
Prayer meetings, slave, 136, 138
Prescott, Lt. Alfred, 184
Price commissioners, 38
Price fixing, 38, 41–42, 65; and impressment, 47
Price gouging. *See* Speculation
Prior, James, 168
Prior, John, 168
Profiteering. *See* Speculation

Promissory notes, 3, 47, 50. *See also* Barter system; Currency
Prostitution, 54, 83
Prussia, 118
Pulaski County, Ga., 32
Purchasing agents. *See* Confederate Commissary Bureau
Putnam County, Ga., 22, 73, 78, 100

Quartermasters, 48, 49
Quincy, Fla., 126, 131, 146
Quitman, Ga., 65, 73, 106, 144–50
Quitman County, Ga., 20, 97, 133, 173

Rable, George, 198n.13
Race: equality and, 10, 133; white unity and, 11
Racism, 133
Railroads, 41, 65, 80, 83, 180, 211n.32; and cotton smuggling, 32; and poor relief, 53, 56, 68; and speculation, 33
Randolph, Sec. of War George, 47
Randolph County, Ga., 13, 28, 143, 188
Rappahannock River, 150
Redpath, James, 136
Reilly, Martin, 59
Republican Party, 12, 17
Reynolds, Gen. A. W., 184–85
Rich Man's War: Class, Caste, and Confederate Defeat in the Lower Chattahoochee Valley, 196n.1
Richmond, Va., 3, 39, 80
Richmond County, Ga., 56, 99, 116, 160
Riley, Harrison W., 18
Riots, 62, 65, 80–89, 193, 198n.13, 211n.32, 211n.33, 212n.48
Road to Disunion, 9
Robinson, Chapell Levy, 134
Robinson (planter), 133
Rogers, Alonzo, 163
Rome, Ga., 168
Roots of Southern Populism: Yeoman Farmers and the Transformation of the Georgia Upcountry, 1850–1890, 195n.1, 196n.2
Rose Dew Island, Ga., 157
Rosenfeldt, Isadore, 116

Rosenwald and Brother, 83
Rountree, L. D., 188
Rudé, George, 211n.33
Russell, Martha, 58
Rutherford, John, 119
Rutledge, Stephen, 7

Salisbury, N.C., 80
Saltworks, 140
Sam (slave), 148, 223n.49
Sanders, Joseph, 6
Sandwich, M. H., 64
Savannah, Ga., 3, 28, 34, 52, 54, 58, 59, 62, 64, 75, 78, 80, 88, 100, 103, 104, 109, 111, 114, 134, 135, 171, 184, 186, 187, 219n.34; city council of, 86; city court of, 115; Confederate state court at, 217n.5
Savannah and Gulf Railroad, 145
Saville, Ga., 171
Scaggs, Harvell, 134
Scaggs, William, 134
Scarlett Doesn't Live Here Anymore: Southern Women in the Civil War Era, 198n.13
Schley County, Ga., 72
Scotland, 118
Scott, Gen. Winfield, 28
Scruggs, William, 46, 189
Secession, 1, 200n.14; and class tensions, 12, 200n.12; opposition to, 13–16, 20, 133, 197n.4; planter pressure for, 15; popular ratification of, 15, 18. *See also* Georgia (secession convention in)
Second Battalion Partisan Rangers, 97
Second Georgia Cavalry, 174
Second Georgia Infantry Regiment, 21, 103
Secret Yankees: The Union Circle in Confederate Atlanta, 197n.3
Seddon, James, Secretary of War, 103
Self-mutilation, 75
Sellars, Joseph E., 122
Seward, James L., 186–87
Shackleford, J.H.B., 39, 47
"Shanghai Brooks," 82
Sharecroppers, 196n.2, 223n.49

Sharpsburg, Battle of, 92, 191, 196n.1, 214n.21
Sheffield, John, 161
Sheffield, West, 189
Shenandoah, 6
Sherman, Tex., 80
Sherman, Gen. William T., 163, 179, 180, 181, 184, 187
Shoots, Giles, 134
Shugg, Roger W., 195n.1
Simmons, Deputy Sheriff Lewis, 170
Sirmons, Charles, 161
Sisk, Singleton, 14
637th Militia District, 122
Sixth Georgia Infantry Regiment, 100
Skulking, 98
Slave patrols, 71, 72, 96, 137, 138, 141, 143, 144
Slavery: defense of, 135; expansion of, 16; white, 11
Slavery and Freedom, 197n.2
Slaves, 131, 168; conscription of, 190; defiance of, 138–39, 174; escaped, 139–41, 182, 183; hopes for emancipation of, 12; and hunger, 138; impressment of, 52, 53; and rebellion, 12, 71, 72, 73, 132–35, 137, 143, 144–50; as soldiers, 73, 189–91
Slave traders, 140
Sloan, William, 117
Smith, Allen, 227n.56
Smith, Arch, 41
Smith, B. D., 87
Smith, B. J., 100
Smith, Cean Carver, 198n.13
Smith, J. T., 182
Smith, Col. Milton A., 173
Smith, Rev. O. L., 148
Smith, Reuban W., 121
Smuggling, 3, 25, 33, 188
Sneed, William, 52
Snell, Daniel, 89
Snell, Sarah, 89
Snelling, David R., 157–58
Snelling, Elizabeth Lester, 157
Snelling, William, 157
Social Circle, Ga., 50

Sociology for the South, or the Failure of Free Society, 11
Soldier Camp Island, 164
Solomon, Verily, 98
Southerners All, 197n.2
South vs. the South, The, 199n.20
Southwestern Railroad, 33, 37
Southwest Judicial Circuit, 118, 209n.74
Southworth, Porter, 163
Spain, James W., 146, 150
Spalding County, Ga., 44, 53
Speculation, 4, 33, 35, 37–41, 45, 48, 49, 57, 59, 61, 68, 73, 80, 83, 84, 87, 98, 111, 119, 124, 129, 146, 178, 193, 194, 196n.1, 205n.46
Speight, T. E., 191
Spies. *See* Espionage
Springfield, Ga., 141
Stalnaker, Joseph W., 148
Standard, Diffee, 35
Starvation, 29, 34, 46, 59, 77, 84, 90, 100, 162. *See also* Food; Hunger; Malnutrition
State rights, 96, 120, 123, 129, 130, 216n.4, 230n.41
State Rights in the Confederacy, 230n.41
Steamboats, 53
Steam Mill, Ga., 189
Steinhatchee River, 146
Stephens, Vice Pres. Alexander H., 13, 35, 189
Stephens, John, 105
Stephens, Linton, 30
Stephens County, Ga., 72
Stewart County, Ga., 13, 72, 76, 123, 124, 138, 160, 173
Still, William, 199n.20
Stills, 40–41
St. Joseph's Bay, Fla., 140
St. Marys, Ga., 136
Stockton, Ga., 86, 99
Stow, Capt., 40
Stroup (merchant), 86
Styles, Col. Cary W., 105, 109–11, 174
Substitution, 2, 92, 97–98, 107, 109, 220n.56; class disparity in, 98; cost of,

213n.13; repeal of, 99, 129. *See also* Confederate Conscription Act; Conscription; Exemptions
Suffrage, 152–53
Sumner, William, 66
Sumter County, Ga., 27, 62, 77, 102, 118, 122, 137
Superior courts, 52, 119; Bibb County, 117, 120, 218n.19; Brooks County, 144, 223n.48; Chatham County, 113, 114, 115, 217n.5; Dougherty County, 43, 137, 173; Elbert County, 97, 120, 121, 130; Richmond County, 116; Sumter County, 62; Thomas County, 85–86, 108
Sutherland, Daniel E., 196n.1, 197n.3
Swainsboro, Ga., 66
Sylvia (slave), 139–40

Talbot County, Ga., 13, 121
Taliaferro County, Ga., 11, 61
Talking Rock, Ga., 85
Tallahassee, Fla., 106, 146
Tanneries, 56
Tap Roots, 6
Tara Revisited: Women, War, and the Plantation Legend, 198n.13
Tattnall County, Ga., 163, 186
Tatum, Georgia Lee, 195n.1, 197n.3
Taxation, 45, 46, 52, 56, 86, 105; income tax, 51; poll tax, 63, 152; property tax, 61–62, 63. *See also* Impressment
Tax in kind. *See* Taxation
Taylor, Hudson, 170
Taylor County, Fla., 146, 147
Taylor County, Ga., 54
Tenants, 196n.2
Terrell County, Ga., 26, 41, 123, 124
Thayer, Eli, 136
Third Georgia Infantry Regiment, 160
Thirteenth Georgia Infantry Regiment, 106
Thomas, Judge Grigsby E., 123
Thomas, Jefferson, 99
Thomas, Judge Thomas W., 97, 113, 120, 121, 129, 130
Thomas County, Ga., 47, 78, 85–86, 106, 107, 108, 122, 137, 138, 161, 186, 219n.34
Thomaston, Ga., 14, 64, 185
Thomasville, Ga., 57, 80, 85, 106, 122, 132, 146, 171, 186–87, 219n.34
Thompson, Peter L., 97
Thread, 38, 56, 58, 66, 68. *See also* Cloth; Wool; Yarn
Thurman, Susan, 76
Tift, Nelson, 41–44
Tift Hall, 42
Tillery, Francis B., 72–73
"To go, or not to go," 179–80
Tolls, 42–43
Toombs, Robert, 15, 28, 46, 53
Tory gangs. *See* Layout gangs
"To the Planters of Georgia," 53
Toward a Patriarchal Republic: The Secession of Georgia, 200n.12
Trade unions, 60
Troup Artillery, 140
Troup County, Ga., 55, 58, 139, 140, 174
Tucker, Rodolphus, 117
Turner, Capt. James P., 106
Twelfth Georgia Infantry Regiment, 21
Twenty-first Georgia Infantry Regiment, 100, 214n.21
Twenty-ninth Battalion Georgia Cavalry, 174, 177
Twenty-sixth Georgia Infantry Regiment, 109–10
Twenty slave law, 2–3, 6, 92, 94, 99, 126
Twiggs County, Ga., 104
Tyler, Martha, 67

Unionism, 1, 2, 18–20, 52, 85, 115, 133, 134, 147, 155, 157–59, 160, 163, 165, 166, 180, 183, 184, 185, 187, 193, 197n.3
Union Missionary Baptist Church, 213n.1
Union Primitive Baptist Church, 87
Union ticket, 152
Unruly Women: The Politics of Social and Sexual Control in the Old South, 195n.1
Upson County, Ga., 15, 16, 163, 167, 185
U.S. Mint, 18
U.S. troops, 134, 144, 163, 180

Valdosta, Ga., 4, 61, 62, 65, 80, 85, 86–87, 110, 171, 188
Vann's Valley, Ga., 75
Vason, David A., 41
Vickery, Elias, 144, 222n.44
Vickery, Jesse, 144
Vickery, John, 144–50, 174, 223n.49
Vicksburg, Battle of, 157
Vigilance committees, 132, 134. *See also* Committees of Public Safety; Police Patrols; Slave Patrols
Virginia's Private War: Feeding Body and Soul in the Confederacy, 196n.1
Volunteer Force of the United States Army from Georgia, 163
Voting. *See* Elections; Suffrage

Wages, 58; soldier's pay, 74
Walker, Col. A. C., 160
Walker County, Ga., 13, 18, 164, 168, 180
Wall, "Old Man" Bill, 176
Walls, Mrs. James B., 104
Walton County, Ga., 40, 185
Ware County, Ga., 65, 66, 105, 109, 172, 174, 177, 184
Waresboro, Ga., 109–10
War of Another Kind: A Southern Community in the Great Rebellion, 196n.1
Warren, J. W., 190
Warren, William, 127–8
Warren (slave), 148
Warren County, Ga., 116
Washington County, Ga., 100, 219n.34
Watkins, Sam, 3
Watson, Thomas A., 157
Watts, Attorney Gen. Thomas, 47
Wayne, Adj. Gen. Henry C., 105, 106, 108, 141, 144, 168, 173–4. *See also* Georgia Adjutant General's Office
Wayne County, Ga., 184
Weapons, 23, 85, 93; and deserters, 167; lack of, 17; and slaves, 136
Webster County, Ga., 123, 124–25, 173
Weeks, Romulus, 134
Welch, Lt. George, 163–64
Wells, James Madison, 6
Welsh, Mary, 86
Western and Atlantic Railroad, 46
West Point, Ga., 140
Wheeler, Pauline L., 73
White County, Ga., 165–66, 167
Whites: competition of, with slave labor, 11; and escaped slaves, 140, 141; and interracial trading, 141; and slave rebellion, 132–34, 135, 144–50; socioeconomic inequality among, 9–11. *See also* Labor; Poor whites; Race; Slaveholders; Women
Whites, LeeAnn, 198n.13
White Sulfur Springs, Ga., 174
Whitfield County, Ga., 47, 65, 67
Why the South Lost the Civil War, 199n.20
Widow's Appeal, The, 79–80
Wilbur, Col. A., 115
Wilcox County, Ga., 169, 172, 186
Wiley, Bell, 195n.1
Wilkes County, Ga., 52, 104
Wilkinson County, Ga., 102, 169
William (slave), 140
Williams, Mrs. Aliff, 76
Williams, David, 196n.1
Williams, F. P., 103
Williams, Jeremiah J., 106
Williams, Sheriff J. J., 176
Wilson, Jack, 176
Wilson, Jeremiah, 40
Wilson, John K., 132
Wimpy, John A., 160
Windsor, Alfred H., 117
Windsor, Robert, 117
Wisenbaker, Thannie, 85
Within the Plantation Household: Black and White Women of the Old South, 198n.13
Wofford, Jake, 167
Wofford, Gen. W. T., 184
Women, 37, 38, 39, 41, 44, 48, 65, 66, 67, 69, 70, 71, 198n.13; and crime, 80, 82, 187; and farm management, 73, 74; and honor, 83–84, 88; and impressment, 50, 54, 87; labor, 57–59; riots, 62, 80–89. *See also* Needle women
Wood, Stephen G. W., 134

Wood, William, 21
Woodward, C. Vann, 198n.13
Woody, John, 160, 182
Wool: factories, 38; material, 57. *See also* Cloth; Thread; Yarn
Worrell, Judge Edmund H., 121
Worth County, Ga., 123, 136, 170, 171, 173, 176, 183
Württemberg, 117

Wylly, Capt. Thomas, 172

Yarn, 38, 66, 70, 82, 87. *See also* Cloth; Thread; Wool
Yellow Creek, 64
Yeoman, 196n.2
"Yeoman Discontent in the Confederacy," 195n.1
Yulee, E., 86

David Williams, a native of Miller County, Georgia, is professor of history at Valdosta State University, Georgia. He is author of numerous books and articles, including *Johnny Reb's War: Battlefield and Homefront* and *Rich Man's War: Class, Caste, and Confederate Defeat in the Lower Chattahoochee Valley*.

Teresa Crisp Williams, a native of Columbus, Georgia, is administrative coordinator of the Graduate School and instructor of history at Valdosta State University. She has published articles in the *Georgia Historical Quarterly* and is a contributor to *The Encyclopedia of the American Civil War*.

David Carlson, a native of Valdosta, Georgia, is a doctoral candidate in history at Emory University. He has published articles in the *Georgia Historical Quarterly* and is a contributor to *The Encyclopedia of the American Civil War*.

www.ingramcontent.com/pod-product-compliance
Lightning Source LLC
Chambersburg PA
CBHW022108150426
43195CB00008B/318